QUESTIONS & ANSWERS:
WILLS, TRUSTS & ESTATES

QUESTIONS & ANSWERS:
WILLS, TRUSTS & ESTATES

Multiple-Choice and Short-Answer Questions and Answers

THIRD EDITION

Thomas M. Featherston, Jr.
Mills Cox Professor of Law
Baylor Law School

 LexisNexis

ISBN: 978-0-7698-9625-0

eBook ISBN: 978-0-7698-9628-1

> NOTE TO USERS
> To ensure that you are using the latest materials available in this area, please be sure to periodically check the LexisNexis Law School web site for downloadable updates and supplements at www.lexisnexis.com/lawschool.

Editorial Offices

121 Chanlon Rd., New Providence, NJ 07974 (908) 464-6800

201 Mission St., San Francisco, CA 94105-1831 (415) 908-3200

www.lexisnexis.com

MATTHEW◆BENDER

TABLE OF CONTENTS

PREFACE TO THE THIRD EDITION

The law governing wills, trusts, and estates in the United States finds its origins primarily in the common law of England. Today, it is increasingly based on statutory law. It is also largely "state law" oriented. Each state has its own set of rules, procedures, statutes, and case law. While there are many common denominators, the law can, and frequently will, differ from state to state. Some of these differences are significant.

To address this reality, most of the problems in this book are to be solved using the law of the hypothetical state of X. It is assumed that X has adopted both the Uniform Probate Code (1990, with amendments through 2011) and the Uniform Trust Code (2000, with amendments through 2011). Throughout the book, the Uniform Probate Code and the Uniform Trust Code are abbreviated "UPC" and "UTC," respectively. Occasionally, some questions will instruct the student to assume that a particular provision of one of the uniform acts is not part of the law of X or that another relevant statute is to be interpreted a certain way.

If neither the Uniform Probate Code nor the Uniform Trust Code provides the "answer," it is assumed that X's courts have adopted a generally accepted principle of the law of wills, trusts and estates. These generally-accepted principles may be the positions taken in a relevant Restatement of the Law published by the American Law Institute or explained in a recognized hornbook or treatise, such as UNDERSTANDING TRUSTS AND ESTATES by ROGER W. ANDERSEN (2013), or PRINCIPLES OF WILLS, TRUSTS & ESTATES by WILLIAM M. McGOVERN, SHELDON F. KURTZ AND DAVID M. ENGLISH (2012). At times, reference will be made to the "old reliables" like BOGERT ON TRUSTS (1987) and ATKINSON'S LAW OF WILLS (1953).

Also, in recognition of the differences in states' laws, most answers will also attempt to explain how the result may differ in a state that does not follow the position taken by the Uniform Probate Code, the Uniform Trust Code or the "majority" case law rule. Regardless of the state law that the student has learned in class, the key issues are identified, and it is hoped that the relevant answer is discussed for each question.

Further, the practical application of this area of the law continues to evolve. Today, fewer assets pass through probate administration than in the not too distant past. Increasingly, wealth transfers take the form a nonprobate or nontestamentary disposition. The revocable trust has become a popular "will substitute" in many states. Lawyers practicing in this area of law spend increasing amounts of time coordinating the disposition of the client's life insurance, retirement benefits and bank accounts with the client's key planning document — either the client's will or revocable trust. Consequently, many of the questions in this edition reflect this growing trend.

Accordingly, a primary purpose of this book is to test the student's practice-oriented understanding of this area of the law. This book supplements the student's casebook and includes questions and answers in eleven main subject areas (plus a final exam) that correspond to basic topics covered in a typical wills, trusts, and estates course. Unfortunately, space does not allow for the coverage of every topic. For example, future interests and the administration of trusts and estates are not addressed as their own topics. However, some future interest and administration issues are integrated into some questions.

When answering most questions, it is suggested that the student (i) identify the type of disposition in question (testamentary, inter vivos, nonprobate, etc.); (ii) identify the parties involved (transferor, transferees, creditors, assignees, etc.); (iii) determine the effective date of the disposition (date of delivery, date of death, date of possession, etc.); (iv) understand the issue presented (who gets what, when, and how); and (v) apply to the facts the appropriate substantive principle (the relevant statute or case law precedent).

In order to focus questions on specific issues, unless otherwise instructed, or the question itself suggests the contrary, the student should assume as follows:

- There are no administration expenses or creditors' claims that affect the proper conclusion. For example, if a question asks about the proper distribution of an intestate's estate, simply divide the assets described assuming there are no estate administration expenses or debts of the decedent.

- There are no individuals relevant to determining the proper distributees other than those specifically identified.

- That none of the property is community property unless the question directs your attention to a potential problem. Also, ignore homestead, exempt property, and family allowance rights. Also assume relevant state law has abolished the common law doctrines of dower and curtesy.

- That a decedent's will was valid and duly admitted to probate. If the question recites that an individual died testate, assume there are no problems with the will, unless the question directs your attention to a potential problem.

- That all trusts are valid, irrevocable express trusts. If the question describes a trust that a settlor has established, assume the trust is valid and enforceable, unless the question directs your attention to the trust's validity, enforceability, or revocability.

- That individuals are not married and/or are alive at all relevant times. For example, if the question states that an individual died, assume he or she was single unless the question directs your attention to a potential problem. If the question states an individual was survived by a child, assume that the child is living at all times relevant to any legal analysis involved in the question.

It is not the intent of the author to raise questions concerning whether a couple (opposite sex or same sex) is validly married. The validity of a marriage is typically a matter of the law of the state where the couple is domiciled, but the state of domicile usually recognizes a marriage as valid, if valid where the ceremony was performed or where the couple was previously domiciled. Similarly, it has not been the author's intent to address whether domestic partners or parties to a civil union (or any other similar relations) assume or should assume the status of being "married". Again, that determination is a matter of a particular state's law. Accordingly, this edition assumes that the couple in question has that status of being married under applicable law. For discussion purposes, terms like "spouse" and "marriage" are used to refer to the individuals who have that status and the relationship resulting from that status.

Finally, for any questions involving federal transfer taxes, the student should assume that the American Taxpayer Relief Act of 2012 is in effect as of January 1, 2013 (i.e., that the annual exclusion for gift tax purposes is $14,000 and that the available exemption amount for transfer tax purposes is $5.25 million.) The student should also assume that the State of X does not have either an estate or inheritance tax.

Prof. Tom Featherston
November 15, 2013

ABOUT THE AUTHOR

Thomas M. Featherston, Jr., is the Mills Cox Professor of Law at Baylor University's School of Law in Waco, Texas. He earned his J.D. with highest honors from Baylor in 1972. After graduation, he entered private practice in Houston, Texas from 1973 through 1982. He is Board Certified in Estate Planning and Probate Law by the Texas Board of Legal Specialization (originally certified in 1979). He joined the Baylor Law School faculty in 1982, and in 1990, he was appointed to the Mills Cox Chair.

Professor Featherston was elected as an Academic Fellow of the American College of Trust and Estate Counsel in 1991 and a Fellow of the American Bar Foundation in 1993. He is active in both the State Bar of Texas and the American Bar Association. He is a past chair of the Real Estate, Probate and Trust Law Section of the State Bar of Texas and has served on the governing council of the Real Estate, Trust and Estate Law Section of the American Bar Association. He is also the Trusts and Estates Articles Editor for *Probate & Property*, an ABA publication, and is a co-author of West's *Texas Practice Guide — Probate*. He is a frequent author and lecturer in the areas of trusts, estates, marital property, fiduciary administration and other related topics, the subjects that he teaches at Baylor Law School. In 2009, he was honored as the *Distinguished Texas Probate and Trust Attorney* by the Real Property, Probate and Trust Law Section of the State Bar of Texas.

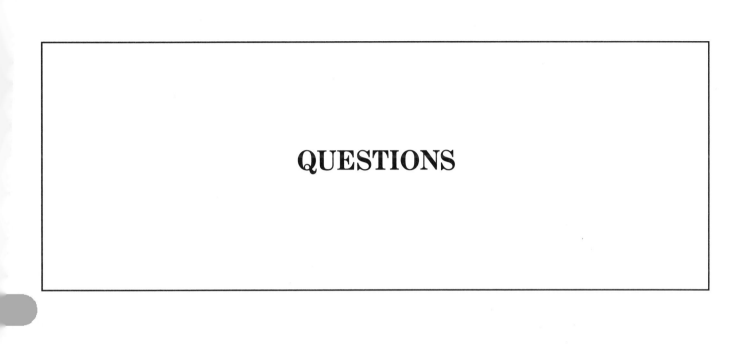

QUESTIONS

SURVIVING SPOUSES, FORMER SPOUSES, AND OMITTED CHILDREN

1.   S1 and S2 were married for 10 years. During the marriage, S1 acquired real and personal property located in the state where they resided; all assets were titled in S1's name. S1 recently died. S1's valid will has been admitted to probate, and the will leaves all of S1's property to C, the adult child of S1 and S2.

    Assuming all debts and taxes have been satisfied, which answer best describes S2's interest in the described assets?

ANSWER:

Note: Except where specifically indicated, answer the remaining questions in Chapter 1 ignoring a surviving spouse's homestead, exempt property, and family allowance rights and assuming the state where they reside is a non-community property state that has adopted the Uniform Probate Code.

2.   Refer to Question 1, but assume S1's will leaves Greenacre to S2 and the "rest, residue, and remainder of my property" to C. Assuming all debts and taxes have been satisfied, which answer best describes the most likely disposition of S1's estate?

    (A) Greenacre passes to S2, and the remaining assets pass to C.

    (B) Greenacre passes to S2, and the remaining assets are shared equally by S2 and C.

    (C) Greenacre passes to S2, and the remaining assets pass 30% to S2 and 70% to C.

    (D) The value of Greenacre is deducted from S2's share of S1's estate.

3.   Refer to Question 1, but assume S1's will leaves all of S1's property to S2. Assuming all debts have been satisfied, which answer best describes the interest of C in the described assets?

    (A) S2 succeeds to the entire estate.

    (B) C is entitled to an intestate share of the estate, and S2 owns the balance.

    (C) An amount necessary for C's support during formal administration may be set aside for C, and S2 owns the balance.

    (D) An amount necessary for C's support for the remainder of C's lifetime is set aside for C, and S2 owns the balance, if any.

4.   Refer to Question 3. Assuming that C is a minor at the time of S1's death, how would your answer in Question 3 differ?

ANSWER:

5.   S1 and S2 were married for one year. Prior to and during the marriage, S1 acquired real and personal property; all assets were owned by S1 and titled in S1's name. S1 recently died. S1's valid will has been admitted to probate, and the will leaves Greenacre to C and the "rest, residue, and remainder of my property" to S2. C is S1's adult child from a prior marriage. Assuming all debts and taxes have been satisfied, which answer best describes the most likely disposition of S1's estate?

(A)   Greenacre passes to C, and S2 owns to the balance.

(B)   Greenacre is shared equally by C and S2, and S2 owns the balance.

(C)   S2 must elect to take either S2's elective share or only what is devised to S2 in the will.

(D)   C must elect to take C's intestate share or Greenacre.

6.   S1 and S2 were married for over 20 years. S1 recently died. S1's valid will has been admitted to probate, and the will leaves S1's estate to C. C is S1's adult child from a prior marriage. Also assume that, at the time of death, S1 was a participant in a pension plan provided by S1's employer. S1's employer also provided each employee with a group life insurance policy as part of its employee benefit package. The employer's records indicate that S1 had not signed the appropriate forms necessary to designate the beneficiaries of the plan and policy in the event of S1's death. Which answer best describes the most likely disposition of the death benefits payable by reason of the pension plan and life insurance policy?

(A)   The death benefits pass as part of the probate estate to C.

(B)   The death benefits pass nonprobate to S2.

(C)   The insurance proceeds pass as part of the probate estate to C, and the plan benefits pass nonprobate to S2.

(D)   The plan benefits pass as part of the probate estate to C, and the insurance proceeds pass nonprobate to S2.

7.   Refer to Question 6, but assume S2, not S1, has died with a valid will that has been admitted to probate. S2's will leaves all of S2's property to S2's child by a prior marriage. Explain the most likely effect S2's death will have on S1's pension plan.

ANSWER:

8. S1 and S2 were married. S1 died recently. S1's original will left all of S1's property equally to S2 and C, S1's adult child by a prior marriage. However, S1 revoked the described will shortly before S1 died and then validly executed a new will leaving "all of my property" to P, S1's friend. This will has been admitted to probate. Assuming all debts and taxes have been satisfied, which answer best describes the most likely disposition of S1's estate.

    (A) P succeeds to the assets.

    (B) S2 takes S2's elective share, C takes an intestate share, and P inherits the balance.

    (C) S2 takes S2's elective share, and P inherits the balance.

    (D) C takes an intestate share, and P inherits the balance.

9. Refer to Question 8 and assume S1 also signed a form provided by S1's employer that changed the beneficiary of S1's ERISA regulated pension plan from S2 to P. Which answer best describes the most likely disposition of the pension plan's death benefit?

    (A) It is payable to P.

    (B) It is payable to P and C.

    (C) It is payable to C.

    (D) None of the above.

10. T died recently. T was survived by T's spouse, S, and T's parents, M and F; T never had any children. T's will was validly executed prior to T's marriage to S; T never changed the will. It devises T's entire estate to M and F. What is the most likely disposition of T's estate?

ANSWER:

11. Refer to Question 10. What would your answer be if the will had been executed during the marriage of T and S?

    (A) The will can be admitted to probate; the entire estate passes to M and F.

    (B) The will cannot be admitted to probate; the entire estate passes to S.

    (C) The will can be admitted to probate; S will be entitled to S's elective share, if any, and M and F will succeed to everything else.

    (D) The will cannot be admitted to probate; the estate will be shared by S, M, and F.

12. O died recently. O was survived by O's spouse, S, and their two minor children, C1 and C2. O's will, which was executed after O married S but before the births of C1 and C2, leaves all of O's property to S. Which answer best describes the most likely disposition of O's estate?

(A) The will can be admitted to probate; the entire estate passes to S.

(B) The will cannot be admitted to probate; the entire estate passes to C1 and C2.

(C) The will cannot be admitted to probate; S, C1, and C2 share the estate.

(D) The will can be admitted to probate, but C1 and C2 will be entitled to an intestate share of the estate, and the balance of the entire estate passes to S.

13. Refer to Question 12. How would your answer differ if the will had been executed following the births of C1 and C2?

(A) The will can be admitted to probate; the entire estate passes to S.

(B) The will cannot be admitted to probate; the entire estate passes to C1 and C2.

(C) The will cannot be admitted to probate; S, C1, and C2 share the estate.

(D) The will can be admitted to probate, but C1 and C2 will be entitled to an intestate share of the estate, and the balance of the estate passes to S.

14. S1 died recently. S1 was survived by S1's spouse, S2, and their minor child, C1. S1's will, which was executed after S1 married S2, but before the birth of C1, leaves all of S1's property to S2. It was also executed before the birth of C2, a child born of an extramarital affair of S1 and P; C2 also survived S1. Which answer best describes the most likely disposition of S1's estate?

(A) The will can be admitted to probate; the entire estate passes to S2.

(B) The will cannot be admitted to probate; the entire estate passes to C1 and C2.

(C) The will can be admitted to probate, but C1 and C2 will be entitled to an intestate share of the estate, and the balance of the entire estate passes to S2.

(D) The will can be admitted to probate, but C2 will be entitled to an intestate share of the estate, and the balance of the entire estate passes to S2.

15. T died recently. T was survived by T's parents, M and F. T was divorced from T's spouse, S, two years prior to T's death. After the divorce, T did not change the will that T had executed while married to S and that left all of T's property to S. What is the most likely disposition of T's estate?

ANSWER:

16. O and S were divorced last year after 10 years of marriage. O died intestate recently and was survived by O's parents, M and F. Two of the more significant assets existing at the time of O's death were two savings accounts. The bank's records indicate that the first account is a "joint account with survivorship rights" in the names of O and S. The second account is "payable on O's death" to S. Apparently, O forgot to change the deposit

QUESTIONS & ANSWERS: WILLS, TRUSTS & ESTATES

QUESTIONS & ANSWERS: WILLS, TRUSTS & ESTATES
7

agreements with the bank after the bitter divorce even though O was awarded ownership of both accounts as part of the divorce settlement and did not have an obligation to leave S's name on the accounts. Which answer best describes the most likely disposition of the accounts?

(A) Both accounts pass nonprobate to S.

(B) The joint account passes to M and F, and the POD account passes nonprobate to S.

(C) The POD account passes to M and F, and the joint account passes nonprobate to S.

(D) Both accounts pass to M and F.

17. Refer to Question 16 and assume that there were also an insurance policy on O's life and a pension plan provided by O's employer. The policy was owned by O and still made payable at O's death to S. The death benefit of the pension plan was also still payable to S. Apparently, O forgot to change the beneficiary designations after the bitter divorce even though O was awarded the policy and plan as part of the divorce settlement and was not obligated to designate S as the beneficiary of either the policy or plan. What is the most likely disposition of the death benefits?

ANSWER:

1.   O died recently. Immediately prior to O's death, O owned fee simple title to certain real and personal property. In addition to those assets, O owned a life estate in Blackacre; A owned the remainder interest. O also owned a remainder interest in Whiteacre; B owned the life estate. A and B were not related to O, and both A and B survived O. O died intestate, and as O's sole heir at law, H, a cousin, inherited O's entire probate estate. Assume O also owned (i) a savings account entitled "O payable on O's death to C" and (ii) an insurance policy on O's life payable at O's death to D. Both C and D were friends of O who survived O.

What interest, if any, is H likely to acquire in Blackacre, Whiteacre, the savings account and the life insurance policy?

ANSWER:

2.   Refer to Question 1. How would your answers differ if O had died with a valid will that had been admitted to probate leaving "all my property" to O's friend, F?

(A) My answers would not change.

(B) F acquires the remainder interest in Whiteacre but acquires no interest in Blackacre, the account, or the policy.

(C) F acquires the account but acquires no interest in Blackacre, Whiteacre, or the policy.

(D) F acquires the proceeds of the policy but acquires no interest in Whiteacre, Blackacre, or the account.

3.   Refer to Question 2. How would your answers differ if A, B, C, and D had died before O?

(A) My answers would not change.

(B) F acquires Whiteacre but acquires no interest in Blackacre, the account or the policy.

(C) F acquires Whiteacre, the account, and the policy but no interest in Blackacre.

(D) F acquires the account and the policy but acquires no interest in Whiteacre or Blackacre.

4.   Refer to Question 3, but assume that C and D survived O but died two days after O.

Which answer best describes the interest, if any, F is most likely to acquire in the savings account and the life insurance policy?

    (A) F acquires ownership of the account and the policy proceeds.

    (B) F acquires ownership of the account but no interest in the policy or its proceeds.

    (C) F acquires ownership of the policy and its proceeds but no interest in the account.

    (D) F acquires no interest in the policy, its proceeds, or the account.

5.   Refer to Question 3, but assume that C and D died before O, but each was survived by a child. Which answer best describes the interest, if any, F is most likely to acquire in the savings account and the life insurance policy?

    (A) F acquires ownership of the account and the policy proceeds.

    (B) F acquires ownership of the account but no interest in the policy or its proceeds.

    (C) F acquires ownership of the policy and its proceeds but no interest in the account.

    (D) F acquires no interest in the policy, its proceeds, or the account.

6.   Refer to Question 5, but assume that C and D were O's grandchildren. Which answer best describes the interest, if any, F is most likely to acquire in the savings account and the life insurance policy?

    (A) F acquires ownership of the account and the policy proceeds.

    (B) F acquires ownership of the account but no interest in the policy or its proceeds.

    (C) F acquires ownership of the policy and its proceeds but no interest in the account.

    (D) F acquires no interest in the policy, its proceeds, or the account.

7.   L, a single individual, took out a life insurance policy on himself. The policy named B1 as the beneficiary to receive the proceeds on L's death. Several years later, L signed and delivered to the insurance company the company's change-of-beneficiary form in which L named B2 rather than B1 as the beneficiary. Neither of the beneficiary designation forms was witnessed or otherwise executed in compliance with the statutory formalities for a will. L died intestate, survived by both B1 and B2. Neither B1 nor B2 is an intestate heir of L. Which of the following best describes the proper disposition of the insurance proceeds?

    (A) The policy proceeds are probate assets to be distributed to L's heirs.

    (B) The policy proceeds are payable to B2.

    (C) The policy proceeds are payable to B1.

    (D) B1 owned the policy and is entitled to the proceeds.

8.   Refer to Question 7. How would the results differ if L had validly executed a will that specifically devised the policy and its proceeds to L's alma mater, Big State University. Would L's dying testate affect the result?

ANSWER:

9. O owned and lived on Blackacre, the family farm. O's grandson, GS, operated the farming activities. O wanted GS to have Blackacre after she died because she believed he would continue to operate the family farm. To encourage GS, she conveyed Blackacre to GS in a deed reserving a life estate for herself, but conveying the remainder to GS. GS died before O. Under the terms of his will, he left his entire estate to his wife, S. After GS died, O executed a will leaving the farm to her granddaughter, GD. Assuming both S and GD survived O, who gets the farm?

    (A) GD because GS did not survive O.

    (B) GD because O's will revoked the earlier gift to GS.

    (C) S because she inherited GS's remainder interest in the farm.

    (D) GD, unless the deed was executed in compliance with the statutory formalities for wills, in which case, S.

10. Refer to Question 9, but assume that O, rather than conveying GS the remainder interest, executed and recorded a valid deed conveying the farm to O and GS, as joint tenants with rights of survivorship. Explain who gets the farm under those circumstances.

ANSWER:

11. S1 and S2 were married. They had two sons, C1 and C2. S1 purchased an insurance policy on S1's life. The beneficiary designation is "to S2, if S2 survives the insured, otherwise, to the insured's children." S1 has died. S1's will devised "all of my property" to Big State University. S2 and C2 predeceased S1. However, C2 was survived by his daughter, G. Which of the following best describes the proper disposition of the proceeds at S1's death?

    (A) C1 is entitled to receive the proceeds under the terms of the beneficiary designation.

    (B) C1 and G are entitled to receive the proceeds equally.

    (C) C1 and G are entitled to receive the proceeds, 2/3 and 1/3 respectively.

    (D) The proceeds will be paid to S1's probate estate and distributed to Big State University.

12. Refer to Question 11. If S1 also had a joint checking account with C2 and the account provided for rights of survivorship, who would have been entitled to the account at S1's death?

    (A) C1.

    (B) G.

(C) Big State University.

(D) The bank.

13. Two friends, A and B, have a joint savings account at a local bank. A has contributed $1,000 to the account. B has contributed $500. There has been $100 in interest paid. The current balance in the account is $1,600. There have not been any withdrawals from the account. Which of the following is the best statement as to the ownership of the account?

   (A) They each own $800 of the account.

   (B) A owns $1,066.66 and B owns $533.33 of the account.

   (C) A owns $1,050 and B owns $550.

   (D) A owns the account and owes B $500.

14. Refer to Question 13. If A dies intestate, who owns the account?

ANSWER:

15. Refer to Question 14. Assume that A, A's wife, S, and B had been the parties to the account. S had made no contributions or withdrawals. Would the result in Question 14 differ if A died survived by S and B?

ANSWER:

16. Refer to Question 15. If A and S lived together but were not married, how would the account have been owned after A's death?

ANSWER:

17. Refer to Question 16. What would S own when B later dies?

ANSWER:

18. Refer to Question 17. Assume B's probate estate is insufficient to pay B's estate's debts. Is this account subject to those claims?

ANSWER:

19. D opens a bank account and designates that it should pay on D's death to E. D has deposited $5,000, and the account has earned $200 in interest. The total balance is $5,200. What are E's rights to the account before and after D's death?

ANSWER:

20. O had deposited $10,000 into a savings account in O's name "payable on O's death to A" and another $10,000 into a checking account in the names of O and B "with rights of survivorship." O has recently died, survived by A and B. Which answer best explains whether these accounts would be included in O's gross estate for federal transfer tax purposes?

   (A) The checking account and the savings account would be included in O's gross estate.

   (B) Neither the checking account nor the savings account would be included in O's gross estate.

   (C) The checking account, but not the savings account, would be included in O's gross estate.

   (D) The checking account and half of the savings account would be included in O's gross estate.

21. Refer to Question 20. Assume that, at O's death, O also owned two life insurance policies: one is a term policy made payable at O's death to O's estate, and the other is a whole life policy made payable to A. Which answer best explains whether the policies would be included in O's gross estate for federal transfer tax purposes?

   (A) Both policies would be included in O's gross estate.

   (B) Neither policy would be included in O's gross estate.

   (C) The whole life policy, but not the term policy, would be included in O's gross estate.

   (D) The term policy, but not the whole life policy, would be included in O's gross estate.

22. E died recently. Immediately prior to E's death, E had been participating in a 401(k) plan created and funded by E's employer; at the time of E's death, the value of the 401(k) plan was $1,000,000. In addition, E had been voluntarily contributing to another 401(k) plan, which had a value at the time of E's death of $500,000. Prior to E's death, E had designated a child, C, as the beneficiary of both 401(k) plans. Which answer best explains whether the 401(k) plans would be included in E's gross estate for federal transfer tax purposes?

   (A) Both plans would be included in E's gross estate.

   (B) Neither plan would be included in E's gross estate.

   (C) The employer's plan, but not the voluntary plan, would be included in E's gross estate.

   (D) The voluntary plan, but not the employer's plan, would be included in E's gross estate.

1. The client, C, explains that she has recently read several books on avoiding probate. These books describe probate as a corrupt system whose primary beneficiaries are lawyers. The books insist that any reasonable person should avoid probate at all costs and that there are never any benefits to property passing through probate. C also explains that she is a person of "moderate" wealth, recently widowed with three adult children who live in three different states. She is considering moving to one of those states. The solution, as C understands it, is the "living trust." Is C's understanding of probate and living trusts accurate? If not, outline for C a more balanced understanding of the potential advantages and disadvantages of probate compared to "living trusts."

ANSWER:

2. S transferred property to T, in trust, to pay S the income for life, and to distribute the trust estate to B on S's death. S retained the power to revoke or amend the trust. S died intestate, survived by B. B is not S's intestate heir. The trust instrument was not witnessed and was not otherwise executed in compliance with the statutory formalities for a will. Which of the following best describes the distribution of the trust estate at S's death?

(A) S's trust is invalid. The trust estate must pass through the probate system which means that the trust estate passes to S's intestate heirs.

(B) S's trust is a valid testamentary trust. The trust estate passes probate to B.

(C) S's trust is a valid testamentary trust. The trust estate passes nonprobate to B.

(D) S's trust is a valid inter vivos trust, which means that the trust estate passes to B outside of the probate system.

3. Would the result in Question 2 be different if S had declared himself to be the trustee of the property rather than transferring it to a third party as trustee?

ANSWER:

4. O died recently. O was survived by two children, C1 and C2, as well as (i) a great grandchild, GG, the only child of C1's deceased child, G1, and (ii) G2, the only child of C2. O's valid will has been admitted to probate and devises all of O's estate to G2. Several years prior to O's death, O had executed a valid inter vivos irrevocable declaration of trust, whereby O declared himself to be the trustee of Blackacre; F was named as the successor

trustee. At that time, O was married to W. The document was duly recorded in the county where Blackacre is located. The terms of the written trust agreement provide that, for the remainder of O's life, O is to receive all of the trust's income; at O's death, all the income is to be paid to W; and at the death of the survivor of O and W, Blackacre is to be delivered to G1. After the execution of the trust document, but before O died, O and W divorced, and G1 died, survived by G1's spouse, S, and G1's only child, GG. G1's valid will has been admitted to probate and devises all of his property to S. What is the most likely disposition of the trust estate by reason of O's death?

ANSWER:

5. Refer to Question 4. How would your answer differ if the trust agreement, by its own terms, was revocable, but there is no evidence that O ever intended to revoke the trust?

    (A) My answer would not change.

    (B) Because W was no longer O's spouse and G1 predeceased O, Blackacre should be delivered to G2.

    (C) Because O was no longer O's spouse, Blackacre should be delivered to O's heirs at law.

    (D) Because O was no longer O's spouse, Blackacre should be delivered to GG.

6. O died recently. O was survived by two children, C1 and C2, and two grandchildren, G1 and G2. Prior to O's death, O had properly executed a valid, enforceable inter vivos revocable declaration of trust document, whereby O declared O to be the trustee of the trust. The terms of the trust provide that the income and principal could be used for O's health, education, maintenance, and support during the remainder of O's lifetime; at O's death, any real property is to be delivered to G1, and any personal property is to be delivered to G2. There is no evidence that O ever intended to revoke the trust. The trust also provided that, if O was ever unable or unwilling to act, a local bank was named as the successor trustee. At the time the trust document was signed by O, O attached a ten-dollar bill to the trust document. No other assets were made subject to the trust during O's lifetime. Following the execution of the trust document, O validly executed a will, whereby O devised O's entire estate to the bank as the successor trustee of the described inter vivos trust. The significant assets of O's estate at the time of O's death were Blackacre (fair market value $100,000) and common stocks (fair market value $100,000). Neither the will nor the trust document addresses the payment of O's debts following O's death, but there were unsecured debts of $100,000 at O's death. What is the most likely disposition of Blackacre and the stocks by reason of O's death?

ANSWER:

7. Refer to Question 6, but assume that O was married to S at the time O executed the trust agreement and will and also at the time of O's death. Also assume that, prior to O's death, O transferred to himself, as trustee of the trust, $100,000 cash still held in trust at O's death. Which answer best describes the legal advice you should give to S after S explains

to you that S has been apparently disinherited by O?

(A) Don't worry, the trust agreement and will are void.

(B) You are entitled to your marital share of the $100,000, Blackacre, and the stocks.

(C) You are entitled to your marital share of Blackacre and the stocks.

(D) You are entitled to your marital share of Blackacre.

8. S died last week. One year ago, S typed and signed a letter to S's brother, T. In the letter, S wrote that the family farm was being held in an irrevocable trust; S declared that S was serving as the trustee of the family farm and that S would continue to manage the farm as long as S could, paying S all the income from the farm each year. However, the letter explained that if S were ever unable or unwilling to continue as trustee, T would serve as trustee until S died and was to pay S any income the farm produced. At S's death, the terms of the letter direct T, as trustee, to convey the family farm to T, personally. Also, on that same day, S executed a will, which has now been admitted to probate. Under the terms of the will, S's estate is devised to G, the only child of S's only child, C. Despite the letter, record title to the farm remained in S's name, individually. Both G and C survived S. Which answer best describes the most likely disposition of the family farm after S's death?

(A) The family farm passes to G under S's will.

(B) The family farm passes to C as S's intestate heir.

(C) At S's death, the family farm passed to T as a nonprobate asset.

(D) T, as trustee, can convey legal title to T, individually.

9. Refer to Question 8, but assume that the terms of the letter provide that the trust was revocable by S at any time prior to S's death. There is no evidence that S ever intended to revoke the trust. Which answer best describes the most likely disposition of the family farm after S's death?

(A) The family farm passes to G under S's will.

(B) The family farm passes to C as S's intestate heir.

(C) At S's death, the family farm passed to T as a nonprobate asset.

(D) T, as trustee, can convey legal title to T, individually.

10. In 2013, S created a trust by executing an irrevocable trust agreement with S's sister, T. The assets of the trust consist of real and personal property; title is in T's name, as trustee. The beneficiaries are T's adult children, B1 and B2. B1 is entitled to all of the income for the rest of B1's lifetime; at B1's death, T is to deliver the trust estate to B2. After creating the trust, S became very ill and could not work. During S's illness, S fell significantly behind on the payment of many of his debts. Consequently, one of S's creditors has recently obtained a judgment against S and is trying to attach the assets of the trust. Which answer

best describes the legal advice you would give to T?

(A) The trust estate is not reachable by S's creditors unless they are tort creditors.

(B) The trust estate is not reachable by S's creditors.

(C) The trust estate may be reached by S's creditors.

(D) The trust estate is reachable by S's creditors.

11. Refer to Question 10, but assume that the trust agreement by its own terms was revocable by S. Assuming that S has never evidenced any intention to revoke the trust, which answer best describes the legal advice you would give to T?

(A) The trust estate is not reachable by S's creditors.

(B) The trust estate is not reachable by S's creditors unless they are tort creditors.

(C) The trust estate is reachable by S's creditors.

(D) The trust estate may be reached by S's creditors.

12. Refer to Question 11, and also assume that S had just died and that the judgment was obtained by S's creditor against S's personal representative. Which answer best describes the legal advice you would give to T?

(A) The trust estate is not reachable by S's creditors.

(B) The trust estate is reachable by S's creditors.

(C) The trust estate is not reachable by S's creditors unless they are tort creditors.

(D) The trust estate may be reached by S's creditors.

13. O created a trust that is revocable during O's lifetime but becomes irrevocable at O's death. The principal asset of the trust is O's home. O is the trustee. The trust provides that at O's death the home is to be delivered by the successor trustee to O's daughter, C. Which of the following best describes whether O made a gift for federal transfer tax purposes?

(A) O has not made a gift of the home to C. By retaining the power to revoke the trust, O has not parted with dominion and control over the home.

(B) O has made a gift of O's home to C.

(C) O has made a gift of a future interest in O's home to C.

(D) O has parted with dominion and control of O's home, but O has not made a gift.

14. Refer to Question 13. Would your answer be different if, prior to O's death, O resigned as trustee, and by the terms of the trust, C becomes the successor trustee?

ANSWER:

15. Refer to Question 14. At O's death, is O's home included in O's gross estate for federal estate tax purposes?

   (A) No, the home is excluded from the gross estate.

   (B) Yes, the home is included in the gross estate.

   (C) The fair market value of O's retained life estate is included in the gross estate.

   (D) The fair market value of C's remainder interest is included in the gross estate.

16. S created a revocable trust to pay income to S's child, C, for C's lifetime and then on C's death to distribute the principal to C's son, G. S is the original trustee and Big Bank and Trust is the successor trustee. In the current year, the trust has $5,000 of income, which the trustee distributes to C. Which of the following best describes the federal gift tax consequences of the described transactions?

   (A) S made a gift of the trust corpus to C and G when S created the trust.

   (B) S made a gift of a life estate to C when S created the trust.

   (C) S made a gift of $5,000 whenever the income is distributed to C.

   (D) S did not make a gift to C because S has the power to revoke the trust.

17. Refer to Question 16. Which is the best statement as to how the $5,000 income is taxed for federal *income* tax purposes?

   (A) The $5,000 income is taxable to S because he retained the power to revoke the trust.

   (B) The $5,000 income is taxable to S because he retained the power to revoke the trust. However, he will be entitled to a deduction since the $5,000 was distributed to C.

   (C) The $5,000 income is taxable to "the trust." However, "the trust" will be entitled to a deduction for the $5,000 distribution to C.

   (D) C1 will be taxable on the $5,000 income as C received the $5,000 distribution.

18. Refer to Question 16. True or False? Once a revocable trust has been created and funded by the settlor, the law of trusts governs the administration of the trust estate, and S, as trustee, will be held to the same fiduciary standards as Big Bank and Trust, if it were serving as the trustee. Explain your answer.

ANSWER:

19. A testator must have testamentary capacity to validly execute a will. Is testamentary capacity required for the creation and funding of a revocable trust intended to be a will substitute?

ANSWER:

20. A review of a validly executed and funded inter vivos trust agreement reveals that the terms of the agreement do not specify whether the trust is revocable or irrevocable by the settlor. Both the settlor and the trustee ask, "Is it a revocable trust?"

ANSWER:

1.   Explain the concept of testamentary power.

ANSWER:

2.   O, who is not married, died recently survived by two adult children, C1 and C2. In the presence of several friends, a competent O typed a letter addressed to both C1 and C2 stating that at O's death the home and its contents were to pass to C1. O explained to the friends what he was doing and then signed the letter. At all relevant times, O was a competent individual, and O's friends are willing to testify as to O's verbal statements. C1 and C2 did not receive the letter until after O's death. Which answer best explains the most likely disposition of O's home and its contents?

    (A) The house and contents pass to C1 and C2.

    (B) The house and its contents would pass to C1.

    (C) The house but not the contents would pass to C1.

    (D) The contents but not the house would pass to C1.

3.   Refer to Question 2. How would your answer differ if the letter would have been actually delivered to C1 and C2 prior to O's death?

    (A) The house and contents pass to C1 and C2.

    (B) The house and its contents would pass to C1.

    (C) The house but not the contents would pass to C1.

    (D) The contents but not the house would pass to C1.

4.   Refer to Question 2. How would your answer differ if the letter described would have been entirely in O's handwriting and signed by O?

    (A) The house and contents pass to C1 and C2.

    (B) The house and its contents would pass to C1.

    (C) The house but not the contents would pass to C1.

    (D) The contents but not the house would pass to C1

5.   A and B were two competent, unmarried sisters. A and B inherited Blackacre as tenants in common when their parent, O, died. Following O's death, A and B executed a single written document in 2000 meeting the requirements of a valid will. In this document, the first to die devises her interest in Blackacre to the other. In addition, the will devises Blackacre to their niece, C, upon the survivor's death. A has recently died survived by B, C, and D, who is C's mother and the sister of A and B. The family has discovered a validly executed will signed in 2010 by A that devises A's entire estate, including Blackacre, to F, a friend. Which answer best describes the most likely disposition of Blackacre by reason of A's death?

(A)   A's interest passes nonprobate to B.

(B)   B succeeds to A's interest pursuant to the 2000 will.

(C)   F succeeds to A's interest pursuant to the 2010 will.

(D)   F succeeds to A's interest pursuant to the 2010 will, and B has a breach of contract action against A's estate.

6.   Refer to Question 5. What would your answer be if the 2000 will included a provision stating that A and B agreed never to revoke the 2000 will?

ANSWER:

7.   Refer to Question 5. What would your answer be if the 2000 document had been a written agreement signed and acknowledged by A and B before a notary public providing that Blackacre would become the survivor's property upon the first of A or B to die?

(A)   A's interest passes nonprobate to B.

(B)   B succeeds to A's interest upon the probate of the 2000 document.

(C)   F succeeds to A's interest pursuant to the 2010 will.

(D)   F succeeds to A's interest pursuant to the 2010 will, and B has a breach of contract action against A's estate.

8.   S1 and S2 were married but had no children. In 2005, they executed new wills. S1's will leaves all of S1's property to S2, if S2 survives S1; and if S2 predeceases S1, all of S2's property is left to S2's niece, C. S2's will leaves all of S2's property to S1, if S1 survives S2, and if S1 predeceases S2, all of S2's property is left to S2's niece, C. S1 has recently died, and S1's 2005 will has been admitted to probate. S2 is seeking legal advice. S2 now wishes to devise S2's entire estate to D when S2 dies. D is the child of a friend of S2. What answer best describes the legal advice that should be given to S2?

(A)   You are free to devise the entire estate to anyone you choose.

(B)   You can devise the entire estate to D, but C may sue you for breach of contract.

    (C) You can devise the entire estate to D, but C may have a breach of contract action against your estate.

    (D) You cannot devise the entire estate to D. C inherited a remainder interest in S1's estate at S1's death that will become possessory at your death.

9.   Refer to Question 8. How would your answer differ if the 2005 wills both contained provisions stating that S1 and S2 agreed not to revoke the 2005 wills?

    (A) My answer would not change.

    (B) You can devise the entire estate to D, but C may sue you for breach of contract.

    (C) You can devise the entire estate to D, but C may have a breach of contract action against your estate.

    (D) You cannot devise the entire estate to D. C's remainder interest in S1's estate becomes a possessory fee interest when you die.

10.   Refer to Question 9. Which answer best describes the legal advice that should be given to S2 if C had died one week after S1's death? C never married and had no children; C's valid, probated will left C's estate to H.

    (A) You can probably devise the entire estate to anyone you choose.

    (B) You can probably devise the entire estate to D, but H may sue you for breach of contract.

    (C) You can probably devise the entire estate to D, but H may have a breach of contract action against your estate.

    (D) You cannot devise the entire estate to D. C's remainder interest in S1's estate was devised by C to H.

11.   Refer to Question 10. How would your answer differ if C would have been survived by a child, J?

    (A) My answer would not change.

    (B) You cannot devise the entire estate to D. C inherited a remainder interest in S1's estate at S1's death that was devised to H.

    (C) You can devise the entire estate to D, but J may sue you for breach of contract.

    (D) You can devise the entire estate to D, but J may have a breach of contract action against your estate.

12.   A and B were two competent, unmarried brothers who inherited Blackacre as joint tenants, not tenants in common, when their parent, O, died in 1999. Following O's death, A and B executed a single written document in 2000 meeting the requirements of a valid

will. In this document, the first to die devises his interest in Blackacre to the other. In addition, the joint will devises Blackacre to their nephew, C, upon the survivor's death.

A has recently died survived by B, C, and D, who is C's mother and the sister of A and B. The 2000 joint will included a provision stating that A and B agreed never to revoke the 2000 joint will. The family has discovered a validly executed will signed in 2010 by A that devises A's entire estate, including Blackacre, to F, a friend. Which answer best describes the most likely disposition of Blackacre by reason of A's death?

ANSWER:

13. Refer to Question 12. What answer best describes the most likely disposition of Blackacre if A's 2010 will devised Blackacre to F and the rest of A's estate equally to F and B?

   (A) A's interest in Blackacre would pass nonprobate to B.

   (B) A's interest in Blackacre passes nonprobate to B, but B cannot accept any benefits from A's estate unless B conveys A's one-half interest to F.

   (C) A's interest in Blackacre passes nonprobate to B, but B cannot accept any interest in A's estate unless B conveys all of Blackacre to F.

   (D) A's one-half interest in Blackacre passes to F.

14. Refer to Question 13. What would your answer be if B died one week before A, and B's 2005 valid will left all of B's estate to B's spouse, S, who B had married in 2005? B was also survived by a child, B1.

   (A) Blackacre passes to F, and the balance of A's estate passes equally to F and S.

   (B) Blackacre passes to F, and the balance of A's estate passes equally to F and B1.

   (C) The entire estate, including Blackacre, passes to F.

   (D) C will seek specific performance of the original contract between A and B.

15. O's validly executed will left "all of my property" to O's adult child, A. On the same day O executed the will, O changed the beneficiary of a life insurance policy from his deceased spouse to O's other adult child, B. O's most valuable assets are Blackacre and the $1,000,000 life insurance policy. Explain the most likely disposition of both assets upon O's death.

ANSWER:

16. Refer to Question 15. Would your answer differ if the will was executed by O five years after O had changed the beneficiary from O's deceased spouse to B?

ANSWER:

17. O's validly executed will, dated 2010, devised "any and all life insurance on O's life to child A, and the rest, residue and remainder of O's estate to child B." A and B were adults, children of a prior marriage of O. The only life insurance on O's life at the time of O's death was a $1,000,000 policy purchased in 2000 and made payable at O's death to O's spouse. O's spouse S, died in 2009 with a valid will leaving all of S's estate to S's child by a prior marriage, C. Which answer best describes the most likely disposition of the insurance proceeds upon O's death?

(A) The insurance company should pay the $1,000,000 to C as the devisee under S's will.

(B) The insurance company should pay the $1,000,000 to C pursuant to the substituted gift statute.

(C) The insurance company keeps the $1,000,000 since the designated beneficiary died before the insured.

(D) The $1,000,000 becomes part of O's probate estate and passes to A under the will.

18. Refer to Question 17. How would your answer differ if the policy would have been made payable to S, if S survived O, and if not, to B.

ANSWER:

19. S1 and S2 were married and resided in a non-UPC community property state. S1 has recently died. The significant assets are Blackacre, which was S1's separate property, Whiteacre, which was the community property of S1 and S2, and Greenacre, which was the separate property of S2. S1's valid will has been admitted to probate and devises "all of my property" to C, S1's child by a prior marriage. Which answer best explains the likely distributions of the three tracts of land?

(A) Blackacre passes to C; Whiteacre and Greenacre are retained by S2.

(B) Blackacre and Whiteacre pass to C; Greenacre is retained by S2.

(C) Blackacre and one-half of Whiteacre pass to C; S2 retains Greenacre and half of Whiteacre.

(D) One-half of both Blackacre and Whiteacre pass to C; W retains Greenacre and half of both Blackacre and Whiteacre.

20. Refer to Question 19. How would your answer differ if S1's will devised Whiteacre to C and the rest, residue and remainder of S1's interest to S2?

ANSWER:

Note: In this chapter, assume that a party, who would like the court to exercise its "dispensing power" and excuse O's "non-compliance" with the statutory requirements of will execution or revocation, cannot meet the burden of proof required in UPC § 2-503 (or a "substantial compliance" rule in a jurisdiction which has not adopted the Uniform Probate Code). These so-called "harmless error" statutes generally permit a court to admit a will to probate that was not executed with statutory formalities if the proponent can establish by clear and convincing evidence that the testator intended the document to be a will.

1.   What is a will?

ANSWER:

2.   O died recently survived by an adult child, A. O's apparently valid will (*i.e.*, a document in writing signed by O in the presence of three witnesses) leaves all of O's estate to O's live-in caretaker, F. O signed the will shortly after O's medical records indicate that O had been diagnosed with Alzheimer's disease. Which answer best explains whether the document will be admitted to probate?

(A)   The court will deny the will's probate due to the diagnosis of Alzheimer's.

(B)   The court will admit the will to probate unless A proves that O lacked the mental capacity to execute a will.

(C)   The court will admit the will to probate if F can prove that O had the capacity to execute a will, notwithstanding the Alzheimer diagnosis.

(D)   The court will admit the will to probate notwithstanding the diagnosis of Alzheimer's, since during O's lifetime a court had not determined that the Alzheimer's had rendered O incapacitated.

3.   Refer to Question 2. What would your answer be if the will had been executed after A had been appointed the guardian (conservator) of O?

(A)   The court will deny the will's probate due to the guardianship.

(B)   The court will admit the will to probate unless A proves that O lacked the mental capacity to execute a will.

(C)   The court will admit the will to probate if F can prove that O had the capacity to execute a will, notwithstanding the guardianship.

(D)   The court will admit the will to probate, notwithstanding the guardianship.

4.   Refer to Question 3. What would your answer be if shortly after the execution of the will A had been appointed the guardian (conservator) of O?

     (A)   The court will deny the will's probate due to the finding of incapacity in the guardianship proceeding.

     (B)   The court will admit the will to probate unless A proves that O lacked the mental capacity to execute a will.

     (C)   The court will admit the will to probate if F can prove that O had the capacity to execute a will, notwithstanding the guardianship.

     (D)   The court will admit the will to probate, notwithstanding the guardianship.

5.   Refer to Question 4. What would your answer be if one of the factors which motivated A to proceed with the guardianship of O was A's concern about an improper sexual relationship between O and F?

     (A)   If O had testamentary capacity, evidence of an improper relationship between O and F is irrelevant.

     (B)   Evidence of the improper relationship can only be used in the determination of O's testamentary capacity.

     (C)   Even if O had testamentary capacity, the will is invalid if A can prove F improperly influenced O during the execution of the will.

     (D)   Even if O had testamentary capacity, the will is still valid if F can prove that F did not improperly influence O during the execution of the will.

6.   O died recently survived by an adult child, A, and O's grandchild, B. O's apparently valid will (*i.e.*, a document in writing signed by O in the presence of three witnesses) leaves all of O's estate to O's grandchild, B. Assuming O had testamentary capacity, what would your answer be if O had been physically too weak to sign O's full name on the will and had written only O's first name rather than O's first and last names in the place provided in the will for the testator's full signature?

ANSWER:

7.   Refer to Question 6. What would your answer be if O had been physically too weak to sign even O's first name and had just been able to place an "X" in the place provided in the will for the testator's signature?

     (A)   Since O did not sign O's full name, the will cannot be admitted to probate.

     (B)   Even though O did not sign O's full name, the will can be admitted to probate.

(C) Even though O did not sign even part of O's full name, the will may be admitted to probate.

(D) Since O did not sign even part of O's name, the will cannot be admitted to probate.

8. Refer to question 6. What would your answer be if O had been physically too weak to sign the will in any way and asked one of the witnesses to sign the will on O's behalf? The witness signed O's name in the place provided in the will for the testator's signature while O was in the same room, but O was not in a position to actually see the witness sign the will.

(A) Since O did not sign his full name, the will cannot be admitted to probate.

(B) Since O did not sign anything, the will cannot be admitted to probate.

(C) Even though O did not sign anything, the will may be admitted to probate.

(D) I need to research the question.

9. O died recently survived by an adult child, C. O's apparently valid will (*i.e.*, a document in writing signed by O in the presence of three witnesses) leaves all of O's estate to O's live-in significant other, G. Assuming O had testamentary capacity, what would your answer be if the witnesses did not know the document they signed was O's will at the time they signed the will?

ANSWER:

10. Refer to Question 9. Assuming the witnesses knew the document was a will, how would your answer differ if the witnesses were not actually present when O signed the will?

(A) Since the witnesses did not see O sign the will, the will cannot be admitted to probate.

(B) Even if the witnesses did not see O sign the will, the will can be admitted to probate.

(C) Even if the witnesses did not see O sign the will, the will may be admitted to probate.

(D) I need to research the question.

11. Refer to Question 10. How would your answer differ if each witness signed the will but not while the other two witnesses were present?

ANSWER:

12. O died recently survived by an adult child, A. O's apparently valid will (*i.e.*, a document in writing signed by O in the presence of three witnesses) leaves all of O's estate to O's friend, F. Assuming O had testamentary capacity, if the witnesses observed a bedridden O sign the will before the witnesses signed the will on a table with their backs to O so that O was unable to observe them sign the will, is the will valid?

(A) Since O did not see the witnesses sign the will, the will cannot be admitted to probate.

(B) Even though O could not see the witnesses sign the will, the will can be admitted to probate.

(C) Even though O could not see the witnesses sign the will, the will may be admitted to probate.

(D) I need to research the question.

13. Refer to Question 12. How would your answer differ if the witnesses observed O sign the will but they did not sign the will until shortly after O's death?

ANSWER:

14. Refer to Question 12. O died recently survived by an adult child, C, and a grandchild, B. O's apparently valid will (*i.e.*, a document in writing signed by O in the presence of witnesses) leaves all of O's estate to O's grandchild, B. Assuming O had testamentary capacity, how would your answer differ if there had been only two witnesses rather than three?

(A) Since there were only two witnesses, the will cannot be admitted to probate.

(B) Because there were at least two witnesses, the will can be admitted to probate.

(C) Because there were at least two witnesses, the will may be admitted to probate.

(D) I need to research the question.

15. Refer to Question 14. How would your answer differ if the will form used by a non-lawyer friend of O who typed the will provided for O to sign the will only in a blank space in the first sentence of the will (*i.e.*, "I, _____, hereby declare this document to be my last will.")? The witnesses signed at the end of the document.

(A) Since a will must be signed at its end by the testator, the will cannot be admitted to probate.

(B) Even if the testator did not sign at the end of the will, the will can be admitted to probate.

(C) Even if the testator did not sign at the end of the will, the will may be admitted to probate.

(D) I need to research the question.

16. O died recently survived by three descendants — two adult children, C1 and C2, and C1's child, G. In 2000, O, being disappointed in C2, executed a valid attested will prepared by O's lawyer that left O's estate to C1. Shortly before O's death, a fully competent O e-mailed the lawyer. In the e-mail, O explained that O was now extremely disappointed in both C1 and C2 and that O wanted all of O's property to pass to G when O died. O then instructed

the lawyer in the e-mail to "formalize" O's wishes. The lawyer prepared a new will for O leaving all of O's estate to G, but O died before O had an opportunity to execute the new will. Who is most likely to succeed to O's estate under the circumstances?

ANSWER:

17. Refer to Question 16. What would your answer be if O's message to the lawyer would have been in a typewritten letter dated by O, signed by O, and mailed by O to the lawyer?

   (A) C1 and C2.

   (B) C1

   (C) G

   (D) C2 and G.

18. Refer to Question 16. What would your answer be if the message to the lawyer would have been in a handwritten note written by O, dated by O, and signed by O and then mailed to the lawyer?

   (A) C1 and C2.

   (B) C1.

   (C) G.

   (D) C2 and G.

19. Refer to Question 16. What would your answer be if, following O's death, a typewritten document, dated shortly before O's death and signed only by O, was found in O's safe deposit box, along with the original of the 2000 will? The document simply stated, "At my death I leave all my property to G."

   (A) C1 and C2.

   (B) C1.

   (C) G.

   (D) C2 and G.

20. Refer to Question 19. What would your answer be if the document found in the safe deposit box would have been entirely in O's handwriting, dated by O, and signed by O, all shortly before O's death?

ANSWER:

21. Refer to Question 20. What would your answer be if the handwritten document signed by O had been written by O on hotel stationery? The date was filled in by O at the top of the page immediately below the name and address of the hotel, where the preprinted form provided "_____ ___, 20__ ." O filled in the month and day and the last two digits of the year.

    (A) C1 and C2.

    (B) C1.

    (C) G.

    (D) C2 and G.

22. O died recently survived by two adult children, A and B. In 2010, O, being disappointed in B, executed a valid attested will prepared by O's lawyer that left O's estate to A. However, the 2010 will was discovered after O's death in O's safe deposit box with an "X" marked across the signature of O. Who is likely to receive O's estate?

ANSWER:

23. O died recently survived by his only descendants — two adult children, C1 and C2, and C1's child, G. In 2000, O, being disappointed in C2, executed a valid attested will prepared by O's lawyer that left O's estate to C1. O's lawyer retained the original of the 2000 will. O later telephoned the lawyer explaining that O wanted all of O's property to go to G when O died and instructed the lawyer to (i) retrieve the 2000 will from the firm's vault and destroy it and (ii) draft a new will leaving all of O's property to G? The lawyer immediately photocopied and then destroyed the 2000 will and later prepared the new will, but O did not sign it before O died. Who is likely to receive O's estate?

    (A) C1 and C2.

    (B) C1.

    (C) G.

    (D) C2 and G.

24. Refer to Question 23 What would your answer be if O had validly executed the new will leaving all of O's property to G and O had physically destroyed the 2000 will? However, shortly prior to O's death, upset over the news that G, a U.S. Marine, had been killed in action in Afghanistan, O destroyed the will in favor of G. Unfortunately, O died prior to receiving the news that G had not died but had been taken prisoner and had just been rescued.

ANSWER:

25. O died recently survived by one adult child, C, and several cousins. In 1990, because O was estranged from C, O validly executed a typewritten, witnessed will leaving all of O's estate to a friend, A. In 2000, O validly executed a new typewritten, witnessed will expressly revoking all prior wills and leaving all of O's property to another friend, B. Before O's death, while O was angry with B, and while several friends were present, a competent O intentionally destroyed the 2000 will by tossing it in a fire in the fireplace and told the friends that O wanted the estate to pass to A when O died. The 1990 will is still located in O's safe deposit box. O had never reconciled with C. Which answer best describes who is most likely to succeed to O's estate?

(A) C.

(B) A.

(C) B.

(D) The cousins.

26. Refer to Question 25. Who is likely to succeed to O's estate if the 2000 will had not expressly revoked all earlier wills and had simply left all of O's estate to B?

(A) C.

(B) A.

(C) B.

(D) The cousins.

27. Refer to Question 26. Who is likely to succeed to O's estate if the 2000 document had not been a typewritten witnessed will, but a document entirely in O's handwriting and signed by O.

(A) C.

(B) A.

(C) B

(D) The cousins.

28. Refer to Question 25. Who is likely to succeed to O's estate if, after the 1990 will had been executed, O had left the original 1990 will with the lawyer, and the lawyer destroyed the 1990 will in 2001 when the lawyer was cleaning out the lawyer's file room? The lawyer will testify that the lawyer thought retention of the original was unnecessary because the 1990 will had been revoked when the 2000 will was executed by O.

ANSWER:

29. O died recently survived by one adult child, C, and several siblings. In 1990, because O was estranged from C, O validly executed a typewritten, witnessed will leaving all of O's estate to a friend, A. The original 1990 will has not been found. O's lawyer will testify that, after the 1990 will had been executed, O took the original, explaining that O was going to place the original in O's desk at home. Which answer best describes who is most likely to succeed to O's estate?

(A) C.

(B) A.

(C) The oldest sibling.

(D) All the siblings.

30. Refer to Question 29. Who is likely to succeed to O's estate if the evidence reveals that a competent but bedridden O had not personally destroyed the 1990 will but had asked O's nurse to destroy the will? The nurse found the 1990 will in a desk in O's study, returned to the bedroom, and while O was watching, tore the will into multiple pieces and tossed the 1990 will into a trash can.

(A) C.

(B) A.

(C) The oldest sibling.

(D) All the siblings.

31. O died recently. O was survived by O's two adult children, C1 and C2, and C1's child, G. Shortly before O died, angry with both children, a competent O phoned O's lawyer to prepare a will leaving all of O's property to G. The lawyer prepared the will and phoned O to advise that the will was ready for execution. Dependent on C1 for transportation, O asked C1 to take O to the lawyer's office in order to take care of "a few matters." Unknown to O, C1 had overheard O's telephone conversation with the lawyer and continued to postpone the trip to the lawyer's office. O died without ever executing the will. There were no earlier wills. What is the most likely disposition of O's estate?

ANSWER:

32. O died recently, survived by one child, C, and C's two children, G1 and G2. Shortly before O died, while C was out of town, G1, using physical threats, forced a competent but physically weak, O to sign a typewritten will that G1 had prepared. Two of G1's friends were present and signed the will as the witnesses. The will purports to devise O's estate to G1 and G2. One of the witnesses has had a change of heart and is willing to testify as to what occurred. Which answer best explains the most likely disposition of O's estate?

(A) The will can be admitted to probate; G1 and G2 take.

(B) The will cannot be admitted to probate; C takes.

(C) The will can be admitted to probate, but C may take the entire estate anyway.

(D) The will can be admitted to probate, but C may take G1's half of the estate.

33. O died recently survived by O's two children, C1 and C2, and C2's child, G. O had validly executed a will leaving all of O's property to G at a time when a competent O was angry with both children. Shortly prior to O's death, having been threatened with physical harm by C1, a competent but bedridden O directed a nurse to retrieve the will from the study. The nurse brought the will to O, and O tore the will into many pieces. Unknown to C1, the nurse had overheard C1's physical threats. Which answer best explains the most likely disposition of O's estate?

(A) The will can be admitted to probate; G takes.

(B) The will cannot be admitted to probate; C1 and C2 take.

(C) The will cannot be admitted to probate, but G may take the entire estate.

(D) The will cannot be admitted to probate, but G may take C1's half of the estate.

34. O died recently survived by a child, C, and C's two children, G1 and G2. O had validly executed a will whereby O left O's entire estate to G1 and G2. Shortly prior to O's death, a competent but bedridden O directed O's nurse to retrieve the will from O's desk located in O's study so that O could destroy the will. Unknown to O, G1 overheard O's instructions to the nurse and substituted a photocopy of the will for the original will before the nurse could retrieve it. Neither O nor the nurse noticed the "switch." O died shortly after destroying the photocopy of the will. Which answer best explains the most likely disposition of O's estate?

(A) The will may be admitted to probate; G1 and G2 take.

(B) The will cannot be admitted to probate; C takes.

(C) The will can be admitted to probate, but C may take.

(D) The will may be admitted to probate, but C may take G1's half of the estate.

35. O died recently. O was survived by O's children, C1 and C2, and O's grandchildren, G1 and G2. O had validly executed a typewritten witnessed will leaving all of O's property to G1 and G2. Near the time O was diagnosed with Alzheimer's, O, in the presence of two family friends, destroyed the will, explaining to the friends that O had reconciled with C1 and C2. Explain the most likely disposition of O's estate.

ANSWER:

36. Refer to Question 35 and assume that O had testamentary capacity and that O had not destroyed the old will but had, in O's own handwriting, written the following note, "I hereby

revoke all prior wills and leave all my property to C1." O signed the note while two family friends watched, explaining O had reconciled with C1. Which answer best explains who is likely to succeed to O's estate?

(A) G1 and G2.

(B) C1 and C2.

(C) C1 and G2.

(D) C1.

37. Refer to Question 36. What would your answer be if the note written and signed by O would have simply said, "I revoke all of my prior wills"?

(A) G1 and G2.

(B) C1 and C2.

(C) C1 and G2.

(D) C1.

38. O died recently. O was survived by O's spouse, S, and O's parents, M and F; O never had any children. O's will was validly executed prior to O's marriage to S; O never changed the will. It devises O's entire estate to M and F. Did O's marriage to S revoke the will?

ANSWER:

39. Refer to Question 38. How would your answer differ if the will had been executed during the marriage of O and S?

(A) The will can be admitted to probate; the entire estate passes to M and F.

(B) The will cannot be admitted to probate; the entire estate passes to S.

(C) The will can be admitted to probate; S will be entitled to S's marital share, if any, and M and F will succeed to everything else.

(D) The will cannot be admitted to probate; the estate will be shared by S, M, and F.

40. O died recently. O was survived by O's parents, M and F. O was divorced from O's spouse, S, two years prior to O's death. After the divorce, O did not change the will that O had executed while married to S and that left all of O's property to S. What is the most likely disposition of O's estate?

ANSWER:

1.　Explain how will interpretation differs from will construction.

ANSWER:

2.　O died recently. O was survived by an independent adult child, C. O's valid, probated will leaves to C all of O's property, including personal property and unimproved real property. After O's death, the court-appointed personal representative determined that the fair market value of O's estate was $100,000. It was also determined that O owed unsecured contractual creditors $25,000 and tort creditors $50,000; the expenses of O's last illness were $25,000. Which answer best explains how O's assets will likely be distributed?

(A)　All of the assets will be sold to pay the creditors.

(B)　Only the personal property can be sold to pay the creditors on a pro rata basis.

(C)　All of the assets will be sold to pay the tort creditors and the last illness expenses.

(D)　Only the personal property can be sold in order to pay the tort creditors and the last illness expenses on a pro rata basis.

3.　Refer to Question 2. How would your answer differ if C was a minor at the time of O's death?

ANSWER:

4.　Refer to Question 2. How would your answer differ if O had also been survived by S, O's second spouse who was not a parent of C, and the only real estate owned by O was the home where O and S resided?

(A)　The home will likely be sold to pay the creditors.

(B)　The home will not be sold to pay the debts, and C will inherit the home.

(C)　The home will not be sold to pay the debts, and S will inherit the home.

(D)　The home will not be sold to pay the debts and will be owned by C, but S will have a right to live there.

5.　O died recently. O was survived by two independent adult children, S and D. O's valid will has been admitted to probate; it simply states, "I devise my home to S and the rest, residue, and remainder of my estate to D." At the time of O's death, the significant assets of the estate consisted of the home (fair market value of $100,000) and shares of a New York Stock Exchange company (fair market value of $100,000). The only debt or expense of O's estate is a note signed by O and secured by the home; the outstanding balance of the debt at the time of death was $50,000. The will does not direct how the decedent's debts are to be paid. Which answer best explains the most likely disposition of O's estate?

(A) S receives the home, subject to the outstanding indebtedness, and D receives all of the shares of stock.

(B) S receives the home, free of any indebtedness, and D receives only the shares of stock remaining after enough shares are sold to pay the debt.

(C) Half of the debt should be paid by S, or out of the sales proceeds of the home, and the other half of the debt should be paid out of the sales proceeds of part of the stock.

(D) The answer depends on the decisions the creditor makes after O's death.

6. Refer to Question 5. How would your answer differ if the $50,000 debt was not a note secured by the home but an unsecured debt of $50,000 owing by O at the time of O's death?

(A) S receives the home, free of any indebtedness, and D receives only the stock remaining after the debt is paid.

(B) D would receive the stock, and the home would be sold in order to pay the debt with S receiving the balance of the proceeds of the sale after the debt is paid.

(C) Half of the debt should be paid by S, or out of the sales proceeds of the home, and the other one-half of the debt should be paid by D, or out of the sales proceeds of part of the stock.

(D) The answer depends on the intention of the creditor after O's death.

7. O died recently. O was survived by three independent adult children, A, B, and C. At the time of O's death, O's estate consisted of O's home and the home's contents (fair market value of $100,000), stocks and bonds (fair market value of $100,000), and $100,000 cash. At the time of O's death, there were outstanding unsecured debts of $100,000. O's valid will has been admitted to probate, and the will devises the home and its contents to A, $100,000 to B, and the rest, residue, and remainder of O's estate to C. Which of the described assets should be used by the executor to satisfy the debts?

ANSWER:

8. Refer to Question 7, but assume the will devises $100,000 to B, the stocks and bonds to C, and the rest, residue, and remainder of O's estate to A. Which answer best describes the assets the executor should use to satisfy the debts?

(A) The home and its contents.

(B) Cash.

(C) The stocks and bonds.

(D) A third of the home and its contents, a third of the cash and a third of the stocks and bonds.

9. Refer to Question 7, but assume the will devises $100,000 to B and the rest, residue, and remainder of O's estate to A and C. Which answer best describes the assets the executor should use to satisfy the debts?

(A) Cash.

(B) Half of the home and its contents and half of the stocks and bonds.

(C) The home and its contents.

(D) The stocks and bonds.

10. O died recently. O was survived by three independent adult children, A, B, and C. A's valid, probated will, dated 1990, devises all of O's Exxon stock to A, Blackacre to B, and the rest, residue, and remainder of O's estate to C. Following the execution of the will, O sold Blackacre and immediately used the sales proceeds to purchase Whiteacre. O's home was originally located on Blackacre and then he moved into a house on Whiteacre. When Exxon and Mobil merged in 1998, O's Exxon stock was exchanged for shares of stock in ExxonMobil. At the time of O's death, the significant assets of O were Whiteacre, the ExxonMobil stock, and just enough cash to pay O's debts and the administration expenses. Which answer best describes the disposition of the ExxonMobil stock and Whiteacre?

(A) The ExxonMobil stock passes to A, and Whiteacre passes to B.

(B) The ExxonMobil stock passes to A, and Whiteacre passes to C.

(C) The ExxonMobil stock passes to C, and Whiteacre to passes B.

(D) The ExxonMobil stock and Whiteacre pass to C.

11. O died recently. O was survived by O's three independent adult children, A, B, and C. O's valid will has been admitted to probate, and the will devises O's Cadillac to A, $100,000 to B, and the rest, residue, and remainder of O's estate to C. At the time O executed the will, O's significant assets consisted of the Cadillac (fair market value of $50,000), cash ($100,000), stocks and bonds (fair market value of $100,000), and a home (fair market value of $100,000). Immediately prior to O's death, the Cadillac had a fair market value of $25,000; there was no cash remaining, the stocks and bonds had declined in value to only $10,000, and the home had declined in value to $65,000. O died in a one-car automobile accident while driving the Cadillac, and O's insurance company has recently paid O's executor $25,000 in order to "total" the car ($24,000 for replacement value, $1,000 salvage value). The debts, all unsecured, and the administration expenses totaled $50,000. Explain the likely disposition of the remaining assets of O's estate.

ANSWER:

12. O died recently. O was survived by O's three independent adult children, A, B, and C. O's valid will has been admitted to probate. The will directs that $10,000 is to be paid to A, and the rest, residue, and remainder of O's estate is to pass equally to B and C. After the execution of the will and six months prior to O's death, O made a gift of $10,000 to A and another gift of $10,000 to B. At the time of O's death, O's estate consisted primarily of cash with a total value of $100,000 after the debts were paid. Which answer best describes the most likely disposition of the remaining assets of O's estate?

(A) $10,000 to A, $45,000 to B, and $45,000 to C.

(B) $50,000 to B and $50,000 to C.

(C) $10,000 to A, $40,000 to B, and $50,000 to C.

(D) $45,000 to B and $55,000 to C.

13. Refer to Question 12, but assume that the $10,000 "given" to B was actually a loan by O that had not been repaid by B prior to O's death and that O's estate is insolvent (*i.e.*, O's debts exceed the described assets by $10,000). Which answer best describes the effect the outstanding loan will have on the administration of O's estate?

(A) It has no effect; O's death extinguished the debt.

(B) B must repay the entire debt.

(C) B must repay half of the debt.

(D) B must pay A $10,000.

14. Refer to Question 13, but assume that, at the time of O's death, O's estate was solvent (*i.e.*, the value of the non-exempt liquid assets exceed the debts by more than $10,000). Which answer best describes the effect the outstanding loan will have on the administration of O's estate?

(A) It has no effect; O's death extinguished the debt.

(B) B must repay the entire debt.

(C) B must repay half of the debt.

(D) Although B does not have to repay the debt, B's share of the estate will be reduced by half of the amount of the debt.

15. Refer to Question 13, but assume that the loan from O to B occurred more than ten years prior to O's death. What effect would the outstanding loan have on the administration of O's estate?

(A) It has no effect.

(B) B must repay the entire debt.

    (C) B must repay half of the entire debt.

    (D) Although B does not have to repay the debt, B's share of the estate will be reduced by half of the amount of the debt.

16.   Refer to Question 14, but assume that the loan from O to B occurred more than 10 years prior to O's death. Which answer best explains the effect the loan will have on the administration of O's estate?

    (A) It has no effect.

    (B) B must repay the entire debt.

    (C) B must repay half of the entire debt.

    (D) Although B does not have to repay the debt, B's share of the estate will be reduced by half of the amount of the debt.

17.   O died recently. At the time O executed O's will, O had three independent adult children, A, B, and C. O's valid will has been admitted to probate, and the will devises Blackacre to A, Whiteacre to B, and the rest, residue and remainder of O's estate to C. A predeceased O. B died one day after O. C died one week after O. O was also survived by several cousins. Each child of O had a valid, probated will that devised that child's estate to that child's spouse. O's children never had any children. What is the most likely disposition of O's estate?

ANSWER:

18.   Refer to Question 17, but assume that A was also survived by a child, A1, that B was also survived by a child, B1, and that C was also survived by a child, C1. A1, B1, and C1 are adults. Which answer best describes the most likely disposition of O's estate?

    (A) Blackacre passes to A's spouse and A1; Whiteacre passes to B's spouse and B1; the rest, residue, and remainder passes to C's spouse.

    (B) Blackacre passes to A1; Whiteacre passes to B1; the rest, residue, and remainder passes to C1.

    (C) Blackacre passes to A1; Whiteacre passes to B's spouse; the rest, residue, and remainder passes to C's spouse.

    (D) Blackacre passes to A1; Whiteacre passes to B1; the rest, residue, and remainder passes to C's spouse.

19.   Refer to Question 17, but assume that A, B, and C all died before O died. The children's spouses survived O. Which answer best describes the most likely disposition of O's estate?

    (A) Blackacre passes to A's spouse; Whiteacre passes to B's spouse; the rest, residue, and remainder passes to C's spouse.

(B)   Blackacre passes to A's spouse; Whiteacre passes to B's spouse; the rest, residue, and remainder passes to the cousins.

(C)   Blackacre and Whiteacre pass to the cousins; the rest, residue, and remainder passes to C's spouse.

(D)   The entire estate passes to the cousins.

20.   O died recently. O was survived by O's independent adult daughter, D. At the time O executed O's will, O had a close friend, F, who had three children, A, B, and C. O's valid will has been admitted to probate and devises Blackacre to A, Whiteacre to B, and the rest, residue, and remainder of the estate to C. A, B, and C predeceased O. The wills of A and B devised that child's estate to that child's surviving spouse. Each of A, B, and C had a child. What is the most likely disposition of O's estate following formal administration?

ANSWER:

21.   O died recently. O was survived by an independent adult child, D. Another child of O, S, died several years before O died; S was survived by S's children, A, B, and C. O's valid will has been admitted to probate and simply says, "I devise all of my property equally to A, B, and C." A died one day before O died; A was survived by A's spouse, who is the sole beneficiary of A's will, and A's child, A1. B died one day after O died; B was survived by B's spouse, who is the beneficiary of B's will, and B's child, B1. C survived O. Which answer best explains the most likely disposition of O's estate?

(A)   The entire estate passes to C.

(B)   A third passes to A's spouse, a third passes to B's spouse and a third passes to C.

(C)   A third passes to A1, a third passes to B1 and a third passes to C.

(D)   Two-thirds pass to C and D, and one-third passes to C.

22.   Refer to Question 21, but assume A and B were not survived by any children. Which answer best describes the most likely disposition of O's estate?

(A)   The entire estate passes to C.

(B)   A third passes to A's spouse, a third passes to B's spouse and a third passes to C.

(C)   One-third passes to B's spouse, and two-thirds pass to C.

(D)   One-third passes to C, and two-thirds pass to D and C.

23.   Refer to Question 21. How would your answer differ if S would have had another child after the execution of the will and before S died? This child, E, survived O.

(A)   My answer would not change.

    (B) E and C would share a third of the estate.

    (C) E and C would share a half of the estate.

    (D) A1, B1, C, and E would share the estate equally.

24. O died recently. O was survived by an independent adult child, D. Another child of O, S, died several years before O died; S was survived by S's children, A, B, and C. O's valid will has been admitted to probate and simply says, "I devise all of my property to my grandchildren." A died one day before O died; A was survived by A's spouse, who is the sole beneficiary of A's will, and A's child, A1. B died one day after O died; B was survived by B's spouse, who is the beneficiary of B's will, and B's child, B1. C survived O. Which answer best describes the most likely disposition of O's estate?

    (A) A third passes to A1, a third passes to B1 and a third passes to C.

    (B) A third passes to A1, a third passes to B's spouse and a third passes to C.

    (C) The entire estate passes to C.

    (D) Two-thirds pass to D, and one-third passes to C.

25. Refer to Question 24. How would your answer differ if S would have had another child, E, before S died, and E had survived O?

    (A) My answer would not change.

    (B) E and C would share a third of the estate.

    (C) E and C would share a half of the estate.

    (D) A1, B1, C, and E would share the estate equally.

26. Refer to Question 24, but assume that O's will states, "I devise all of my property to my grandchildren who survive me." What is the most likely disposition of the estate?

ANSWER:

27. O died recently. O was survived by an independent adult child, D. Another child of O, S, died several years before O died; S was survived by S's children, A, B, and C. O's valid will has been admitted to probate and simply says, "I devise all of my property to my grandchildren." A died one day before O died; A was survived by A's spouse, who is the sole beneficiary of A's will. B died one day after O died; B was survived by B's spouse, who is the beneficiary of B's will. C survived O. Which answer would best describe the most likely disposition of O's estate?

    (A) The entire estate passes to C.

    (B) Two-thirds pass to D, and one-third passes to C.

(C)   One-half passes to D, and one-half passes to C.

(D)   One-third passes to A's spouse, one-third passes to B's spouse and one-third passes to C.

28.   O died recently. O was survived by an independent adult child, D. Another child of O, S, died several years before O died; S was survived by S's stepchildren, A, B, and C, the children of S's spouse by a prior marriage. O's valid will has been admitted to probate and simply says, "I devise all of my property to A, B and C." A died one day before O died; A was survived by A's spouse, who is the sole beneficiary of A's will, and A's child, A1. B died one day after O died; B was survived by B's spouse, who is the beneficiary of B's will, and B's child, B1. C survived O. S never adopted A, B, and C. Which answer best describes the most likely disposition of O's estate?

(A)   The entire estate passes to D.

(B)   Two-thirds pass to D, and one-third passes to C.

(C)   One-third passes to A1, one-third passes to B1 and one-third passes to C.

(D)   The entire estate passes to C.

29.   How would your answer in Question 28 differ if (i) O's will would have devised the estate to "O's grandchildren," and (ii) A, B, and C had survived O by 120 hours? Witnesses will testify that O referred to A, B, and C as "grandchildren" and treated them as "grandchildren" even after S's death. Which answer best describes the most likely disposition of O's estate?

ANSWER:

30.   O died. O was survived by O's only child, C, an independent adult, and C's only child, G. O's valid will has been admitted to probate and devises Blackacre to G and the rest, residue, and remainder of O's estate to a charity. Due to G's serious financial difficulties, G filed a valid disclaimer in the probate proceedings of O's estate. G was not married and did not have any children. What is the likely disposition of Blackacre?

ANSWER:

31.   O died recently. O was survived by O's only child, D, an independent adult. A, B, and C were friends of O. O's valid will has been admitted to probate, and the will provides that (i) the stock certificates located in O's safe deposit box are devised to A, (ii) the jewelry listed on O's homeowner's insurance policy is devised to B, (iii) any other personal property is to be distributed by the executor pursuant to the instructions the testator intends to leave in a memo that will be attached to the will, and (iv) the rest, residue, and remainder of O's estate is devised to D. A memo was attached to the will at the time O died. The memo was dated several months after the execution of the will and indicated that certain described items of tangible personal property were to be delivered to C by the executor. This memo

was typewritten and signed by O. Which answer best describes the most likely disposition of the stock certificates located in the safe deposit box, the jewelry listed on the insurance policy, and the items of personal property described in the memo?

(A) The stock, jewelry, and personal property pass to D.

(B) The stock passes to A; the jewelry passes to B; and the other items of tangible personal property pass to C.

(C) The stock passes to A; the jewelry passes to B; and the other items of tangible personal property pass to D.

(D) The stock passes to A, and the jewelry and the other items of tangible personal property pass to D.

32. O died recently. O was survived by O's independent adult child, C, and C's child, G. O's valid will has been admitted to probate. O's will devises Blackacre to F, a friend of O, and the rest, residue, and remainder of O's estate to a charity. However, other friends of both F and O will testify that O and F had orally agreed, prior to O's execution of the will, that F would manage Blackacre for C during C's lifetime, paying C any income generated, and that at C's death, F would convey Blackacre to G. What is the most likely disposition of Blackacre?

ANSWER:

33. Refer to Question 32, but assume that the agreement between O and F had been memorialized in a written agreement signed by both F and O at the time the will was signed. What is the most likely disposition of Blackacre?

(A) An express trust has been created with F, as trustee, and C and G, as the beneficiaries.

(B) F acquired fee simple title to Blackacre since the terms of the agreement are not in the will.

(C) C, as O's sole heir, or the charity will have the court impose a resulting trust on F in favor of C since O's attempt to create an express trust failed.

(D) The court will impose a constructive trust on F in favor of C and/or G in order to avoid unjust enrichment by F.

34. Refer to Question 32, but assume O's will had devised Blackacre to "F as trustee." Which answer best describes the most likely disposition of Blackacre?

(A) An express trust has been created with F, as trustee, and C and G, as the beneficiaries.

(B) The charity will acquire fee simple title to Blackacre since the terms of the agreement are not in the will.

    (C) C, as O's sole heir, will have the court impose a resulting trust on F in favor of C since O's attempt to create an express trust failed.

    (D) The court will impose a constructive trust on F in favor of C and/or G in order to avoid unjust enrichment on the part of F and/or the charity.

35. Refer to Question 34 and assume that O's will had devised Blackacre to "F as trustee" but there is no evidence of (i) any agreement existing between O and F prior to O's death related to the disposition of Blackacre or (ii) what O intended F to do with the property. Which answer best describes the most likely disposition of Blackacre following O's death?

    (A) An express trust has been created with F, as trustee, and the charity, as the beneficiary.

    (B) The charity acquired fee simple title to Blackacre.

    (C) C, as O's sole heir, will have the court impose a resulting trust on Blackacre in favor of C.

    (D) F acquired fee simple title to Blackacre.

36. O died recently. O was survived by O's independent adult child, C, and C's child, G. O's valid will has been admitted to probate. O's will devises Blackacre to "F in trust for C and G," and the rest, residue and remainder of O's estate to a charity. However, other friends of both F and O will testify that O and F had orally agreed, prior to O's execution of the will, that F would manage Blackacre for C during C's lifetime, paying C any income generated, and that at C's death, F would convey Blackacre to G. What is the most likely disposition of Blackacre?

ANSWER:

37. Refer to Question 36, but assume that there is no evidence of (i) any agreement existing between O and A prior to O's death related to the disposition of Blackacre or (ii) what O intended F to do with the property. Which answer best describes the most likely disposition of Blackacre following formal administration of O's estate?

    (A) An express trust has been created with F, as trustee, and C and G, as the beneficiaries.

    (B) The charity acquired fee simple title to Blackacre.

    (C) C, as O's sole heir, will have the court impose a resulting trust on Blackacre in favor of C.

    (D) C and G acquired fee simple title.

38. O died recently survived by G, the only child of O's sister-in-law, C. O's valid will has been admitted to probate. O's will devises Blackacre to F, a friend of O, and the rest, residue and remainder of O's estate to a charity. Friends of both F and O will testify that O and F had

orally agreed, prior to O's execution of the will, that F would manage Blackacre for C during C's lifetime, paying C any income generated, and that at C's death, F would convey Blackacre to G. C died one day prior to O. C was survived by a spouse, S, as well as G and one other child of C, G2. C's valid will has been admitted to probate and devises all of C's property to S. Which answer best describes the most likely disposition of Blackacre following formal administration of O's estate?

(A) An express trust has been created with F, as trustee, and G, as beneficiary.

(B) F acquired fee simple title to Blackacre since the terms of the agreement are impossible to complete.

(C) G and G2, as O's heirs, will have the court impose a resulting trust on F in favor of G and G2 since O's attempt to create an express trust failed.

(D) G will have the court impose a constructive trust on F in favor of G in order to avoid unjust enrichment by F.

39. Refer to Question 38, but assume both C and G died prior to O. C was survived by C's spouse, S, and C's valid will has been admitted to probate and devises all of C's property to S. G was survived by G's spouse, GS, and one child, GG; G's valid will has been admitted to probate and devises all of G's property to GS. Which answer best describes the most likely disposition of Blackacre following formal administration of O's estate?

(A) GS will have the court impose a constructive trust on F to avoid unjust enrichment.

(B) GG will have the court impose a constructive trust on F to avoid unjust enrichment.

(C) The charity will have the court impose a constructive trust on F to avoid unjust enrichment.

(D) F retains the fee simple title.

40. Refer to Question 38, but assume both C and G survived O and F died one day prior to O. F was survived by F's spouse, S, and one child, F1. F's valid will has been admitted to probate and devises all of F's property to S. What is the most likely disposition of Blackacre following the administration of O's estate?

(A) C and G will have the court impose a constructive trust on F's spouse to avoid unjust enrichment.

(B) C and G will have the court impose a constructive trust on F's child to avoid unjust enrichment.

(C) C will have the court impose a resulting trust on the charity since the attempt to create an express trust failed.

(D) The charity acquired Blackacre.

41. Refer to Question 38, but assume C, G and F survived O. You are F's lawyer. F has

informed you that F acknowledges that F and O had the oral agreement but that F does not want to assume the responsibility of managing Blackacre for C and G. Which answer best describes the legal advice that should be given to F under these circumstances?

(A) You can disclaim, and the title will vest in the charity.

(B) You can disclaim, and the title will vest in C.

(C) You can accept the legal title to Blackacre and then simply convey Blackacre to C and G.

(D) You can disclaim, and the court will appoint a successor trustee to manage the express trust.

42. Refer to Question 41, but assume that the property subject to the oral agreement and devised to F in O's will was common stock in a publicly-held corporation, not Blackacre. What advice should be given to F?

ANSWER:

IDENTIFICATION OF HEIRS/INTESTATE SUCCESSION

1. Is it possible that the property of a decedent may pass by intestate succession to the decedent's heirs even though the decedent had a validly executed, unrevoked will at the time of death?

ANSWER:

2. O died recently. O was not married and did not have any children. O was survived by O's parents, M and D, as well as S1 and S2, two other children born to M and D, and two other siblings, S3, who is D's child from a prior marriage, and S4, who is M's child from a prior marriage. O executed a will that leaves all of O's property to F, a friend. O had not had any contact with the members of O's family for years due to the family's disapproval of O's relationship with F. F has filed the will for probate. Which answer best describes the members of O's family who have standing to contest the will?

    (A) M and D.

    (B) S1, S2, S3, and S4, as well as M and D.

    (C) S1 and S2, as well as M and D.

    (D) Proof of the strained relationship of O to O's family revokes the family's standing to contest the will.

3. O died recently. O was not married and did not have any children or siblings. O was survived by O's divorced parents, H and W. H is currently married to W2, and W is currently married to H2. Additionally, the parents of H, W, W2, and H2, as well as siblings of H, W, W2, and H2, plus a number of descendants of those siblings, survived O. O had maintained a close relationship with O's parents and their spouses and extended families, but O executed a will prior to O's death which leaves all of O's property to F, a friend. F has filed the will for probate. Which answer best describes the members of O's extended family who have standing to contest the will?

    (A) H, W, W2, and H2, their parents, and the descendants of their parents.

    (B) H, W, their parents, and the descendants of their parents.

    (C) H, W, and their parents.

    (D) H and W.

4. Refer to Question 3. How would your answer differ if, following the divorce of O's parents, O had been adopted by W's second husband, H2, in order for O to be covered by H2's medical and dental insurance coverage at work?

    (A) My answer would not change.

    (B) Only W would have standing.

    (C) H, W, and H2 would have standing.

    (D) W and H2 would have standing.

5. Refer to Question 4, but assume H died intestate after O was adopted by H2 but before O died. Which answer best describes the identity of H's heirs?

    (A) O.

    (B) O and H's parents.

    (C) H's parents.

    (D) H's parents and siblings.

6. Refer to Question 4, but assume (i) H2 had two children from a prior marriage, S1 and S2, and (ii) W died intestate, survived by O, H2, S1 and S2. Discuss the likely distribution of W's estate.

ANSWER:

7. Refer to Question 6. How would your answer differ if H2 had not adopted O?

    (A) O inherits the entire estate.

    (B) H2 inherits the entire estate.

    (C) H2 inherits the first $300,000, and H2 and O share the excess.

    (D) H2 inherits the first $150,000, and H2 and O share the excess.

8. O died recently. O's divorced parents, H and W, did not survive O. O was survived by one sibling, S1, who was also born to H and W. O was also survived by two other siblings: S2, who is H's child from a prior marriage, and S3, who is W's child from a subsequent marriage. W's second husband, H2, had a child from a prior marriage, S4. O was raised in the home of W and H2 with S1 and S4. Identify O's heirs.

    (A) S1, S2, S3, and S4.

    (B) S1, S2, and S3.

    (C) S1 and S2.

(D) S1.

9. O died intestate recently. O was survived by a parent, P. Additionally, a twice-divorced O was also survived by a child from O's first marriage, C1; another child born to O during O's second marriage; C2; and a child born to O's second spouse during a prior marriage of that spouse, C3, who lived with O during the second marriage. C1, C2, and C3 are still minors and still in the custody of their respective surviving parents. Which answer best describes O's heirs?

(A) P, C1, C2, and C3.

(B) P, C1, and C2.

(C) C1, C2, and C3.

(D) C1 and C2.

10. Refer to Question 9. How would your answer differ if, in addition to C1 and C2, it was rumored that O had fathered a non-marital child born out of wedlock prior to even meeting O's first wife; this child is C4, who is now an adult? O never even met C4 and had not had any contact with C4's mother for years.

ANSWER:

11. O died recently without a will. O had four children born during O's two marriages, both of which ended in divorce over twenty years ago while all four children were minors. O's first spouse was awarded custody of the two older children. O's second spouse was awarded custody of the two younger children. The children were C1, C2, C3, and C4. C1 died one day prior to O; C2 died the same day as O; C3 died one day after O; and C4 died one week after O. The children never married and did not have any children of their own. Which answer best describes the identity of O's heirs?

(A) C1, C2, C3, and C4.

(B) C2, C3, and C4.

(C) C3 and C4.

(D) C4.

12. Refer to Question 11, but assume that C2 was married to S2, and they had one child, G2; C3 was married to S3, and they had one child, G3; and C4 was married to S4, and they had one child, G4. Each of C2, C3, and C4 had a valid, probated will leaving his or her property to his or her spouse. Following the payment of all debts and taxes, which answer best describes those who will actually take possession of O's estate?

(A) S2, S3, and S4, equally.

(B) G2, S3, and S4, equally.

    (C) G2, G3, and S4, equally.

    (D) G2, G3, and G4, equally.

13.   Refer to Question 12. How would your answer differ if C2's wife was pregnant at the time of the deaths of both O and C2; this child, G5, was born six months later. In addition, before O's death, C3 had adopted G6, a child of S3 by a prior marriage.

    (A) G5 would share equally with G2 one-third of the estate, but G6 is excluded.

    (B) G6 would share equally with G3 one-third of the estate, but G5 is excluded.

    (C) G5 would share equally with G2 one-third of the estate, and G6 would share equally with G3 one third of the estate.

    (D) G5 would share equally with G2 one-third of the estate, and G6 would share with G3 one-third of the estate, but G3 would receive twice as much of that one third as G6.

14.   Refer to Question 13 but assume that C1, C2, C3, and C4 all died before O. Who will take possession of O's estate following formal administration?

ANSWER:

15.   Refer to Question 14, but assume that G4 also died before O, and G4 was survived by G4's child, GG. Which answer best describes who will take possession of O's estate following formal administration?

    (A) O's estate would be distributed equally to G2, G5, G3, and G6.

    (B) O's estate would be distributed 4/9 to G2 and G5; 4/9 to G3 and G6; and 1/9 to GG.

    (C) O's estate would be distributed 1/3 to G2 and G5; 1/3 to G3 and G6; and 1/3 to GG.

    (D) O's estate would be distributed 1/5 to each of G2, G5, G3, G6, and GG.

16.   O died recently. O's closest living relatives at the time of O's death were A, the first cousin of O's mother, and B, a child of a great uncle of O's father. Which answer best describes the identity of O's heirs at law?

    (A) A and B.

    (B) A.

    (C) B.

    (D) The state where O resided.

17.   Refer to Question 16 and assume that, in addition to A and B, O was survived by C, the child of O's deceased first cousin. Which answer best describes who succeeds to O's probate

estate?

(A) The state where O resided.

(B) The state and C.

(C) C.

(D) The first cousin's estate.

18. Refer to Question 16. How would your answer differ if C were a citizen of a foreign country residing in that country?

ANSWER:

19. O died recently without a will. O never married but had two non-marital children. The children are A and B, and they both survived O. The children have never married and do not have any children. Prior to O's death, O conveyed Blackacre to B. There is no evidence that B paid any consideration for Blackacre. Discuss the effect, if any, the conveyance has on the distribution of O's probate estate.

ANSWER:

20. O died recently without a will. O had two children born of O's only marriage, which ended when O's spouse died years ago. The children were C1 and C2. C1 died one month before O, and C2 died one month after O. C1 was married to S1, and they had one child, G1. C2 was married to S2, and they had one child, G2. Each child had a valid, probated will leaving his or her property to his or her spouse. Identify O's heirs.

(A) C2.

(B) C2 and S1.

(C) C2 and G1.

(D) C2 and C1's estate.

21. Refer to Question 20. Following the payment of all debts and taxes by the personal representative of O's estate one year later, which answer best describes those who will actually be entitled to the distribution of O's estate?

(A) S2 and S1, equally.

(B) S2 and C1, equally.

(C) S2 and G1, equally.

(D) G2 and G1, equally.

22. Refer to Question 20 and assume that one year prior to O's death, O had conveyed Blackacre to C2. Which answer best describes the effect the conveyance would have on C2's share in O's probate estate?

    (A) C2's share of the estate would not be affected.

    (B) C2's share of the estate would be reduced by the value of Blackacre.

    (C) C2 would be barred from sharing in the estate.

    (D) C2's estate would have to reimburse O's estate for one-half of the value of Blackacre.

23. Refer to Question 22, but assume that Blackacre had been conveyed to C1, not C2. Which answer best describes the effect the conveyance will have on G1's share of the estate?

    (A) G1's interest in the estate would not be affected.

    (B) G1's share of the estate would be reduced by the value of Blackacre.

    (C) G1 would be barred from sharing in the estate.

    (D) G1 would have to reimburse O's estate for one half of the value of Blackacre.

24. Refer to Question 22 and assume that, prior to the death of O, O had conveyed Blackacre to G2, not C2. Which answer best describes who succeeds to O's estate after the completion of formal administration?

    (A) S2's interest in the estate would not be affected.

    (B) S2's share of the estate would be reduced by the value of Blackacre..

    (C) S2 would be barred from sharing in the estate.

    (D) S2 would have to reimburse O's estate for one-half of the value of Blackacre.

25. Refer to Question 24, but assume that C2 also died one month before O and that O conveyed Blackacre to G2 two months before O died. What effect does the conveyance have on G2's share of the estate?

ANSWER:

26. O died intestate recently. O had two children born of O's only marriage, which ended in divorce years ago. The children were C1 and C2. C1 died one month before O, and C2 died one month after O. Both children's valid wills left their estates to their respective spouses. There were no grandchildren. Prior to O's death, C1 assigned C1's "interest in O's estate" to an unrelated third party. Explain the proper disposition of O's estate.

    (A) The assignment has no legal effect on the distribution of O's estate. C2 is the only heir.

(B)   The interest in O's estate that would have passed to C1's spouse had it not been for the assignment passes to the third-party assignee.

(C)   The interest in O's estate that would have passed to C1's spouse had it not been for the assignment passes to the third-party assignee if the third-party assignee paid good and valuable consideration for the assignment.

(D)   The third party has a claim against O's estate as a creditor if the third-party assignee paid good and valuable consideration for the assignment.

27.   Refer to Question 26. How would you answer differ if, following O's death, but prior to C2's death, C2, not C1, would have assigned C2's "interest in O's estate" to an unrelated third party.

(A)   My answer would not change; the assignment has no legal effect on the distribution of O's estate.

(B)   The interest in O's estate that would have been distributed to C2's spouse had it not been for the assignment should be distributed to the third-party assignee.

(C)   The interest in O's estate that would have been distributed to C2's spouse had it not been for the assignment passes to the third-party assignee if the third-party assignee paid good and valuable consideration for the assignment.

(D)   The third party assignee has a claim against O's estate as a creditor if the third-party assignee party paid good and valuable consideration for the assignment.

28.   Refer to Question 27. What effect would the assignment have if C2's assignment had occurred prior to O's death?

ANSWER:

29.   Refer to Question 26. How would your answer differ if there had not been an assignment, but a creditor of C1 had a judgment lien against C1 at the time of C1's death?

(A)   My answer would not change; the lien cannot attach to any part of O's estate.

(B)   The creditor can attach the one-half interest that would have passed to C1's spouse.

(C)   The creditor can attach the one-half interest that would have passed to C1's spouse if the original debt was tortious in nature.

(D)   The creditor has a claim against O's estate.

30.   Refer to Question 29. How would your answer differ if C1 would not have died until one day after O?

(A)   The lien cannot attach to any part of O's estate.

(B) The creditor can attach C1's one-half interest.

(C) The creditor can attach C1's one-half interest, if the original debt was tortious in nature.

(D) The creditor has only an unsecured claim against O's estate.

31. Refer to Question 30. What would your answer be if C1 would have survived O by one week before C1 died?

(A) The lien cannot attach to any part of O's estate.

(B) The creditor can attach the one-half interest that would be distributed to C1's spouse.

(C) The creditor can attach the one-half interest that would be distributed to C1's spouse if the original debt was tortious in nature.

(D) The creditor has only an unsecured claim against O's estate.

32. O died recently without a will. O had two children born of O's only marriage, which ended when O's spouse died years ago. The children were C1 and C2. C1 survived O, and C2 died one month after O. C1 has a child, G1. C2 was survived by a child, G2. Following O's death, a qualified disclaimer of C2's interest in O's estate was properly filed in the probate proceedings of O's estate by C2's personal representative because a creditor of C2 had filed a large judgment lien against C2 prior to O's death. What is the legal effect of the disclaimer on C2's interest in O's probate estate?

ANSWER:

33. Refer to Question 32, but assume that (i) the judgment lien did not exist and (ii) the disclaimer was filed in order for C2's one-half interest in O's estate to pass to G2 for transfer "tax" purposes. Which answer best describes the federal transfer consequences, if any, of the disclaimer?

(A) There are no transfer tax consequences.

(B) If C2 filed the disclaimer, it would be considered a gift to G2 of C2's interest in O's estate. If the executor filed the disclaimer, C2's one-half interest in O's estate would be included in C2's gross estate for federal transfer tax purposes.

(C) If C2 filed the disclaimer, there would be no transfer tax consequences. If the executor filed the disclaimer, C2's one-half interest in O's estate would be included in C2's gross estate for federal transfer tax purposes.

(D) If C2 filed the disclaimer, it would be considered a gift to G2 of C2's one-half interest in O's estate. If the executor filed the disclaimer, there would be no transfer tax consequences.

34. Refer to Question 32 and assume that C1 had borrowed $12,000 from O and had not repaid

the debt prior to O's death. What effect does the $12,000 debt have on C1's interest in O's estate?

ANSWER:

35. Refer to Question 32 and assume that C1 and a family friend discovered O had died when C1 and the friend took breakfast to O as they had done every day for several months. C1 and the friend entered O's house through the back door directly into O's kitchen using a key O had given to C1. Upon entering the kitchen, C1 and the friend found an envelope with C1's name on it; they opened the envelope and discovered $10,000 in cash and an unrecorded deed signed by O whereby O conveyed O's house to C1. After opening the envelope, C1 and the friend discovered O had died the night before. Which answer best explains the likely disposition of the house and the $10,000?

(A) Both the house and the $10,000 pass as part of O's probate estate.

(B) Because O made a gift to C1 of the house and the $10,000, the house and the $10,000 belong to C1 and are not part of the probate estate.

(C) Since O made a gift to C1 of the $10,000, but not the house, the $10,000 is not part of the probate estate, but the house is part of O's probate estate.

(D) Since O made a gift to C1of the house, but not the $10,000, the house is not part of the probate estate, but the $10,000 is part of O's probate estate.

36. Refer to Question 32, but assume that C1 murdered O. Which answer best describes the effect of C1's crime on the disposition of O's estate?

(A) The fact that C1 murdered O disqualifies C1 as an heir, and the half of the estate to which C1 would have been entitled is forfeited to the state where O resided.

(B) The fact that C1 murdered O disqualifies C1 as an heir, and the half of the estate to which C1 would have been entitled passes to G1.

(C) The fact that C1 murdered O disqualifies C1 as an heir, and the half of the estate that C1 would have been entitled passes to G2.

(D) The only legal remedy of G2 is to impose a constructive trust on C1 to avoid unjust enrichment.

1.   True or False? An express trust is a legally recognizable entity for state law purposes. Explain your answer.

ANSWER:

2.   O conveyed Blackacre to O's cousin, F. After the conveyance, O told G that, at the time of the conveyance, O and F had orally agreed that F would manage Blackacre until O's death; at that time, F would convey Blackacre to O's grandchild, G. G is the only child of C, who is O's only child. G also says that O told G that F had also agreed to pay to O any income generated by Blackacre during O's lifetime. The deed was duly recorded; no income had been generated since the conveyance, and O has recently died intestate. Record legal title is in F's name. F denies that F had any agreement with O concerning what F was to do with the property. Which answer best describes the most likely disposition of Blackacre following O's death?

      (A)   G can have the court enforce the terms of the oral express trust.

      (B)   F retains Blackacre since the oral express trust is unenforceable.

      (C)   C will have the court impose a resulting trust on F in favor of C since O's attempt to create an express trust failed.

      (D)   G will have the court impose a constructive trust on F in favor of G because F breached the oral agreement.

3.   Refer to Question 2, but assume that other friends of O were present at the time of the original transaction between O and F, and they are willing and able to testify as to the oral agreement. What is the most likely disposition of Blackacre by reason of O's death?

ANSWER:

4.   Refer to Question 3, but assume F admits that F and O had the oral agreement but says F will not abide by the agreement since it was not in writing. Which answer best describes the most likely disposition of Blackacre following O's death?

      (A)   G can have the court enforce the terms of the oral express trust.

      (B)   F retains Blackacre since the oral express trust is unenforceable.

    (C)   C will have the court impose a resulting trust on F in favor of C since O's attempt to create an express trust failed.

    (D)   G will have the court impose a constructive trust on F in favor of G because F breached the oral agreement.

5.   Refer to Question 3, but assume that F was also O's long-time accountant and financial advisor. Which answer best describes the most likely disposition of Blackacre following O's death?

    (A)   G will ask the court to enforce the terms of the oral express trust.

    (B)   F retains Blackacre since the oral express trust is unenforceable.

    (C)   G will have the court impose a constructive trust on F in favor of G.

    (D)   C will have the court impose a resulting trust on F in favor of C.

6.   O assigned AT&T common stock certificates to O's cousin, F. At the time of the assignment, O and F had orally agreed that F would hold the stock until O's death; at that time, F would assign the stock to O's grandchild, G. G is the only child of C, who is O's only child. F had also agreed to pay to O any dividends paid by AT&T during O's lifetime. O has recently died intestate. The stock has been registered in F's name. F now denies that F had any agreement with O concerning what F was to do with the stock after O's death. However, friends of both O and F were present at the time of the original transaction and are willing and able to testify that there was the oral agreement. Which answer best describes the most likely disposition of the shares of stock by reason of O's death?

    (A)   G will have the court impose a constructive trust on F in favor of G because F breached the oral agreement.

    (B)   G will have the court enforce the terms of the oral express trust.

    (C)   C will have the court impose a resulting trust on F in favor of C because O's attempt to create an express trust failed.

    (D)   F retains the stock since the oral express trust is unenforceable.

7.   O conveyed Blackacre to O's friend, "F, as trustee." At the time of the conveyance, O and F had orally agreed, in the presence of credible, disinterested witnesses, that F would manage Blackacre until O's death; at that time, F would convey Blackacre to O's grandchild, G. G is the only child of C, who is O's only child. F had also agreed to pay to O any income generated by Blackacre during O's lifetime. The deed was duly recorded; no income had been generated since the conveyance, and O has recently died intestate. F now claims that F is not required to convey the property to G since the terms of the agreement were not in writing. Which answer best describes the most likely disposition of Blackacre by reason of O's death?

    (A)   G will have the court enforce the terms of the oral express trust.

(B) G will have the court impose a constructive trust on F in favor of G because F breached the oral agreement.

(C) C will have the court impose a resulting trust on F in favor of C because O's attempt to create an express trust failed.

(D) F will retain Blackacre since the oral express trust is unenforceable.

8. Refer to Question 7, but assume that (i) there is no admissible evidence of the terms of the oral agreement between O and F concerning what F was to do with the property and (ii) the duly recorded deed conveyed Blackacre to "F, as trustee for G." Which answer best describes the most likely disposition of Blackacre by reason of O's death?

(A) Fee simple title is vested in C.

(B) Fee simple title is vested in G.

(C) F owns the legal title, and G owns the equitable interests.

(D) F owns the legal title, and C owns the equitable interests.

9. S conveyed Blackacre to T. At the time of the conveyance, T and S had orally agreed that T would manage Blackacre until S's death; at that time, T would convey Blackacre to S's grandchild, G. G is the only child of C, who is S's only child. The deed was duly recorded. Record legal title is in T's name. T acknowledges the oral agreement T had with S. However, a creditor of T has obtained a judgment against T and is seeking to satisfy the judgment by attaching Blackacre. Assuming the relevant statute of frauds does not require a trust of real property to be in writing, what legal advice should be given to T?

ANSWER:

10. Refer to Question 9. How would your answer in Question 9 differ if the relevant statute of frauds requires a trust of real property to be in writing?

ANSWER:

11. Refer to Question 9, but assume that a writing signed by T and S evidencing the creation of the trust and its terms has been discovered. However, a creditor of T has a judgment against T and is seeking to satisfy the judgment by attaching Blackacre. Which answer best describes the legal advice that should be given to T?

(A) You can convey Blackacre to G pursuant to your agreement with O notwithstanding the judgment against you.

(B) You can convey Blackacre to C pursuant to the agreement with O, but the creditor will have it set aside as a transfer in fraud of creditors.

    (C)   You can allow the creditor to attach Blackacre notwithstanding your agreement with O.

    (D)   The creditor can attach Blackacre regardless of what you decide to do.

12.   O and F, a friend of O, entered into a written trust agreement signed by both O and F. Following the execution of the trust agreement, O conveyed Blackacre to F; record legal title is in F's name. The terms of the trust agreement direct F to manage Blackacre until O's death; at that time, F is to convey Blackacre to O's grandchild, G. O died intestate recently. G died following the conveyance to F, but prior to O's death. Also assume G died intestate and was survived by G's parents, C (O's child) and M. G never married and had no descendants. C and M are divorced. Which answer best describes the most likely disposition of Blackacre by reason of O's death?

    (A)   C will have the court to impose a resulting trust on F in favor of C.

    (B)   C will ask the court to enforce the terms of the express trust.

    (C)   C and M will ask the court to enforce the terms of the express trust.

    (D)   F retains fee simple title.

13.   Refer to Question 12, but assume that the terms of the written express trust directed F to deliver Blackacre at O's death to G, if G survived O. Which answer would most likely describe the disposition of Blackacre by reason of O's death?

    (A)   F retains fee simple title.

    (B)   C will have the court to impose a resulting trust on F in favor of C.

    (C)   C will have the court enforce the terms of the express trust.

    (D)   C and M will have the court enforce the terms of the express trust.

14.   O died recently. O was survived by a child, C, and O's grandchild, G, a child of another child of O who predeceased O. O's valid will has been admitted to probate and devises 1,000 shares of the common stock of a publicly held corporation to C "with the request that C deliver the shares to G, if G graduates from college"; the rest, residue, and remainder of O's estate is devised to a charity. G was 18 at the time of O's death and had not yet graduated from high school. Which answer best explains the likely disposition of the shares of stock by reason of O's death?

    (A)   C is the trustee of an express trust for the benefit of G.

    (B)   G will have the court to impose a constructive trust on C in favor of G to avoid unjust enrichment.

    (C)   The charity will have the court impose a resulting trust on C in favor of G, since O's attempt to create an express trust failed.

(D) C owns the stock.

15. Refer to Question 14, but assume that O's will devises the 1,000 shares to "C to be delivered to G when G graduates from college." Which answer best explains the likely disposition of the shares of stock by reason of O's death?

    (A) C is the trustee of an express trust for the benefit of G.

    (B) G will have the court to impose a constructive trust on C in favor of G to avoid unjust enrichment.

    (C) The charity will have the court impose a resulting trust on C in favor of G, since O's attempt to create an express trust failed.

    (D) C owns the stock.

16. Refer to Question 15, but assume G died after the will was executed by O but before O died. G had not yet graduated from college. Which answer best explains the likely disposition of the shares of stock by reason of O's death.

    (A) C is the trustee of an express trust for the benefit of G's heirs.

    (B) The charity owns the stock.

    (C) The charity will have the court impose a resulting trust on C in favor of the charity because O's attempt to create an express trust failed.

    (D) C owns the stock.

17. O died intestate recently. O was survived by child, C, and grandchild, G, the child of C. Prior to O's death, O told several friends that O was holding Blackacre as trustee for the benefit of G, and when G reached age 21, O was going to convey legal title to G. Record legal title then and now is in O's name. There is no written evidence of O's stated intent. When O died, G was age 18. C now claims Blackacre as O's heir. Assuming the statute of frauds does not require a trust of real property to be in writing, what is the most likely disposition of Blackacre by reason of O's death?

ANSWER:

18. Refer to Question 17, but assume that the property involved in the controversy is 1,000 shares of stock in a publicly held corporation. Which answer best explains the most likely disposition of the 1,000 shares of stock?

    (A) The court should appoint a successor trustee of the express trust to manage the stock until G attains age 21.

    (B) The trust is unenforceable; the stock passes to C.

(C) G will have the court impose a constructive trust on C to avoid unjust enrichment by C.

(D) The personal representative of O's estate should retain the stock until G attains age 21 and then deliver it to G.

19. Refer to Question 17, but assume a written memorandum stating O's intent and signed by O has been discovered. Record legal title to Blackacre remains in O's name. Which answer best describes the most likely disposition of Blackacre by reason of O's death?

(A) The court should appoint a successor trustee of the express trust to manage Blackacre until G attains age 21.

(B) The trust is unenforceable; Blackacre passes to C.

(C) G will have the court impose a constructive trust on C to avoid unjust enrichment by C.

(D) The personal representative of O's estate should retain Blackacre until G attains age 21 and then deliver Blackacre to G.

20. Refer to Question 19, but assume shortly prior to O's death O had conveyed Blackacre as a gift to O's friend, F. F was unaware of the trust. Which answer best describes the legal advice you would give to G?

(A) That's life; there's nothing you can do.

(B) You should file suit against O's estate for breach of fiduciary duty.

(C) You should have the court impose a constructive trust on F because O breached a fiduciary duty.

(D) You should file suit against F for conspiring with O to breach a fiduciary duty.

21. O died recently. O was survived by O's adult child, C, and G, the adult child of C. Prior to O's death, in a written document signed by O, O declared that O was serving as the trustee of Blackacre and explained that O would manage Blackacre so long as O was willing and able to do so; if O would ever be unable or unwilling to continue to serve as trustee, O's friend, F, would serve as trustee until O's death. The document also provides that F, as trustee, was to convey Blackacre to F at the time of O's death. Additionally, prior to O's death, O or F, whoever was serving as trustee, was to pay to O any income Blackacre generated. The terms of the written document also provide that the trust was irrevocable. O's valid will, executed the same day as the described written document, has been admitted to probate and devises all of O's estate to G. Record title to Blackacre stayed in O's name until O died. Which answer best describes the most likely disposition of Blackacre by reason of O's death?

(A) Because the document was not executed with testamentary formalities, Blackacre passes to G.

(B) Because the document was not executed with testamentary formalities, Blackacre passes to C.

(C) Blackacre passes to F by reason of O's death.

(D) F, as trustee, can convey legal title to F, individually.

22. Refer to Question 21, but assume that the terms of the described written document provide that the trust was revocable by O at any time prior to O's death. There is no evidence that O ever intended to revoke the trust. Which answer best describes the most likely disposition of Blackacre by reason of O's death?

(A) Because the document was not executed with testamentary formalities, Blackacre passes to G.

(B) Because the document was not executed with testamentary formalities, Blackacre passes to C.

(C) Blackacre passes to F by reason of O's death.

(D) F, as trustee, can convey legal title to F, individually.

23. O created a valid, enforceable irrevocable express trust last year by a written agreement. The assets of the trust consist of real and personal property. The trustee is T; the beneficiaries are C and G. C is entitled to all of the income for the rest of C's lifetime; at C's death, T is to deliver the trust estate to G. A creditor of O has recently obtained a judgment against O and is trying to attach the assets of the trust. Which answer best describes the legal advice you would give to T?

(A) The trust estate is not reachable by O's creditors.

(B) The trust estate is not reachable by O's creditors unless they are tort creditors.

(C) The trust estate may be reached by O's creditors.

(D) The trust estate is reachable by O's creditors.

24. Refer to Question 23, but assume that the trust agreement by its own terms was revocable by O; however, O has never evidenced any intention to revoke the trust. Which answer best describes the legal advice you would give to T?

(A) The trust estate is not reachable by O's creditors.

(B) The trust estate is not reachable by O's creditors unless they are tort creditors.

(C) The trust estate may be reached by O's creditors.

(D) The trust estate is reachable by O's creditors.

25. Refer to Question 24, and also assume that O had just died and that the judgment was obtained by O's creditor against O's personal representative. Which answer best describes

the legal advice you would give to T?

(A) The trust estate is not reachable by O's creditors.

(B) The trust estate is not reachable by O's creditors unless they are tort creditors.

(C) The trust estate may be reached by O's creditors.

(D) The trust estate is reachable by O's creditors.

26.   Refer to Question 23, but assume that the irrevocable trust agreement was pursuant to an oral understanding between O and T. Which answer best describes the legal advice you would give to T under the circumstances?

(A) The trust estate is not reachable by O's creditors.

(B) The trust estate is not reachable by O's creditors unless they are tort creditors.

(C) The trust estate may be reached by O's creditors.

(D) The trust estate is reachable by O's creditors.

27.   Refer to Question 23, but assume that the creditor was a creditor of T, not O, and has obtained a judgment against T arising out of a situation totally unrelated to the trust property. Which answer best describes the legal advice that you would give to T in view of these circumstances?

(A) The trust estate is not reachable by your creditors.

(B) The trust estate is not reachable by your creditors unless they are tort creditors.

(C) The trust estate may be reachable depending upon the facts and circumstances.

(D) The trust estate is reachable to satisfy your creditors.

28.   Refer to Question 27, but assume that the trust agreement was pursuant to an oral agreement between O and T, and T wishes to protect the interests of C and G. What legal advice would you give to T?

ANSWER:

29.   S created a valid, enforceable, irrevocable express trust last year by a written agreement. The assets of the trust consist of real and personal property. The trustee is T; the beneficiaries are C and G. C is entitled to all of the income for the rest of C's lifetime; at C's death, T is to deliver the trust estate to G. A former business associate of C has obtained a judgment against C related to a business transaction unrelated to the trust while the trust was in existence. Which answer best describes the legal advice you would give to T under the circumstances?

(A) The trust estate can be attached to satisfy the debt.

(B) Trust income can be attached to satisfy the debt.

(C) Trust income can be attached only if the claim is tortious in nature.

(D) The trust income cannot be attached to satisfy the debt.

30. Refer to Question 29, but assume that the trust agreement only authorizes T to distribute to C as much income as T, in T's discretion, determines is appropriate. Which answer best describes the legal advice you would give to T under the circumstances?

(A) The trust estate can be attached to satisfy the debt.

(B) Trust income can be attached to satisfy the debt.

(C) Trust income can be attached only if the claim is tortious in nature.

(D) The trust income cannot be attached to satisfy the debt.

31. Refer to Question 29, but assume that T, according to the terms of the trust agreement, can only distribute to C such amounts of income as are necessary for C's health, education, maintenance, or support. Which answer best describes the legal advice you would give to T under the circumstances?

(A) The trust estate can be attached to satisfy the debt.

(B) Trust income can be attached to satisfy the debt.

(C) Trust income can be attached only if the claim is tortious in nature.

(D) The trust income cannot be attached to satisfy the debt.

32. Refer to Question 31, but assume the creditor is a hospital that provided medical services to C. Which answer best describes the legal advice you would give to T under the circumstances?

(A) The trust estate can be attached to satisfy the debt.

(B) Trust income can be attached to satisfy the debt.

(C) Trust income can be attached only if the creditor has exhausted C's individual assets.

(D) The trust income cannot be attached to satisfy the debt.

33. Refer to Question 29, but assume that the creditor is a creditor of G, not C, and has a judgment against G. Which answer best describes the legal advice that should be given to T under the circumstances?

(A) The trust estate can be attached to satisfy G's debt.

(B)   G's interest in the trust estate can be attached to satisfy G's debt.

(C)   The trust estate must be sold in order to pay the debt.

(D)   The trust income can be attached.

34.   Refer to Questions 29 and 33. How would your answers differ if the trust agreement included a provision stating expressly that the beneficiaries' interests in the trust could not be attached in order to satisfy any debt of a beneficiary?

ANSWER:

35.   Refer to Question 33, but assume that the only provision in the trust agreement relating to creditors of beneficiaries is one that provides that, if a creditor of C ever attempts to attach C's interest, the interest terminates and passes to G; if a creditor of G ever attempts to attach the interest of G, the interest terminates and passes to a charity. Which answer best describes the legal advice you give T under those circumstances?

(A)   The provision is valid; the trustee should terminate the trust by delivering the property to the charity.

(B)   The provision is valid; the trustee should terminate the trust by delivering the property to C.

(C)   The provision is valid; G's interest has passed to the charity.

(D)   The provision is not valid; the creditor can attach G's interest in the trust.

36.   O was the settlor of a valid, enforceable irrevocable express trust. The trustee is T; the beneficiaries are two adults, C and G. According to the terms of the trust agreement, C is entitled to all of the trust income for the rest of C's lifetime; at C's death, the trustee is to distribute the trust estate to G. T has recently learned that C has assigned C's interest in the trust to Q. Q is demanding that the trustee distribute the trust income to Q. Which answer best describes the legal advice that should be given to T?

(A)   The assignment is valid; you should distribute the income to Q as long as C is alive.

(B)   The assignment is void; you should continue to pay C for the remainder of C's lifetime.

(C)   Since the assignment is not enforceable against the trust, you should continue to pay the income to C for the rest of C's lifetime.

(D)   C's interest in the trust has terminated; the remaining trust assets should be delivered to G.

37.   Refer to Question 36, but assume that the trust agreement only authorizes T to deliver to C as much income as C needs for C's health, support, education, or maintenance. Which answer best describes the legal advice that should be given to T?

(A)   The assignment is valid; you should pay all the income to Q for the rest of C's lifetime.

(B)   The assignment is valid; you should distribute to Q whatever income you would have distributed to C for C's health, support, education, or maintenance.

(C)   The assignment may be valid if Q paid C good and valuable consideration in exchange for the assignment.

(D)   The assignment may be valid if Q provided services for C's health, support, education, or maintenance.

38.   Refer to Question 36, but assume that the trust agreement authorized T to distribute to C only as much income as T, in T's discretion, deems appropriate. What legal advice should be given to T under the circumstances?

ANSWER:

39.   Refer to Question 36, but assume that it was G, not C, who assigned G's interest in the trust estate to Q. Which answer best describes the legal advice that should be given to T under the circumstances?

(A)   The assignment is void; you should continue to pay the income to C and deliver the trust estate to G when C dies.

(B)   The assignment is valid; T should deliver the trust estate to Q now.

(C)   The assignment is valid; T should deliver the trust estate to Q when C dies.

(D)   The assignment is enforceable only against G; you should continue to pay the income to C and deliver the trust estate to G when C dies.

40.   Refer to Question 39, but assume the trust agreement includes a provision that prohibits both voluntary and involuntary assignments of beneficial interests by beneficiaries. Which answer best describes the legal effect of the assignment?

(A)   The assignment is unenforceable against T who can deliver the trust estate to G when C dies.

(B)   The assignment is valid; T should deliver the trust estate to Q when C dies.

(C)   The assignment is valid only if Q paid good and valuable consideration for the assignment.

(D)   The assignment is voidable at the election of G.

41.   Refer to Question 36, but assume that both C and G assigned their interests in the trust estate to T, not Q. Which answer best explains the most likely disposition of the trust estate under those circumstances?

(A) The assignment can be set aside by O.

(B) The assignment is valid; T is now the beneficiary of the trust.

(C) The assignment is valid; T acquires fee simple title to the trust estate.

(D) The assignment may be voidable by C and G.

42. O created a valid, enforceable irrevocable express trust. T is the trustee; C and G are the beneficiaries. The trust agreement provides that T is to pay to C only as much income as T, in T's discretion, determines is appropriate, as long as C is alive; at C's death, T is to deliver the remaining trust estate to G. T has been making distributions of income to C. C believes the amount is not enough; G believes the amount is too much. Which parties have standing to challenge the distributions made by T?

ANSWER:

43. Refer to Question 42. How would your answer differ if the terms of the trust granted the trustee "absolute, uncontrolled discretion"?

(A) T is not answerable to the beneficiaries.

(B) The court will have to substitute its judgment for that of T's judgment.

(C) T must prove that T did not abuse T's discretion.

(D) C or G must prove that T abused T's discretion.

44. Refer to Question 42, but assume that the trust agreement authorized T to distribute to C only as much income as was necessary for C's health, support, education, or maintenance. Which answer best describes the burden of proof in litigation involving the appropriate amount?

(A) T must prove that T did not abuse T's discretion.

(B) T must prove the amount distributed was needed for C's health, support, education, or maintenance.

(C) C or G must prove the amount was not the amount needed for C's health, support, education, or maintenance.

(D) G or C must prove that T abused T's discretion.

1. Explain the difference between general powers of appointment and non-general powers of appointment.

ANSWER:

2. O created a valid, enforceable irrevocable express trust. The terms of the written trust agreement direct the trustee, T, to pay the income to A for the rest of A's lifetime; at the time of A's death, T is directed to deliver the trust estate to A's children if A appoints to them by will. In default of appointment, T is to deliver the trust estate to a charity. At the time the trust was created, A had three children, C1, C2, and C3. Following the creation of the trust, A validly executed a will in which A expressly appoints the trust estate to C1 and C2. Which answer best describes the current beneficiaries of the trust?

    (A) A.

    (B) A, C1, C2, C3, and the charity.

    (C) A and the charity.

    (D) A, C1, C2, and the charity.

3. Refer to Question 2, but assume A has recently died, survived by A's children, C1, C2, and C3. A's will has been admitted to probate. Which answer best describes who is likely to succeed to the trust estate by reason of A's death?

    (A) The charity.

    (B) C1 and C2.

    (C) C1, C2, and the charity.

    (D) C1, C2, and C3.

4. Refer to Question 2 and assume A's will has been admitted to probate, but also assume that the will does not make any reference to A's power of appointment or the trust estate; it simply devises all of A's property to A's children. Which answer best describes the most likely disposition of the trust estate?

    (A) T should distribute it to the charity.

    (B) T should distribute it to A's children.

    (C) The children can have the court impose a constructive trust on the charity to avoid unjust enrichment.

    (D) The children can have the court impose a resulting trust on the charity to avoid unjust enrichment.

5.   Refer to Question 3, but assume the will described in Question 2 does not comply with a technical requirement of the relevant wills act. What is the most likely disposition of the trust estate?

ANSWER:

6.   What would be your answer in Question 3 if A had executed a new will in which A expressly revoked the will described in Question 2 and exercised the power of appointment in favor of S, the spouse A had married shortly before A's death. The will also devised A's probate estate to S.

ANSWER:

7.   Refer to Question 3, but assume A never executed a will and died intestate. Which answer best describes the most likely disposition of the trust estate?

    (A) T should distribute it to the charity.

    (B) T should distribute it to the children.

    (C) The children can have the court impose a constructive trust on the charity to avoid unjust enrichment.

    (D) The children can have the court impose a resulting trust on the charity to avoid unjust enrichment.

8.   O died years ago. O's valid will was admitted to probate and devised Blackacre to A for life, remainder to such person or persons as A appoints by will, including A's estate, and, in default of appointment, to a charity. A died recently survived by A's spouse, S, and A's child, C. A's valid, probated will specifically appoints Blackacre to C and devises all of A's estate to S. Which answer best describes the most likely disposition of Blackacre?

    (A) It passes to the charity.

    (B) It passes to C.

    (C) It passes to C, subject to S's marital share.

    (D) It passes to the charity, subject to S's marital share.

9. Refer to Question 8, but assume A's will simply devises all of A's property to C. There is no reference in A's will to Blackacre or A's power of appointment. Which answer best describes the most likely disposition of Blackacre by reason of A's death?

    (A) It passes to C.

    (B) It passes to C, subject to S's marital share.

    (C) It passes to the charity.

    (D) It passes to the charity, subject to S's marital share.

10. Refer to Question 8, but assume C predeceased A survived by C's parents, A and S. What is the most likely disposition of Blackacre?

ANSWER:

11. Refer to Question 8, but assume C predeceased A survived by C's spouse, CS, and C's child, CC. Which answer best explains the most likely disposition of Blackacre by reason of A's death?

    (A) It passes to CC.

    (B) It passes to CS.

    (C) It passes to S.

    (D) It passes to the charity.

12. Refer to Question 8, but assume that, at the time of A's death, A's liabilities exceeded A's assets. Explain the rights of A's creditors, if any, in and to Blackacre?

ANSWER:

13. A created 10 years ago an irrevocable valid inter vivos express written trust declaration with A as trustee. At the time the trust was created, A was solvent and remained solvent right after the trust was funded. The terms of the trust declare the trust to be a "spendthrift" trust and authorize A to distribute to A as much income and/or principal as A needs for A's health, support, education, or maintenance. In addition, A may appoint all or any part of the trust estate to any one or more of A's children by deed during A's lifetime or at A's death by A's will. At the time of A's death, the successor trustee is to distribute any remaining trust assets to a charity. No trust assets have been distributed to A or A's children. A is now in financial difficulties due to bad investments made last year. A's creditors are seeking assets to attach. Creditors of A are seeking your legal advice about the trust and its trust estate. Which answer best describes the legal advice you should give the creditors?

    (A) You cannot reach any part of the trust estate.

(B) You may be able to reach whatever assets A may distribute to A's children.

(C) You may be able to attach only what A distributes to himself.

(D) You can attach all or any part of the trust estate.

14. Refer to Question 13, but assume that A's parent created the trust for the benefit of A. What legal advice would you give A's creditors? Would that advice differ if the trust agreement included a "spendthrift" provision?

ANSWER:

15. Refer to both Questions 13 and 14 and assume A's financial difficulties were resolved prior to A's death. At A's death, will the trust estates of the two trusts be included in A's gross estate for federal estate tax purposes?

(A) Both trust estates will be included in A's gross estate.

(B) Both trust estates will be excluded from A's gross estate.

(C) The trust estate described in Question 13 is excluded and the other is included.

(D) The trust estate described in Question 14 is excluded and the other is included.

1. Politicians debate the advisability of the government imposing a "death tax." Republicans typically argue in favor of its repeal; Democrats typically favor its retention. Explain what is the "death tax."

ANSWER:

2. O died. O's valid will was admitted to probate 10 years ago and devised Blackacre to A for life, remainder to such of A's children as A appoints by will, and in default of appointment, to another child of O, B. The rest, residue, and remainder of O's estate was devised to B. Additionally, during O's lifetime, O had created a valid irrevocable inter vivos express trust which directed the trustee, T, to pay the income to A during A's lifetime; at A's death, T is directed to distribute the principal to anyone, including A's estate, as A may appoint by will, and in default of appointment, to Big State University. A died with a valid will expressly exercising both powers in favor of A's children. Which answer best explains whether Blackacre and the trust estate of the trust are included in A's gross estate for federal transfer tax purposes?

    (A) Both Blackacre and the trust estate will be included in A's gross estate.

    (B) Neither Blackacre nor the trust estate will be included in A's gross estate.

    (C) Blackacre, but not the trust estate, will be included in A's gross estate.

    (D) The trust estate, but not Blackacre, will be included in A's gross estate.

3. Refer to Question 2, but assume A died intestate, survived by A's spouse, S, and A's children. Which answer best explains whether Blackacre and the trust estate of the trust will be included in A's gross estate for federal transfer tax purposes?

    (A) Both Blackacre and the trust estate will be included in A's gross estate.

    (B) Neither Blackacre nor the trust estate will be included in A's gross estate.

    (C) Blackacre, but not the trust estate, will be included in A's gross estate.

    (D) The trust estate, but not Blackacre, will be included in A's gross estate.

4. Refer to Question 3. Assume that the trust estate has a fair market value of $10,000,000. Will the inclusion of the trust estate in A's gross estate generate any federal transfer tax liability?

ANSWER:

5.   Refer to Question 3. A's probate estate includes A's home and its contents, A's auto, and A's investments. State law directs that the home, its contents, and the auto are to be set aside for S's use during formal administration. Which probate assets are included in A's gross estate?

    (A) The entire probate estate.

    (B) The investments, but not the home and its contents and the auto.

    (C) The investments and the auto, but not the home and its contents.

    (D) None of the probate estate since A died intestate.

6.   Refer to Question 5. How would your answer differ if A had a valid will that devised A's probate estate to A's spouse, S?

ANSWER:

7.   S created two valid, enforceable irrevocable inter vivos express trusts. B is the trustee of the first trust, and as trustee of the trust, B is authorized to distribute to B such amounts of the income and principal as B needs for B's health, support, education, or maintenance. At B's death, the successor trustee is directed to deliver the remaining trust estate to anyone in the world who B appoints, other than B's estate or creditors, and in default of appointment, to B's sibling, R. S created the second trust with B as trustee. According to the terms of the second trust agreement, B, as trustee, can distribute to B such amounts of income and principal as B needs for B's comfort or welfare. At B's death, the successor trustee is directed to deliver any remaining trust estate of the second trust to R. B has recently died, intestate, survived by B's children, C1 and C2. Which answer best explains whether the trust estates of the two trusts will be included in B's gross estate for federal transfer tax purposes?

    (A) Both trust estates will be included in B's gross estate.

    (B) Neither trust estate will be included in B's gross estate.

    (C) The trust estate of trust one, but not of trust two, will be included in B's gross estate.

    (D) The trust estate of trust two, but not of trust one, will be included in B's gross estate.

8.   O created a valid irrevocable inter vivos express trust with Big Bank and Trust serving as trustee. The terms of the written trust agreement direct the trustee to pay to B all of the income and such amounts of principal as the trustee determines is appropriate for B's comfort or welfare; at B's death, the bank is directed to deliver the trust estate to the children of B. Additionally, when O died, O's valid will was admitted to probate and devised certain property to the bank with directions for the bank to pay to B such amounts of

income or principal as the bank, in its discretion, determines is appropriate; at B's death, the bank is directed to deliver any remaining trust estate to B's children. B died recently and was survived by B's spouse, S, and two children, C1 and C2. Which answer best describes whether the trust estates of the inter vivos trust and the testamentary trust will be included in B's gross estate for federal transfer tax purposes?

(A) The trust estates of both trusts will be included in B's gross estate.

(B) The trust estates of both trusts will not be included in B's gross estate.

(C) The trust estate of the inter vivos trust, but not the testamentary trust, will be included in B's gross estate.

(D) The trust estate of the testamentary trust, but not the inter vivos trust, will be included in B's gross estate.

9. S1 died recently. S1 was survived by S1's spouse, S2, and two adult children, A and B. S1's valid will has been admitted to probate and devises S1's entire probate estate to S2. At the time of S2's death, S1 owned (1) several tracts of real estate; (2) certain common stocks; (3) numerous items of tangible personal property; and (4) a checking account. The value of the probate estate at S1's death is $6,000,000. The gross estate for transfer tax purposes consists entirely of these probate assets. Estimate the amount of federal estate tax that will be due by reason of S1's death.

ANSWER:

10. Refer to Question 9. If S2 dies later in the same year with a gross estate for estate tax purposes of $8,000,000 (the $6,000,000 S2 inherited from S1, plus $2,000,000 S2 already owned), estimate the amount of federal estate tax that will be due.

ANSWER:

11. O died recently. Prior to O's death, O had conveyed to A, a child of O, a remainder interest in Blackacre, expressly retaining a life estate. In addition, O had conveyed to B, another child of O, an executory interest in Whiteacre that becomes possessory at O's death. Both deeds were duly recorded prior to O's death. Which answer best explains whether Blackacre and Whiteacre will be included in O's gross estate for federal transfer tax purposes?

(A) Both Blackacre and Whiteacre will be included in O's gross estate.

(B) Neither Blackacre nor Whiteacre will be included in O's gross estate.

(C) Whiteacre, but not Blackacre, will be included in O's gross estate.

(D) Blackacre, but not Whiteacre, will be included in O's gross estate.

12. Refer to Question 11 and assume also that O had deposited $10,000 into a savings account in O's name "payable on O's death to A" and another $10,000 into a checking account in the names of O and B "with rights of survivorship." Which answer best explains whether these accounts would be included in O's gross estate for federal transfer tax purposes?

   (A) The checking account and the savings account would be included in O's gross estate.

   (B) Neither the checking account nor the savings account would be included in O's gross estate.

   (C) The checking account, but not the savings account, would be included in O's gross estate.

   (D) The savings account and one half of the checking account would be included in O's gross estate.

13. Refer to Question 11, but assume that, at O's death, O owned two life insurance policies. One is a term policy made payable at O's death to O's estate, and the other is a whole-life policy made payable to A at O's death. Which answer best explains whether the policies would be included in O's gross estate for federal transfer tax purposes?

   (A) Both policies would be included in O's gross estate.

   (B) Neither policy would be included in O's gross estate.

   (C) The whole-life policy, but not the term policy, would be included in O's gross estate.

   (D) The term policy, but not the whole-life policy, would be included in O's gross estate.

14. Refer to Question 13, but assume that (i) four years prior to O's death, O had assigned the ownership of the term policy to B (who then changed the beneficiary to B) and (ii) two years prior to O's death, O had assigned the ownership of the whole-life policy to A. Will the policies be included in O's gross estate for federal transfer tax purposes?

ANSWER:

15. Refer to Question 14, but also assume that, in addition to assigning the life insurance policies to A and B, O had also given shares of common stock worth $500,000 to each of A and B when O had assigned the policies. Which answer best explains whether the shares of stock would be included in O's gross estate for federal transfer tax purposes?

   (A) The stock given to both A and B would be included in O's gross estate.

   (B) The stock would not be included in O's gross estate.

   (C) The stock given to A, but not B, would be included in O's gross estate.

   (D) The stock given to B, but not A, would be included in O's gross estate.

16. O died recently. O was survived by two children, A and B, and three grandchildren, G1, G2, and G3. O's gross estate for federal transfer tax purposes has been valued at $6,000,000. At the time of O's death, O owed to third parties debts secured by real estate included in O's gross estate of $600,000 and unsecured debts of $100,000. Which answer describes the proper amount that can be deducted from O's gross estate to determine the amount of O's taxable estate for federal transfer tax purposes?

    (A) $700,000.

    (B) $600,000.

    (C) $100,000.

    (D) None.

17. Refer to Question 16 and also assume that the expenses of O's last illness amounted to $30,000, O's funeral expenses amounted to $10,000, and the expenses incurred in the administration of O's estate are $10,000. Estimate the amount of federal estate taxes that will be due.

ANSWER:

18. S1 married S2 shortly before S1 died. S1 was survived by S2 and S1's adult child by a prior marriage, C. S1's will has been admitted to probate and devises property valued at $6,000,000 to S2, property valued at $4,000,000 to C, and property valued at $10,000,000 to Big State University. Which answer best describes the amount that can be deducted from S1's gross estate to determine the amount of S1's taxable estate for federal transfer tax purposes?

    (A) $6,000,000.

    (B) $4,000,000.

    (C) $16,000,000.

    (D) $14,000,000.

19. Refer to Question 18, but assume the $6,000,000 was not devised outright to S2, but $1,000,000 was devised to a trustee in trust for S2 with directions for the trustee to distribute to S2 such amounts of income and principal as S2 would need for S2's health, support, education or maintenance. At S2's death, the trustee is to deliver the remaining trust estate to C. The other $5,000,000 was devised in trust to a trustee with directions to pay to S2 all of the trust income for the remainder of S2's lifetime, and at S2's death, the principal is to be delivered to C. Which answer best describes the part, if any, of the $6,000,000 that can be properly deducted from S1's gross estate to determine the amount of S1's taxable estate for federal transfer tax purposes?

    (A) $6,000,000.

    (B) $5,000,000.

    (C) $1,000,000.

    (D) The actuarial value of S2's life estate in $5,000,000.

20.   Refer to Question 19 and explain whether or not the trust estates of the described trusts would be included in S2's gross estate at the time of S2's later death.

ANSWER:

1.   Briefly explain the probate exception to federal jurisdiction of federal courts.

ANSWER:

2.   O, an unmarried resident of the State of X, died recently in X. O was survived by several members of O's family residing in several different states. Immediately prior to O's death, O owned items of tangible personal property (such as household furnishings, jewelry, clothing, and other personal effects) located in a rented apartment in the State of X, an automobile registered and located in the State of X, a checking account at a local branch of a national bank in X, shares of stock in a corporation incorporated in the State of Y, and other items of tangible personal property located in O's parents' house in the State of Z. Which answer best describes the law to apply in determining the proper succession to the described assets?

(A)   Federal law will determine who succeeds to the ownership of the described personal property.

(B)   The law of X determines the succession to the tangible personal property located in X; federal law determines the succession of the bank account; the law of Y governs the succession of the shares of stock; and the law of Z governs the succession of the tangible personal property located in Z.

(C)   The law of X governs not only the succession of the tangible personal property located in X but also the checking account; the law of Y will govern the succession of the shares of stock; and the law of Z will govern the succession of the tangible personal property located in that state.

(D)   The law of X will determine who succeeds to the ownership of the described personal property.

3.   Refer to Question 2 and assume O also owned three tracts of land — one tract located in each of the states of X, Y, and Z. Which answer best describes the law that will govern the proper succession to the three tracts?

(A)   The law of X governs the succession of all three tracts.

(B)   The law of X governs the succession of the land in X; the law of Y will govern the succession of the land in Y; and the law of Z will govern the succession of the land in Z.

(C)   Federal law governs the succession of the three tracts to the extent of any inconsistencies existing among the laws of X, Y, and Z.

(D)   Federal law governs the succession of all three tracts of land because O and the heirs resided in different states.

4.   O, an unmarried resident of the State of X, died while vacationing in the State of Y. In addition to the tangible personal property in O's physical possession at the time of O's death, O owned real and personal property located in the State of X, but O's more valuable assets were real and personal property located in the State of Z. O was survived by several members of O's family who all reside in the State of X. Which answer best describes which states' courts have subject matter jurisdiction over the decedent's property?

(A)   X has exclusive jurisdiction over the assets within its boundaries; Y has exclusive jurisdiction over the assets within its boundaries; and Z has exclusive jurisdiction over the assets within its boundaries.

(B)   X and Z have exclusive jurisdiction over the real property located within their respective boundaries, but X has exclusive jurisdiction over all personal property wherever located.

(C)   Each state has jurisdiction over the assets located within its boundaries, but X also has jurisdiction over the personal property located in Y and Z.

(D)   Each state has jurisdiction over the assets located within its boundaries, but X also has jurisdiction over all assets located in Y and Z.

5.   Refer to Question 4. Which answer best describes which law a court should apply in determining whether the decedent died testate or intestate?

(A)   The law of X.

(B)   X's law for the property located in X; Y's law for the property located in Y; and Z's law for the property located in Z.

(C)   The law of X for all the assets except for the real property located in Z.

(D)   The law of X for all the assets except for the real and personal property located in Z.

6.   O has recently died. O's will was drafted by his lawyer, L. The will names a local bank as executor. O's will disinherited his youngest son, A. The will did not specify why A was disinherited. O and L had several discussions about disinheriting A in which O explained why O wanted to disinherit A. O was married to S, A's mother, when the will was executed, as well as when O died. S was not represented by L. S was upset to learn from the bank that A had been disinherited. L believes that, if S knew the reasons for A's disinheritance, she would not be as upset. O and L never discussed revealing the information after O's death, and L does not believe O would want L to reveal the information for any purpose. Which of the following is the best statement as to L's obligations with respect to the information?

(A) So long as O was living, L was obligated not to disclose confidential information. However, the lawyer-client relationship does not survive death, which means L can now use professional discretion with respect to disclosing the information.

(B) Since A is the object of the information, A may consent to the disclosure by L to S. However, if A does not consent, L may not disclose the information.

(C) Since S was married to O when the will was drafted, S has the right to any information disclosed to L since spouses do not have the right to keep legally relevant information confidential from each other.

(D) Since the bank is the personal representative of O's estate, only the bank has the right to the information and the right to consent to L's disclosure of the information.

7. L is a solo practitioner who has been diagnosed with the early stages of Alzheimer's. L's primary practice area is in probate and estate planning. L has always worked alone. L is concerned as to what would happen to L's clients and their files when L dies or becomes incapacitated, and L has made arrangements with another solo practitioner, a law school classmate, A, to review all of L's files when either event occurs. L's clients have never met A. Does L's arrangement with A violate L's duty to preserve the confidentiality of the clients' information?

(A) Yes, unless her clients have explicitly authorized the arrangement.

(B) No. Unless her clients have explicitly prohibited her from making such an arrangement, L is authorized to make these arrangements since a reasonable client would approve the arrangement to safeguard his or her own interests.

(C) Yes, because A is not a partner, associate or employee of L.

(D) No, unless (i) the client explicitly authorizes the arrangement or (ii) the court approves the arrangement.

8. C makes an appointment with L. L is a lawyer and had never met C until the meeting. C provides L with C's prior estate planning documents and detailed information about C's financial situation. C also explains that C has no close relatives in the community. As C begins discussing C's plans for C's estate, L becomes convinced that C is mentally ill. What should L do under these circumstances?

(A) Based on what L has learned, L may initiate a guardianship or other appropriate protective court proceeding, or L may consult with appropriate third parties who may have the ability to protect C without such a court proceeding, such as C's family or social workers. L may disclose information L learned during discussions with C to the extent necessary to protect C's interests.

(B) C is L's client, and L may not disclose any of the information or use it in a guardianship or similar proceeding without C's consent.

(C) L may initiate a guardianship or other appropriate protective court proceeding with respect to C only if the court approves the disclosure of the information and determines the extent to which disclosing it is necessary to protect C's interests.

(D) Based on what L has learned, L may initiate a guardianship or other appropriate protective court proceeding. However, L may not consult with any third parties other than the appropriate court. L may disclose information L learned during discussions only with the court, but only in the context of a guardianship or other appropriate proceeding, and only to the extent necessary to the proceeding.

9. A is an attorney. A receives a phone call from C. A has represented C on various matters in the past. C explains that C's mother, M, is in a nursing home and that M is physically weak but mentally alert. C explains that M would like to update M's will. A makes an appointment to visit with C and M at the nursing home. During the meeting, A observes that M is unable to rise from the bed or speak much above a whisper. A is not able to understand what M is saying, so A relies on C to explain what M is saying about the changes M would like in her will. When C explains something to A, C turns to M and asks, "Mom, is that right?" M invariably shakes her head that it is. Part of what M apparently wants to change in her will relates to ongoing litigation with M's siblings involving some real estate. Through C, M tells A several facts that have not been revealed in the litigation but are prompting M to change M's estate plan. Does C's presence during these discussions affect the applicability of A's attorney-client evidentiary privilege with M?

(A) Since C is a third party present during the disclosure of the information, there is no attorney-client privilege with respect to the information.

(B) Since both C and M are A's clients, the attorney-client privilege remains applicable to the information.

(C) Since C's participation in the discussion between A and M is necessary to A's representation of M, the attorney-client privilege remains applicable to the information.

(D) C's participation in the discussion has prevented the attorney-client relationship from being formed between A and M.

10. Refer to Question 9. Later during the meeting, C relays M's desire to disinherit D, M's only other child — a change that would directly benefit C. Again, M shakes her head in approval. A is personally aware of the justified reasons for M wanting to disinherit D. What should A do under the circumstances?

ANSWER:

11. S1 and S2 are married. S1 made an appointment with an attorney, L, to discuss estate planning. At the initial meeting, S1, S2, and L discuss the estate planning in detail but never discuss who L represents. In the absence of an agreement otherwise, who does L represent?

(A) The lawyer is presumed to represent S1 and S2 jointly.

(B) L is presumed to represent S1 and S2 separately.

(C) L is presumed to represent S1 and S2 jointly and separately.

(D) L represents the client who made the appointment.

12. Refer to Question 11. What should L explain to S1 and S2 about the ethical rules of jointly representing a married couple in estate planning?

ANSWER:

13. Refer to Question 11. After L begins working on the couple's joint estate plan, S1 calls L. In the course of the conversation, S1 reveals that S1 committed adultery three years before and that S2 does not know of the affair. Does L have a duty to disclose this information to S2?

(A) Yes, because L must disclose to each of them the content of all communications with the other.

(B) No, if L concludes the communication is not relevant to the legal representation.

(C) No, because it is confidential information provided by L's client.

(D) Yes, unless S2 has waived the right to be provided information S1 provides to the lawyer.

14. Refer to Question 13. The estate planning involves coordinating the clients' nonprobate and probate assets. In order to minimize legal fees, S1 and S2 had agreed with L that they would each be responsible for making any changes necessary to coordinate their respective nonprobate assets with the agreed upon estate plan and that L would have no responsibility with respect to the nonprobate assets. In the same telephone conversation, S1 tells L not to tell S2, but S1 has changed the beneficiary of one life insurance policy to S1's paramour. What should L do with respect to this information?

(A) As S1 is the client and has instructed L to keep the information confidential, L must not reveal it to S2.

(B) L should discuss with S1 L's need to disclose this information to S2 or withdraw from the representation unless S1 discloses it.

(C) L should withdraw from representation and refuse to discuss the matter any further with either S1 or S2.

(D) S1 and S2 agreed that L would have no responsibility for the nonprobate assets. Thus, L has no responsibility to disclose any information related to the nonprobate assets.

15. C is L's client. L has been C's attorney for many years. Each year on L's birthday, C gives L a gift. Is it ethical for L to accept such gifts?

    (A) No, because lawyers may not accept gifts from clients.

    (B) Yes, so long as L does not suggest the gift or engage in any type of undue influence to obtain the gift.

    (C) No, because it is presumptively fraudulent.

    (D) Yes, because there are no restrictions on social gifts or other activities between lawyers and their clients.

16. Refer to Question 15. During an appointment to update C's estate planning, C tells L that C would like for the will to include a $50,000 gift to L as appreciation for L's kindness over the years. L tries to tell C that this is not necessary, but C insists. What would you do if you were L?

ANSWER:

17. Refer to Question 16, but assume that the discussion concerning the $50,000 bequest did not happen, but that C wants to remove C's daughter as the designated executor of C's estate and name L as the executor of C's estate. What would you do if you were L?

ANSWER:

18. E is the executor of O's estate. E has approached an attorney, A, to assist E during the estate administration process. Absent any agreement otherwise, who would be A's client?

    (A) E.

    (B) O's estate.

    (C) The beneficiaries of O's estate.

    (D) E and the beneficiaries of O's estate.

19. Refer to Question 18. Assume A is E's child who has recently passed the bar exam and needs clients to pay off A's student loans. What should A do under the circumstances?

ANSWER:

20. Refer to Question 19, but assume that A is not E's child, but is E's law partner. E is an insurance defense lawyer with the firm and a sibling of O. What would you do if you were A?

ANSWER:

21.   C hires an attorney, A, to draft C's will. A had not met A prior to the first appointment. Since A becomes so familiar with C's estate during the estate planning process, C asks A to serve as the executor of C's estate. Is it ethical for A to draft a will naming A as the executor of the estate?

(A)   Yes, so long as while serving as executor A does not charge the estate for being both the executor and the executor's attorney.

(B)   No, because A cannot draft a will in which A receives any substantial interest.

(C)   Yes, but A should make sure C understands there is no necessity of A being named and discuss with C what A's fees would be, including any fees as attorney and not just as executor.

(D)   No, unless the will requires that A serve as executor without compensation.

22.   Refer to Question 21. Assume that C would like A to serve as a trustee of a testamentary trust created in C's will for O's children. If the will contains an exculpatory clause for trustees, will a court enforce it if A serves as trustee?

ANSWER:

23.   L prepares C's will. After the will is executed, C asks if L would keep the will in the firm's vault for safekeeping. Is it proper for the firm to retain the will?

ANSWER:

PRACTICE FINAL EXAM

PRACTICE FINAL EXAM

1. T died recently. T was survived by T's parents, M and F. T was divorced from T's spouse, S, two years prior to T's death. After the divorce, T did not change the validly executed will that T had signed while married to S and that included a pecuniary bequest of $10,000 to K, S's child by a prior marriage. What effect did the divorce have on the pecuniary bequest of $10,000 to K?

ANSWER:

2. B1 and B2 were brothers and had owned investment real estate as joint tenants with rights of survivorship since prior to B1's marriage to S. Under B1's valid will, his entire probate estate is devised to B1's spouse, S. B1 has recently died. Which of the following best describes the proper disposition of the land?

    (A) S receives B1's interest in the real estate. However, it is subject to the claims of B1's creditors.

    (B) S receives B1's interest in the real estate free and clear of B1's creditors' claims.

    (C) B2 receives B1's interest in the real estate. However, it is subject to the claims of B1's creditors.

    (D) B2 receives B1's interest in the real estate free and clear of B1's creditor's claims.

3. S conveyed Blackacre to S, in trust, to pay S the income for life, and for the trust estate to pass to B at S's death. S retained the power to revoke or amend the trust. S died intestate, survived by B. B is not S's intestate heir. The recorded deed was not witnessed and was not otherwise executed in compliance with the statutory formalities for a will. Which of the following best describes the distribution of the trust estate at S's death?

    (A) S's trust is invalid. The trust estate must pass through the probate system which means that the trust estate passes to S's intestate heirs.

    (B) S's trust is a valid testamentary trust. The trust estate passes probate to B.

    (C) S's trust is a valid testamentary trust. The trust estate passes nonprobate to B.

    (D) S's trust is a valid inter vivos trust. The trust estate passes to B outside of the probate system.

4. A and B were two unmarried cousins. A and B inherited Blackacre as tenants in common when their grandparent, O, died. Following O's death, A and B executed a single written

document in 2000 meeting the requirements of a valid will. In this document, the first to die devises her interest in Blackacre to the other. In addition, the will devises Blackacre to their alma mater, Big State University, upon the survivor's death. A has recently died survived by B. The family has discovered a validly executed will signed in 2010 by A that devises A's entire estate, including Blackacre, to F, a friend. Which answer best describes the most likely disposition of Blackacre by reason of A's death?

(A) A's interest passes nonprobate to B.

(B) B succeeds to A's interest pursuant to the 2000 will.

(C) F succeeds to A's interest pursuant to the 2010 will.

(D) F succeeds to A's interest pursuant to the 2010 will, and B has a breach of contract action against A's estate.

5. O died recently. O was survived by O's spouse, S, and their two minor children, C1 and C2. O's will, which was validly executed after O married S but before the births of C1 and C2, leaves all of O's property to S. Which answer best describes the most likely disposition of O's estate?

(A) The will can be admitted to probate; the entire estate passes to S.

(B) The will cannot be admitted to probate; the entire estate passes to C1 and C2.

(C) The will cannot be admitted to probate; S, C1 and C2 share the estate.

(D) The will can be admitted to probate, but C1 and C2 will be entitled to an intestate share of the estate, and the balance of the entire estate passes to S.

6. O died recently. O was survived by an independent adult child, D. Another child of O, S, died several years before O died; S was survived by S's child, C. O's valid will has been admitted to probate and simply says, "I devise all of my property to my grandchild, C." C, who was married to C's spouse and also the father of two children, C1 and C2, filed a valid disclaimer in the probate proceedings of O's estate, believing it was a way to make a gift to C's children without incurring gift tax. Which answer best describes the effect the disclaimer would have on the disposition of O's estate?

(A) The estate would pass to C's spouse.

(B) The estate would pass to C1 and C2 as distributees under the will.

(C) The estate would pass to C1 and C2, but as a gift by C to C1 and C2.

(D) The estate would pass to D.

7. Refer to Question 6 and assume C actually was a stepchild of S, and the will devised the estate to C. Which answer best describes the effect the disclaimer would have on the disposition of O's estate?

(A) The estate would pass to D.

(B) The estate would pass to D and to C's spouse.

(C) The estate would pass to C's spouse.

(D) The estate would pass to C1 and C2.

8.   O died recently. O was survived by two adult children, C1 and C2. O never signed a will but verbally told a number of friends over an extended period of time that O wanted C1 to have O's home and its contents when O died. At all relevant times, O was a competent individual, and O's friends are willing to testify as to O's verbal statements. No document appearing to be a will was found after O's death. Which answer best explains the most likely disposition of O's home and its contents?

(A) C1 inherits both the home and its contents.

(B) C1 inherits the contents but not the home.

(C) C1 inherits the home but not the contents.

(D) C1 and C2 inherit both the home and the contents.

9.   Refer to question 8. How would your answer differ if, moments before O died, a still-competent O told O's doctor and two nurses that O really did want C1 to have O's home and its contents when O died?

(A) My answer would not change.

(B) C1 inherits both the home and its contents.

(C) C1 inherits the contents but not the home.

(D) C1 inherits the home but not the contents.

10. Refer to Question 8. How would your answer differ if C1 can produce credible witnesses who will testify that O verbally told C1 that if C1 would drop out of school, return home and care for O in O's declining years, C1 would receive the home and its contents at O's death? C1 did drop out of school, returned home and cared for O until O's death.

ANSWER:

11. Refer to Question 8. How would your answer differ if C1 can produce a written agreement signed by C1 and O, whereby O promised to devise the home and its contents to C1, if C1 dropped out of school, moved in with O and cared for O in O's declining years? C1 did drop out of school, moved in with O and cared for O until O's death.

(A) My answer would not change.

    (B)   The home and its contents passed to C1.

    (C)   The contents, but not the home, passed to C1.

    (D)   C1 would have a claim against O's estate.

12.   O and F, a friend of O, entered into a written trust agreement signed by both O and F. Following the execution of the trust agreement, O conveyed Blackacre to F; record legal title is in F's name. The terms of the trust agreement direct F to manage Blackacre until O's death; at that time, F is to convey Blackacre to O's grandchild, G. Prior to O's death, any income generated was to be delivered to O, but no income was generated. O died recently intestate survived by O's only child, C. G died one day before O, survived by G's spouse, S, and G's only child, GG. G's valid will has been admitted to probate and devises all of G's estate to S. Which answer best describes the most likely disposition of Blackacre by reason of O's death?

    (A)   C will ask the court to impose a resulting trust on F in favor of C.

    (B)   S will ask the court to enforce the express trust on F in favor of S.

    (C)   GG will ask the court to enforce the express trust on F in favor of GG.

    (D)   F retains fee simple title.

13.   Refer to Question 12, but assume, unknown to both O and F at the time of the written agreement and conveyance, G was already dead. Which answer best describes the most likely disposition of Blackacre by reason of O's death?

    (A)   C will ask the court to impose a resulting trust on F in favor of C.

    (B)   C will ask the court to impose a constructive trust on F in favor of C.

    (C)   GG will ask the court to impose a constructive trust.

    (D)   S will ask the court to impose a constructive trust.

14.   Refer to Question 12, but assume that G has not died. Which answer best describes the most likely disposition of Blackacre by reason of O's death?

    (A)   G can have the court enforce the terms of the written express trust.

    (B)   G can have the court impose a constructive trust on F in favor of G.

    (C)   C can have the court to impose a resulting trust on F in favor of C.

    (D)   F retains fee simple title.

15.   Refer to Question 14, but assume that, prior to O's death, O asked F, in a letter delivered to F and signed by O, to convey Blackacre back to O, explaining that O was very disappointed in G and that O did not want G to have Blackacre when O died. F complied with O's request and conveyed Blackacre to O. O then sold Blackacre to X, a good-faith

purchaser. Is F, O's estate or X liable to G by reason of the described transactions?

ANSWER:

16. O created a valid, enforceable irrevocable express trust. The terms of the written trust agreement direct the trustee, T, to pay the income to A for the rest of A's lifetime; at the time of A's death, T is directed to deliver the trust estate to any one or more of O's lineal descendants as A appoints by will. In default of appointment, T is to deliver the trust estate to a named charity. At the time the trust was created, A was not married and did not have any children. Later A married A's spouse who had three children from a prior marriage, C1, C2 and C3. Shortly before A died, A validly executed a will in which A expressly appoints the trust estate to C1, C2, and C3. A's will has been admitted to probate. Which answer best describes who is likely to succeed to the trust estate by reason of A's death?

    (A) The charity.

    (B) C1, C2, C3.

    (C) A's estate.

    (D) O's heirs/devisees.

17. A and B lived together in a long-term committed relationship. They never married, but were the parents of a child, C. A died and was survived by B and C. A's will has been admitted to probate and devises property valued at $6,000,000 to B, property valued at $4,000,000 to C, and property valued at $10,000,000 to Big State University. Which answer best describes the amount that can be deducted from A's gross estate to determine the amount of A's taxable estate for federal transfer tax purposes?

    (A) $6,000,000.

    (B) $4,000,000.

    (C) $10,000,000.

    (D) $16,000,000.

18. Refer to Question 17, but assume A and B were a same-sex couple who were married in the State of Y, a state that permits same-sex marriage. Shortly before A's death, A and B moved to the State of X, a state that does not permit same-sex marriage. Which answer best describes the amount that can be deducted from A's gross estate to determine the amount of A's taxable estate for federal transfer tax purposes?

    (A) $6,000,000.

    (B) $4,000,000.

    (C) $10,000,000.

(D) $16,000,000.

19. O, an unmarried resident of the State of X, died while on a temporary work assignment in the State of Y. In addition to the tangible personal property in O's physical possession at the time of O's death, O owned real and personal property located in State of X, but O's more valuable assets were real and personal property located in the State of Z. O was survived by several members of O's family who all reside in the State of X. Assuming the amount of property (and/or its value) in each state justifies the trouble and expense of a formal administration, describe the states where formal administration of the decedent's estate would be proper.

ANSWER:

20. S created an inter vivos irrevocable trust for the benefit of B. T is the trustee. T hires an attorney, L, to advise T during the administration of the trust. Who is L's client?

(A) The trust.

(B) T.

(C) B.

(D) T and B.

ANSWERS

1. The answer depends on the marital property law of the state where the couple resided since marital property laws vary considerably from state to state. If they resided in a community property state, or a state which has enacted the Uniform Marital Property Act (1983) (thereby enacting the "partnership theory" of marriage), S2 may have owned a half ownership interest in all or a part of the property titled in S1's name; S1 may have owned half of the assets held in S2's name. Only S1's separate property and half interest in the community property passes to C in a community property state. ROGER W. ANDERSEN, UNDERSTANDING TRUSTS AND ESTATES, § 28(A) (5th ed. 2013) (hereinafter "Andersen _____"). In most other states, it appears that the property in question would have been owned by S1 prior to S1's death. While these states have abolished the common law concepts of dower and curtesy, S2 may be entitled to an elective share amount or percentage payable out of the probate estate and other nonprobate transfers. *See* Andersen §§ 28(B), 28(C). In community and non-community property states, the surviving spouse may also have other rights in and to the deceased spouse's estate, such as homestead, exempt property, or family allowance, depending on state law. *See* UPC §§ 2-401–2-405; WILLIAM M. MCGOVERN, SHELDON F. KURTZ, AND DAVID M. ENGLISH, PRINCIPLES OF WILLS, TRUSTS AND ESTATES, § 3.4 (2d ed. 2012) (hereinafter "McGovern _____").

2. **Answer (D) is correct.** Because the couple was married for 10 years, S2's "elective share" is an amount out of the marital property portion of the "augmented estate" of S1 and S2. *See* UPC §§ 2-202, 2-203. Generally, if the value of the property S2 owned prior to S1's death, when added to the value of Greenacre (plus most other assets passing to S2 by reason of S1's death), exceeds that amount, S2 will not receive anything else. If not, the difference is paid out of S1's probate estate and other nonprobate transfers. *See* UPC § 2-209.

   While the results may vary in both UPC and non-UPC states, the surviving spouse may have to elect between what is devised in the will and the elective share amount. See McGovern § 3.7 (p. 179). In a community property state, the residuary estate is typically limited to the decedent's separate property and half of any community property. In those states, the surviving spouse retains the surviving spouse's half of any community property and also inherits what the deceased spouse devised to the surviving spouse. See McGovern § 3.8.

   Answers (A), (B), and (C) are incorrect for the reasons given.

3. **Answer (A) is the correct answer.** C, an adult child, is not entitled to any share of S1's probate estate. Assuming S1's will was executed after C's birth, C is not "omitted" or "pretermitted" as that term is defined in UPC § 2-302.

   Statutes in some non-UPC states may afford C the status of a "pretermitted heir." See Andersen § 29.

   Answer (B) is incorrect. C would be entitled to an intestate share of S1's probate estate only if S1 died intestate. S1 died testate and can devise S1's estate to S2, thereby disinheriting C.

Parents can intentionally disinherit their children in all but one state. Louisiana still retains the civil law concept of "legitime" or "forced heirship" under some circumstances. The "pretermitted child" statute in some non-UPC states may protect C from an unintentional disinheritance, if S1's will does not expressly disinherit C.

Answers (C) and (D) are incorrect. Because C is an adult, neither S1 nor S1's estate following S1's death had a legal obligation to support C, absent a contract which would have created a debt of the estate.

If C were an adult with a disability, the family law of a state may impose some legal obligation on S1's estate to support C following S1's death.

4.   If S1 had a legal obligation to support C and was in fact supporting C, C would have been entitled to a reasonable allowance for C's maintenance during the period of administration. *See* UPC § 2-404. Absent a contractual obligation to the contrary, a general rule of family law is that a parent's legal obligation of support ends at the parent's death. *See* McGovern § 3.3.

States that have not enacted the Uniform Probate Code typically provide for some type of support for minor or dependent children during formal administration. See McGovern § 3.4. Regarding Louisiana's forced heirship rules, see the answer to the immediately preceding question.

5.   **Answer (A) is correct.** Because S1 and S2 were married for one year, S2 may be entitled to an elective share percentage of the augmented estate. However, since S1's will devised to S2 the residuary estate, the value of the residuary, when added to the value of other property received by S2 by reason of S1's death, as well as S2's own property, will likely exceed the elective share amount. *See* UPC §§ 2-202–2-203. *See* Andersen § 28(C)(3).

In a community property state, S2 would not likely retain S2's half of Greenacre and also inherit S1's residuary estate. S2 would be put to an election: (i) retain S2's half of the community assets and disclaim S2's rights under S1's will or (ii) accept S2's rights under S1's will and allow S2's half of Greenacre to pass to C. See McGovern § 3.8; THOMAS E. ATKINSON, HANDBOOK OF THE LAW OF WILLS, § 138 (2d ed. 1953) (hereinafter "Atkinson ____").

Answer (B) is incorrect. S2 did not own an interest in Greenacre at S1's death, and it is likely that Greenacre will not be needed to satisfy S2's elective share percentage.

Answer (C) is incorrect. In some non-UPC states, the surviving spouse may have to elect between what is devised to the spouse in the will or the elective share amount.

Answer (D) is incorrect. An adult child of a prior marriage is not entitled to any share of the probate estate. Since S1's will was presumably executed after C's birth, C is not "omitted" or "pretermitted."

6.   **Answer (C) is correct.** Because S1 failed to designate a third-party beneficiary of the life insurance, the proceeds are payable to S1's personal representative and become part of the probate estate. Like group life insurance, most pensions are subject to ERISA, a federal law which may require all or a portion of the death benefit of the pension plan to be paid to the employee's spouse. Employment Retirement Income Security Act (ERISA) of 1974, 88 Stat. 829 (codified as amended at 29 U.S.C.A. § 1001–1461 (West 2009 & Supp. 2013). *See* McGovern § 3.7 (p. 179). Both death benefits are taken into consideration in determining the augmented estate in order to compute S2's elective share amount. *See* UPC §§ 2-203–2-207.

See Andersen § 28(C).

In a community property state, the surviving spouse may be entitled to half of the proceeds of a community property life insurance policy. See McGovern § 3.8.

Answer (A) is incorrect. ERISA preempts state law as it would otherwise apply to the pension plan.

Answer (B) is incorrect. ERISA does not require the proceeds of a group life insurance policy be made payable to the employee's spouse.

Answer (D) is incorrect for the reasons given.

7.   Since the couple resided in a non-community property state, S2's death does not affect S1's pension plan. If they resided in a community property state, it is likely that S2 had acquired a community property interest in S1's pension plan. However, the United States Supreme Court in *Boggs v. Boggs*, 520 U.S. 833, 117 S. Ct. 1754, 138 L. Ed. 2d 45 (1997), ruled that ERISA preempts state law and prohibits S2 from devising S2's interest in the plan to S2's heirs and/or devisees. *See* McGovern § 3.8 (n. 69).

8.   **Answer (C) is the correct answer.** S2 is entitled to an amount equal to the value of S2's elective share percentage of the augmented estate, less the value of S2's property included in the augmented estate, and P will inherit the balance. *See* UPC §§ 2-202–2-212.

In a community property state, a spouse's testamentary power of disposition is typically limited to the spouse's separate property and half of the community probate property because the surviving spouse retains half of the community property. See McGovern § 3.8.

Answer (A) is incorrect. UPC §§ 2-202–2-212 prevent P from succeeding to the entire probate estate notwithstanding the terms of the will unless the value of S2's property included in the augmented estate exceeds the percentage share amount.

In a non-community property state that has neither adopted the augmented estate concept followed in the Uniform Probate Code nor adopted an elective share system, Answer (A) would be correct.

Answers (B) and (D) are incorrect. C, as S1's heir, is entitled to an intestate share of the probate estate only if S1 died intestate. Since there is a valid will, C does not receive anything.

9.   **Answer D is correct.** The change of beneficiary is likely to be invalid. ERISA requires the participant's spouse to agree to a change of beneficiary. It does not matter if the participant resides in a non-community property state or a community property state. S2 is still likely to receive some death benefit, such as a qualified pre-retirement survivor's annuity under ERISA. *See* McGovern §§ 3.7 (p. 179), 3.9 (p. 200).

Answers (A), (B), and (C) are incorrect for the reasons given.

10.   T's marriage to S after the execution of the will did not revoke the will. *See* UPC §§ 2-508, 2-804. However, S may be entitled to what S would have received had T died intestate. *See* UPC § 2-301. The amount is a factor in determining S's elective share amount as defined in UPC § 2-202.

In a community property state, the surviving spouse is generally entitled to half of any community property. See McGovern § 3.8. The rights of the "forgotten" or "omitted" spouses, if any, in non-UPC states will vary from state to state. In some states, the will may have been revoked by operation of law. See McGovern

§§ 3.6, 5.1.

11.   **Answer (C) is correct.** T generally has the right to devise T's estate to whomever T chooses, subject to S's elective share rights. *See UPC § 2-202.*

In a community property state, a surviving spouse generally retains half of any community probate property. See McGovern § 3.8. In states which have not adopted the Uniform Probate Code and which are not community property states, surviving spouses may have a right to some share of the estate. See McGovern § 3.7.

    Answer (A) is incorrect. S will be entitled to an elective share amount as described above.

    Answers (B) and (D) are incorrect. The will is valid; O did not die intestate.

12.   **Answer (A) is correct.** Because O's will devised all of O's estate to their surviving parent, C1 and C2 will not receive an interest in O's probate estate even though they were omitted from the will. *See UPC § 2-302(a)(1).* Their births did not revoke the will. *See UPC § 2-508.*

In almost every state that has not enacted the Uniform Probate Code, statutes grant "omitted" or "pretermitted" children certain rights in their parents' estates under some circumstances; the details vary from state to state. See McGovern § 3.5.

    Answers (B), (C), and (D) are incorrect for the reasons given.

13.   **Answer (A) is correct.** The "omitted children" provisions of the Uniform Probate Code provide protection from unintended disinheritance under certain circumstances only for children born or adopted after the execution of the will. *See UPC § 2-302.*

The "pretermitted" child statutes in states that have not enacted the Uniform Probate Code vary considerably from state to state. See McGovern § 3.5.

    Answers (B), (C), and (D) are incorrect for the reasons given.

14.   **Answer (D) is correct.** Assuming it is proven that C2 was, in fact, S1's child, C2 will receive an intestate share of O's probate estate since C2 was omitted from the will. *See UPC § 2-302(a)(1).*

In almost every state that has not enacted the Uniform Probate Code, statutes grant marital and non-marital "omitted" or "pretermitted" children certain rights in their parents' estates under some circumstances; the details vary from state to state. See McGovern § 3.5.

    Answer (A) is incorrect. C2 is an "omitted child" and entitled to the share C2 would have received had S1 died intestate.

    Answer (B) is incorrect. The birth of the children after the execution of the will did not revoke the will.

    Answer (C) is incorrect. Since S2 is the surviving parent of C1, C1 is not entitled to an interest in S1's estate.

15.   According to UPC § 2-804(b), the divorce revoked any dispositive provision of T's will in favor of S. Since the will devised all of T's probate estate to S, the probate estate passes by intestate succession to T's heirs. If S is named as the executor of T's estate, the divorce also revoked T's nomination of S as executor. The estate passes intestate to M and F.

Statutes in most non-UPC states would produce the same result, and in some states, even without a statute, case law may work a revocation by operation of law due to the change of circumstances. In a few states, a

QUESTIONS AND ANSWERS: WILLS, TRUSTS & ESTATES

divorce revokes the entire will and not just the provisions in favor of the former spouse. See McGovern § 5.4.

16.   **Answer (D) is correct.** The Uniform Probate Code revokes a pre-divorce beneficiary designation of a transfer-on-death account. As a result, the accounts pass to M and F. *See* UPC § 2-804.

In a state that has not enacted the Uniform Probate Code, or a statute similar to UPC § 2-804, the result may differ. Absent a statute, some courts have allowed the former spouse to enforce the terms of the contract. See McGovern § 5.5.

Answers (A), (B), and (C) are incorrect for the reasons given.

17.   If the policy was not part of O's employee benefit package, the designation of S as beneficiary of the policy was revoked by the divorce. *See* UPC § 2-804. However, notwithstanding state law to the contrary, the designation of S as the beneficiary of a group life policy provided by O's employer or the pension plan may still be enforceable by S despite the divorce. ERISA's preemption clause has been invoked to override state statutes similar to UPC § 2-804 where the death benefit was provided by the employer as part of an employee benefit plan. *Egelhoff v. Egelhoff ex rel. Breiner*, 532 U.S. 141, 121 S. Ct. 1322, 1449 L. Ed. 2d 264 (2001). *See* comment to UPC § 2-804 and McGovern §§ 3.8 (n. 59), 5.5 (n. 71).

Many non-UPC states have statutes similar to UPC § 2-804. Absent a statute, courts have allowed the former spouse to enforce the terms of the contract. See comment to UPC § 2-804.

1. Under the common law, because O owned only a life estate in Blackacre, O's interest in Blackacre terminated at O's death. A's remainder interest became fee simple title by the terms of the original grant, and H inherited no interest in Blackacre. *See* Atkinson § 2.8. Because O's remainder interest in Whiteacre was not expressly made subject to the condition that O survive B, H inherited O's remainder interest, but still subject to B's life estate. *See* Atkinson § 27. Consequently, only O's remainder interest in Whiteacre is part of O's probate estate, which is inherited by H. If the remainder interest in Whiteacre had been held in trust, UPC § 2-707 may reach a different result. *See* Andersen § 45.

    Absent a statute, a disposition of property intended to take effect at the transferor's death, which is not executed with testamentary formalities, must be sustained under the theory of contract, gift, or trust. *See* Atkinson Ch. 4. However, legislation exists in most states that validates many types of nonprobate dispositions of property that become effective at the transferor's death. *See* Andersen Ch. 5. Consequently, while O owned both the savings account and the policy, neither asset is part of O's probate estate at O's death, and H acquired no interest in either asset. The savings account became the property of C at O's death because O had entered into a contract with the bank that controls the disposition of the account. The proceeds of the policy passed to D because of the contract between O and the insurance company. *See* Andersen Ch. 5. The savings account and life insurance policy are examples of "nonprobate" or "nontestamentary" dispositions.

2. **Answer (B) is correct.** O's probate estate includes only O's interest in Whiteacre. Blackacre, the account, and the policy proceeds are not part of the probate estate. Since O's will has been admitted to probate, H has been divested, and F succeeds to the ownership of the assets included in O's probate estate. *See* Atkinson § 1; Andersen Ch. 5.

    Answers (A), (C), and (D) are incorrect. Because O died testate, F succeeded to the ownership of the probate assets in the same way H inherited the assets in the probate estate when O died intestate. Of the four described assets, only O's interest in Whiteacre is included in the probate estate and subject to formal administration.

3. **Answer (C) is correct.** Because O died testate, F succeeded to the ownership of the probate assets in the same way H would have inherited the assets in the probate estate had O died intestate. *See* Atkinson § 1. Of the four described assets, only Blackacre is not included in O's probate estate. When O died, O's interest in Blackacre terminated. A's heirs or devisees own Blackacre because A had a vested remainder. F inherited Whiteacre, the account, and the policy proceeds; these assets became part of O's probate estate and are subject to formal administration. The intended beneficiary must survive the transferor in order to be entitled to the account or insurance proceeds. *See* Andersen Ch. 5.

    Answers (A), (B), and (D) are incorrect. O's probate estate includes Whiteacre, the account, and the policy proceeds because B, C, and D died before O. Blackacre passed to A's successors in interest at O's death because O only had a life estate, which is not included as a part of O's probate estate.

4. **Answer (A) is correct.** The fact that O had entered into contracts with the bank and insurance company that control the dispositions of the assets at O's death did not give C and D ownership interests in the assets during O's lifetime. O retained ownership during O's lifetime. The intended beneficiary must survive the transferor in order to be entitled to the account or insurance proceeds. *See* UPC §§ 6-101, 6-212. *See* Andersen § 18. UPC § 2-702 requires the beneficiary to survive O by 120 hours unless the governing document provides otherwise. The account and proceeds became part of O's probate estate. *See* Andersen § 18(B).

Answers (B), (C), and (D) are incorrect. C and D were "third-party beneficiaries" of contracts prior to their deaths. Their deaths terminated their contractual rights under the contracts. Since C and D had mere "expectancies" and not future interests, the heirs or devisees of C and D did not inherit any interest in the account or policy.

5. **Answer (A) is correct.** The fact that O had entered into contracts with the bank and insurance company that control the dispositions of the assets at O's death did not give C and D ownership interests in the assets during O's lifetime. O retained ownership during O's lifetime. The intended beneficiary must survive the transferor in order to be entitled to the account or insurance proceeds. *See* answer to immediately preceding question. The fact that the intended beneficiary has children is irrelevant if the beneficiary is not related to O. *See* UPC § 2-706. The account and proceeds became part of O's probate estate. *See* Andersen § 45.

Answers (B), (C), and (D) are incorrect. C and D were "third-party beneficiaries" of contracts prior to their deaths. Their deaths terminated their contractual rights under the contracts. Since C and D had mere "expectancies" and not future interests, the heirs or devisees of C and D did not inherit any interest in the account or policy.

6. **Answer (D) is correct.** Because C and D are descendants of O, UPC § 2-706 created substituted gifts in favor of the children of C and D. The assets pass nonprobate to the children. *See* Andersen § 45(B)(2)(b). In a non-UPC state, the relevant statute must be examined to see if it is applicable to nonprobate dispositions.

Answers (A), (B), and (C) are not correct for the reasons given.

7. **Answer (B) is correct.** The proper execution of a life insurance beneficiary designation form creates a contract right in the designated beneficiary to receive the proceeds of the policy at the insured's death. The beneficiary designation confers a contract right on the beneficiary subject to the terms of the policy, which usually reserve to the owner the right to change the beneficiary and require that the beneficiary survive the insured. Since it confers a contract right, life insurance beneficiary designations do not need to comply with the statutory formalities of a will. The proceeds pass to the beneficiary outside of probate pursuant to the terms of the policy. Thus, B2 held the right to collect the proceeds when L died. *See* Andersen § 20.

Answers (A), (C), and (D) are incorrect. Because it is the present assignment of a contract right, a life insurance beneficiary designation does not need to comply with the statutory formalities required for a will. There is no distinction between initial beneficiary designations and subsequent designations. When the insured dies, the proceeds are paid to the current beneficiary pursuant to the terms of the policy.

8.   No, traditionally the terms of the policy control. The most recent beneficiary designation executed in compliance with the terms of the policy conferred the contractual right to receive the proceeds to B2. L's will does not override the terms of the life insurance policy. *See* Andersen § 25. If B2 were a beneficiary under the will, B2 may be put to an equitable election to deliver the proceeds as directed in the will in exchange for the devise to B2 in the will. *See* Atkinson § 138. The Uniform Probate Code expressly prohibits the use of wills to change rights of survivorship or pay-on-death designations in bank accounts. *See* UPC § 6-213(b). Although the Uniform Probate Code does not take a position on the use of wills to change beneficiary designations on other nonprobate assets, the general rule in most jurisdictions is that wills are ineffective to do so. In some jurisdictions, wills have been found to determine the beneficiary of some nonprobate assets. For discussion of these so-called "super wills" see JESSE DUKEMINIER AND ROBERT H. SITKOFF, WILLS, TRUSTS AND ESTATES, 475–476 (9th ed. 2013) (hereinafter "Dukeminier ____").

9.   **Answer (C) is correct.** The deed made a present and irrevocable gift of a nonpossessory future interest to GS. As a lifetime gift, the deed was not a will and did not need to comply with the statutory formalities for a will. It removed the farm from O's probate estate. Since no survivorship language was used, at GS's death his remainder interest passed to S pursuant to his will. *See* Andersen § 17.

   Answer (A) is incorrect. GS's interest in the farm was not conditioned on his surviving O. Survivorship language was not used. O reserved only a life estate, and thus she had no interest in the farm at her death that would pass through probate.

   Answer (B) is incorrect. While revocable deeds are legally permissible, this was not a revocable deed. O made a completed and irrevocable gift to GS. She could not revoke it by her will or otherwise.

   Answer (D) is incorrect for the reasons explained above.

10.   O and GS became joint tenants with rights of survivorship by reason of the deed in most states. At GS's death, his interest in the farm passed nonprobate to O and not under his will to S. When O died, the farm was devised to GD. *See* Andersen § 18.

11.   **Answer (B) is correct.** UPC § 2-706 applies its substituted taker provisions to many nonprobate transfers similar to the way anti-lapse provisions apply to wills under UPC § 2-603. Thus, given the family relationship, G is entitled to receive an equal share of the proceeds. *See* Andersen § 45. Note that the antilapse type provisions in some states do not apply to nonprobate transfers.

   Answer (A) is incorrect because the provisions of UPC § 2-706 apply. Note that the antilapse type provisions in some states do not apply to nonprobate transfers.

   Answers (C) and (D) are incorrect. The substituted taker provisions entitle G to an equal share.

12.   **Answer (A) is correct.** Although the substituted taker provisions of UPC § 2-706 apply to life insurance beneficiary designations and many other types of nonprobate transfers, the

provisions do not apply to interests held in joint tenancy with rights of survivorship or to parties of multi-party joint accounts held with rights of survivorship. *See* UPC § 2-706(a)(2).

Answer (C) is incorrect. Joint accounts with rights of survivorship are nonprobate assets that pass outside the probate system.

Answers (B) and (D) are incorrect for the reasons explained.

13.   **Answer (B) is correct.** The Uniform Probate Code provides that a multi-party account (*e.g.*, a "joint account") is presumed to belong to the parties in proportion to their net contributions, which is the contributions of the parties plus their pro rata share of interest and dividends appropriately reduced by withdrawals. This presumption can be overcome by clear and convincing evidence that one of the parties intended a different result. *See* UPC § 6-211. *See* McGovern § 5.5 (p. 306–307).

       Answers (A), (C), and (D) are incorrect for the reasons explained.

14.   Unless there is specified nonsurvivorship language in the terms of the account, on the death of A, B, as the surviving party, owns the account. *See* UPC § 6-212(a). Some state statutes require specific "survivorship" language in the terms of the account. In those states, the heirs or devisees of the deceased party inherit the owner's interest in the account. *See* Andersen § 18(B).

15.   Yes, as the surviving spouse, S would own the amount A owned immediately before death. *See* UPC §§ 6-211, 6-212(a). *See* Andersen § 18(B).

16.   B and S would each own whatever they owned before A's death plus an equal share of what A owned. *See* McGovern § 5.5 (p. 306–307).

17.   Unless there is specified nonsurvivorship language in the terms of the account, S, as the surviving party, owns the account even though she never contributed to the account. *See* UPC § 6-212(a). *See* Andersen § 18(B). Some state statutes require specific "survivorship" language in the terms of the account. In those states the heirs or devisees of the owner of the account inherit the owner's interest.

18.   Yes, according to UPC § 6-102. *See* Andersen § 18(B).

19.   Before D's death, E has no right to the account. *See* UPC § 6-211(c). However, after D's death, E is entitled to whatever remains in the account. *See* UPC § 6-212(b). *See* McGovern § 5.5 (p. 306–307).

20.   **Answer (A) is correct.** Nonprobate assets are also included in the decedent's gross estate. *See* IRC §§ 2036–2040.

       Answers (B) and (C) are not correct. One cannot avoid inclusion in the gross estate by making this type of nonprobate disposition of the property.

       Answer (D) is not correct. Even though the checking account is in the names of both O and B, 100% of the account is included in O's gross estate because O created and funded the account. *See* IRC § 2040.

21.   **Answer (A) is correct.** An insurance policy on the decedent's life is included in the

decedent's gross estate if (i) the policy is payable to the decedent's probate estate or (ii) the decedent owned the policy immediately prior to death. *See* IRC § 2042.

Answers (B), (C), and (D) are not correct. O owned both policies at the time of death. Accordingly, the proceeds of each are included in the gross estate.

22.   **Answer (A) is correct.** The two plans add $1,500,000 to O's gross estate even though C will have to report the $1,500,000 as income when received. *See* IRC § 2039.

Answers (B), (C), and (D) are not correct. Both plans are included in the gross estate. C will be entitled to an income tax deduction for any estate taxes attributable to the plans. *See* IRC § 691.

1. No, the following issues, factors, and considerations should be discussed with C:

    Comparing Costs. McGovern explains that going through probate with a will may be more expensive than avoiding probate with a revocable trust. The fees of executors and their attorneys may be based on the size of the "probate" estate in some states, and thus the fees can be reduced by nonprobate transfers. There is, however, a growing trend against basing fees simply on the value of the probate estate. Costs are state law specific. The preparation and funding of a revocable trust may be costlier than the preparation of a will in that a revocable trust planning often requires additional work, such as transferring title of assets to the trustee, and these additional expenses could offset some of the contemplated savings in probate costs. Since revocable trusts tend to be more complicated than wills, the legal fees for preparing the revocable trust and administering the trust during the settlor's lifetime are often greater than the fees for simply preparing a comparable will. Thus, whether or not avoiding probate reduces costs depends on each client's situation and can vary from state to state. *See* McGovern § 9.4 (p. 422).

    Delays. McGovern also explains that, while the typical delay associated with probate administration is a source of popular dissatisfaction, its significance should not be exaggerated. The needs of the beneficiaries of the estate during probate administration can be met by family allowances and by partial distributions. Again, the real issue depends on state law. For example, in some states, testamentary trusts are subject to close court supervision, which can create costs and delays, but the number of states in which court supervision of testamentary trusts is required is declining. In most states, trusts, whether revocable or irrevocable, are generally not subject to continuing court supervision. *See* McGovern § 9.4 (p. 422).

    Creditors' Rights. As McGovern explains that, while creditors of the settlor of a revocable trust in some states may not have a right to reach the assets of the revocable trust once the settlor dies, this possible benefit of revocable trusts is no longer true in most jurisdictions. *See* McGovern § 9.4 (p. 422).

    Estate Tax Issues. McGovern also explains that revocable trusts have no real tax advantages. If the settlor retains the power to revoke the trust, the trust income continues to be taxed to the settlor, and the trust property is included in the settlor's gross estate at death. *See* McGovern § 9.4 (p. 423).

    Pour-Over Will. There is still a need for a will that "pours over" into the trust any probate assets not in the trust when the settlor dies. Most individuals using a revocable trust will still need a will to coordinate the various parts of the estate plan. Pour-over wills are used for this purpose. *See* McGovern § 9.4 (p. 423).

    Miscellaneous Issues. Homestead, exempt property and family allowance rights may be affected by placing the estate in a revocable trust prior to the settlor's death. Depending on the jurisdiction, there may be restrictions on testamentary power that do not apply to revocable trusts (*e.g.*, pretermitted child statutes or reduced complications for trustees of inter vivos trusts compared to testamentary trusts). *See* Dukeminier p. 461–465.

2.   **Answer (D) is correct.** S's trust instrument does not need not to be executed in compliance with the statutory formalities required for wills because the trust is not a will. The property subject to S's trust is not probate property at death because it is then no longer owned by S, individually, but rather by the trustee and the beneficiary. An inter vivos trust (unlike a will) is a means to presently transfer ownership during the settlor's lifetime. S transferred legal title to T and a nonpossessory future equitable interest to B when the trust *was created*, not when S died. The fact that B's interest was subject to S's power to revoke or amend the trust, or is subject to a condition of surviving S and may be subject to other conditions, does not make the trust a will (*i.e.*, the trust instrument need not comply with the statutory formalities for wills). *See* Andersen § 2(B).

      Answers (A), (B), and (C) are incorrect for the reasons explained.

3.   No, S's declaration of trust is a present transfer of an equitable nonpossessory future interest to B the same way it would have been had S entered into an agreement of trust with a third party. The identity of the trustee does not affect whether or not the trust must comply with the statutory formalities for wills in order for beneficial interests to pass as a result of the settlor's death. *See* Andersen § 2(B).

4.   Because the express trust was irrevocable, the divorce did not affect W's income interest. *See* UPC § 2-804. However, G1's death terminated G1's interest, and a substituted gift was created in GG. *See* UPC § 2-707. GG will have to survive W to take; if not, GG's contingent remainder interest may fail, and O's reversionary interest in Blackacre may pass to O's successor in interest, presumably the devisee under O's will, G2. *See* Andersen § 45(B)(2)(b).

     The result may differ in a state that has not adopted the UPC approach as it relates to the substituted gift in favor of GG. G1's interest is likely to have been a vested remainder which passed to S when G1 died. See Andersen § 45(B)(2)(c).

5.   **Answer (D) is correct.** The divorce had the effect of revoking W's income interest because the trust was revocable. *See* UPC § 2-804(b). Since G1 died before O, G1's contingent remainder failed, and GG is the substituted taker pursuant to UPC § 2-707(b). See the answer to the immediately preceding question.

     However, in a state that has not adopted the UPC approach, W may still retain her income interest, and G1's vested remainder may have passed to S. See Andersen § 45(B)(1).

     Answers (A), (B), and (C) are incorrect. The substituted taker, GG, survived until the distribution date, O's death.

     In a non-UPC state, S may have succeeded to G1's vested remainder. See Andersen § 45(B)(2)(c).

6.   Because the stocks and Blackacre are probate assets, the executor of O's estate can use them to satisfy O's debts. According to UPC § 3-902, shares of distributees abate without any preference between real or personal property. The stocks and real property should be abated proportionately. After the debts are paid by the personal representative of the estate, what is left should be delivered to the bank to be distributed pursuant to the terms of the trust.

States that have not adopted the Uniform Probate Code approach may provide that personal property should be abated prior to real property within the same classification of devises. See McGovern § 8.4. Accordingly, in a non-UPC state, the stock may need to be sold to pay the debts, and the real property will pass to G1 assuming the state allows testamentary additions to inter vivos trusts. Most states have statutes similar to UPC § 2-511 which do allow probate assets to "pour over" into the trust. If testamentary additions to inter vivos trusts are not allowed, C1 and C2 would succeed to the estate remaining after debts are paid. See McGovern § 6.2.

7.   **Answer (B) is correct.** S is entitled to an elective share amount out of the decedent's net probate estate augmented by the $100,000 in the revocable trust. *See* UPC §§ 2-202, 2-203, 2-205.

The answer may differ in a state that has not adopted the UPC approach. See Andersen § 28(C). For example, in a community property state, the surviving spouse will likely be entitled to half of the community probate assets and be compensated for half of what the decedent contributed to the trust. See McGovern §§ 3.7, 3.8.

Answer (A) is incorrect. The trust is valid.

Answers (C) and (D) are incorrect. The augmented estate consists of the net probate estate and certain nonprobate dispositions.

8.   **Answer (D) is correct.** It appears as if a valid, enforceable express trust was created during S's lifetime even though title remained in S's name until S died. *See* UTC §§ 401, 402. At S's death, T's equitable remainder interest became possessory. *See* Andersen § 12.

Answers (A) and (B) are incorrect. An express inter vivos trust does not need to be executed with testamentary formalities. The family farm passes pursuant to the terms of the trust, not by the will or by intestate succession.

Answer (C) is incorrect. Since S did not change the title to the family farm when the trust was created, the family farm still appears to be a probate asset, and T will need to take steps to establish the existence of the trust and his ownership under the trust.

9.   **Answer (D) is correct.** The facts that there was no transfer of title before S's death and that S retained the power to revoke the trust do not affect the trust's validity. *See* UTC §§ 401, 402. *See* Andersen § 12. Since S did not revoke the apparently valid, enforceable express trust prior to S's death, the terms of the trust control the disposition of the family farm. Since the trust was created by S's declaration of trust, at S's death T's equitable remainder interest became possessory.

Answers (A) and (B) are incorrect. An express trust does not need to be executed with testamentary formalities.

Answer (C) is incorrect. Since S did not change the title to the family farm when the trust was created, the family farm still appears to be a probate asset, and T will need to take steps to establish the existence of the trust and T's ownership under the trust.

10.   **Answer (C) is correct.** If the creation and funding of the trust were a transfer in fraud on S's creditors, the creditors can pursue their claims against the trust estate pursuant to state law on fraudulent transfers. The transfer may also constitute a voidable preference in bankruptcy. *See* comment to UTC § 505. If S did not become insolvent because of the creation of the trust, the trust estate probably is not reachable to satisfy S's debts. UTC § 505 adopts this generally accepted principle. *See* McGovern § 9.8.

Answers (A), (B), and (D) are incorrect for the reasons given.

11.   **Answer (D) is correct.** During the lifetime of the settlor, the trust estate of a revocable trust is subject to claims of the settlor's creditors whether or not the original creation and funding of the trust were fraudulent. *See* UTC § 505(a)(1). The result is likely to be the same in a state that has not adopted the Uniform Trust Code. *See* Andersen § 12(E).

      Answers (A), (B), and (C) are incorrect for the reasons given.

12.   **Answer (B) is correct.** Following the settlor's death, the trust estate of a revocable trust continues to be subject to claims of the settlor's creditors. UTC § 505 adopts this widely accepted principle. *See* Andersen § 12(E) (n. 79). The result may differ in some non-UTC states.

      See GEORGE T. BOGERT, TRUSTS, *§ 148 (6th ed. 1987) (hereinafter "Bogert § ____").*

      Answers (A), (C), and (D) are incorrect for the reasons given.

13.   **Answer (A) is correct.** A donor does not make a gift for federal tax purposes until the donor has parted with all dominion and control. The power to revoke is an explicit reservation of dominion and control to determine what, if anything, C is to receive. *See* Treasury Regulations § 25.2511-2.

      Answers (B), (C), and (D) are incorrect for the reasons given.

14.   No, it is the settlor's retained power of revocation that prevents the transfer from being a completed gift for gift tax purposes. *See* Treasury Regulations §§ 25.2511-2.

15.   **Answer (B) is correct.** The trust estate of a revocable trust is included in the settlor's gross estate. *See* IRC § 2038.

      Answers (A), (C), and (D) are incorrect for the reasons given.

16.   **Answer (C) is correct.** There is no gift for tax purposes when the trust is created because S did not part with dominion and control over the trust estate since S had retained the power to revoke the trust. *See* Treasury Regulations § 25.2511-2. However, whenever a legitimate distribution is made to C pursuant to the trust terms, a gift is made by the settlor to the beneficiary.

      Answers (A), (B), and (D) are incorrect for the reasons given.

17.   **Answer (A) is correct.** Under IRC § 676, the $5,000 is taxable to S because S retained the power to revoke the trust. This is a result of the "grantor trust" income tax rules.

      Answer (B) is incorrect. There is no income tax deduction for gifts.

      Answer (C) is incorrect. Under the grantor trust rules, the settlor (*i.e.*, the "grantor") is taxable on the trust's income, not the trustee (*i.e.*, not the trust).

      Answer (D) is incorrect. The $5,000 distribution to C was a gift to C, and gifts are not taxable to donees. *See* IRC § 102.

18.   Absent specific language to the contrary, trustees of express trusts are held to strict fiduciary standards and can be held personally liable to the trust's beneficiaries for the

breach of those fiduciary duties. *See* UTC § 802(a). *See* Andersen § 12.1. However, if S commits an act of omission or commission in S's role as trustee that otherwise would be a breach of trust, there is nothing C can do while the trust is revocable; the duties of the trustee are owed exclusively to the settlor of the trust. *See* UTC § 603.

19. The same test of mental capacity applies for wills and revocable trusts. *See* UTC § 601. Some states require the mental capacity needed to create and fund any inter vivos trust (*e.g.*, contract capacity). *See* Bogert § 9.

20. The answer depends on the applicable state law. In some states, inter vivos trusts are deemed to be irrevocable unless the settlor expressly retained the right to revoke the trust. In other states, inter vivos trusts are deemed to be revocable unless expressly made irrevocable. UTC § 602(a) adopts the latter view. *See* McGovern § 9.4.

1. Generally, an adult individual with the requisite mental capacity has the right and power to direct how the individual wishes his or her property to be distributed after the individual's death. However, there are limits on the individual's testamentary power. *See* McGovern Ch. 3.

2. **Answer (A) is correct.** O appears to have died intestate. Since the letter was typewritten by O and not signed by the friends, the document does not meet the requirements for a valid will. *See* UPC § 2-502. However, UPC § 2-503 allows a probate court to "excuse a harmless error" and probate a defectively executed document if there is "clear and convincing evidence" that the otherwise defective document represents the decedent's testamentary intent. C1 will likely argue that the letter manifests testamentary intent and for the application of UPC § 2-503.

    Most states do not have a statute similar to UPC § 2-503. See Andersen § 7(B)(4).

    Answers (B), (C), and (D) are not correct. Unless C1 meets the burden of proof required in UPC § 2-503, the letter cannot be admitted to probate. *See* UPC § 2-502.

3. **Answer (A) is correct.** O still appears to have died intestate. Unless the material provisions of the will are in O's handwriting, a testamentary writing that is not acknowledged by the testator before a notary public, or does not include the signatures of two witnesses, cannot be admitted to probate. *See* UPC § 2-502. Delivery is not a prerequisite to a will. However, UPC § 2-503 allows the probate of a defectively executed will if there is "clear and convincing evidence" that the otherwise defective document represents the decedent's testamentary intent.

    Most states do not have a statute similar to UPC § 2-503. See Andersen § 7(B)(4).

    Answers (B), (C), and (D) are not correct. C1 may argue that C2 had agreed with O that C1 was to receive the house and its contents and that the court should impose a constructive trust on C2 to prevent C2 from being unjustly enriched. *See* RESTATEMENT, THIRD, OF TRUSTS § 18 (2003) (hereinafter "Restatement, Third, of Trusts § ___").

4. **Answer (B) is correct.** UPC § 2-502(b) recognizes "holographic" wills. Accordingly, assuming the letter properly manifested O's intent to make a disposition effective at O's death, the will can be admitted to probate, and the house and its contents pass to C1. If not, the letter is not a will, and O died intestate. *See* answers to the preceding questions.

    Some states which have not enacted the Uniform Probate Code have similar statutes. However, a number of states do not recognize holographic wills unless properly witnessed. See McGovern § 4.4.

    Answer (A) is not correct. UPC § 2-502(b) recognizes holographic wills. However, answer (A) would be the correct answer in a number of states.

    Answers (C) and (D) are not correct. In a state which recognizes holographic wills, a properly executed holographic will can devise both real and personal property.

5.   **Answer (C) is correct.** Wills are revocable dispositions of property that take effect upon the testator's death. The execution of a joint will does not create a presumption of a contract not to revoke the will. *See* UPC § 2-514. Accordingly, absent written evidence of a contract, A had the power and the right to revoke the 2000 will, which A did by the execution of the 2010 will. *See* UPC §§ 2-507(c), 2-514.

Many non-UPC states have similar statutes. Absent a statute, the common law of a state may create a presumption that the parties intended to have a contractual will when they executed the joint will. See McGovern § 4.9.

     Answer (A) is incorrect. The 2000 document was intended by A and B to be a will. In order for it to be effective, the 2000 will must be admitted to probate. However, it was apparently revoked by A when A executed the 2010 will.

     Answer (B) is not correct. The 2000 will was revoked. Further, there is no evidence that A ever revoked the 2010 will.

     Answer (D) is not correct. UPC § 2-514 creates a presumption that the 2000 will was not executed pursuant to a contract not to revoke it. Accordingly, unless B can establish that a contract existed pursuant to UPC § 2-514, B is without a cause of action. Even if a contract can be established, A revoked the 2000 will, and B's remedy is typically limited to a breach of contract action. *See* McGovern § 4.9 (p. 279).

6.   The provision in the will stating the material provision of the parties' agreement allows B to enforce the terms of the contract. *See* UPC § 2-514. However, the prevailing view is that A did have the power to revoke the 2000 will, and the 2010 will can be admitted to probate. A's interest in Blackacre passes to F. Consequently, B is typically limited to bringing a breach of contract action against A's estate and/or F and seeking specific performance, the imposition of a constructive trust, or money damages. *See* McGovern § 4.9 (p. 279).

The same result would occur in most other states. However, in some jurisdictions, a contract may not have existed because A did not comply with the terms of the agreement (i.e., A revoked the will and devised the property to F). Under this approach, the agreement was actually an offer by B to be accepted by A, and A did not accept B's offer. Consequently, B has no cause of action.

7.   **Answer (A) is correct.** Assuming that the intent expressed in the 2000 document is not testamentary in nature, but is a valid agreement to create a right of survivorship, A and B converted their tenancy in common into a joint tenancy with rights of survivorship. Andersen § 18(A). Consequently, at A's death, A's interest passed nonprobate to B. A's will only controls the disposition of A's probate estate (*i.e.*, property which would otherwise pass by intestate succession). *See* UPC § 1-201(57).

The same result would likely occur in states that have not enacted the Uniform Probate Code. See Andersen Ch. 5.

     Answer (B) is not correct. The 2000 document was not intended to be a will. If testamentary intent had been evident, UPC § 2-502(a)(3)(B) allows for the testator to acknowledge it before a notary public.

     Answers (C) and (D) are not correct. While the 2010 will devises A's probate estate to F, Blackacre passed nonprobate to B.

8. **Answer (A) is correct.** UPC § 2-514 creates the presumption that the mutual 2005 wills were not contractual. S1's estate passed to S2 when the 2005 will was probated. Absent another written document establishing a contract, S2 has the power and the right to devise the entire estate to anyone, and C would not have a valid cause of action against S2 or S2's estate.

   Many non-UPC states have similar statutes which would create the same result. The result may be different in some states that have not enacted the Uniform Probate Code or a similar statute. In these states, the execution of mutual wills may raise a presumption that a contract does exist. See McGovern § 4.9.

   Answers (B), (C), and (D) are not correct for the reasons given.

9. **Answer (C) is correct.** UPC § 2-514 will allow C to enforce the terms of the contract as the third-party beneficiary of the contract of S1 and S2. However, in most jurisdictions, C cannot stop S2 from executing a new will. *See* McGovern § 4.9. At S2's death, S2's new will can be admitted to probate, and C's remedy typically will be limited to a breach of contract action against S2's estate. C may seek specific performance, a constructive trust, or money damages. A few cases have allowed a suit by the third-party beneficiary of the contract during the promissor's lifetime. *See* McGovern § 4.9.

   Answer (A) is not correct. The provisions of UPC § 2-514 have been met.

   Answer (B) is not correct. A will by its nature is a revocable disposition to take effect at death. Accordingly, a will can be revoked. C's cause of action will not accrue until S2's death.

   Answer (D) is not correct. The terms of the 2005 will did not devise to C a remainder interest.

10. **Answer (A) is correct.** S2's contract with S1 required S2 to devise Blackacre to C when S2 dies. Since a will does not become effective until the testator dies, C's rights under the contract were dependent on C surviving S2. *See* McGovern § 4.9.

    Answers (B) and (C) are not correct. C would have had to survive S2 in order for H to enforce the terms of the contract.

    Answer (D) is not correct. The terms of S1's 2005 will did not devise to C a remainder interest.

11. **Answer (D) is correct.** S1 and S2 agreed not to revoke the 2005 wills, and their contract can be established pursuant to UPC § 2-514. Had C not died, C would likely have been in a position to bring a breach of contract cause of action against S2's estate if S2 revokes the 2005 will. *See* McGovern § 4.9. If S2 does not revoke the 2005 will, at S2's death, C's child, J, may be able to probate S2's 2005 will, and the entire estate would pass to J pursuant to the "antilapse" provisions of UPC § 2-603. Accordingly, if S2 revokes the 2005 will and devises the estate to D, J may have a breach of contract action against S2's estate. D will argue that J was not the intended third-party beneficiary of the contract. However, as Andersen notes, ". . . these contracts are notorious litigation breeders." *See* Andersen § 10 (p. 75).

    Most states that have not enacted the Uniform Probate Code have statutes similar to UPC § 2-603. See McGovern § 8.5.

    Answer (A) is incorrect. UPC § 2-603 may give J a breach of contract action.

    Answer (B) is incorrect. The terms of S1's 2005 will did not devise to C a remainder interest.

> **Answer (C) is incorrect.** Any cause of action J may have will generally not accrue until S2's death. A few cases have allowed a suit during the promissor's lifetime. *See* McGovern § 4.9.

12.   Although a contract not to revoke a will can be established if the provisions of UPC § 2-514 are met, F or the personal representative of A's estate can argue "failure of consideration" as a defense to any breach of contract action brought by C. Because A and B owned Blackacre as joint tenants with rights of survivorship, B acquired A's interest in Blackacre by reason of the form of ownership, not pursuant to A's will. Arguably, B's promise to devise Blackacre to C was not supported by consideration. C will likely argue there was, in fact, consideration, if relevant law permits joint tenants to unilaterally sever the joint tenancy. *See* McGovern §§ 4.8, 4.9.

13.   **Answer (C) is correct.** Although Blackacre passed nonprobate to B due to the survivorship rights associated with the joint tenancy, B is put to an "equitable election," and B cannot accept any benefits under A's will without agreeing, in effect, to convey Blackacre to F. If B accepts any benefits under the will, F will be entitled to Blackacre. C's rights as a third-party beneficiary under the original contract would likely be revoked by the original parties' subsequent modification of the original agreement. *See* Atkinson §§ 40,138.

> **Answers (A), (B), and (D) are incorrect** for the reasons given.

14.   **Answer (B) is correct.** Due to the joint tenancy, A acquired fee simple title to Blackacre by reason of B's death. *See* Andersen § 18. At A's death, Blackacre passes to F, and the residuary estate is divided between F and B1, who takes as a substituted taker for B pursuant to UPC § 2-603(b)(1). Assuming A's promise to B to devise Blackacre to C was not supported by consideration, C appears to be without a legitimate cause of action. If consideration is found, C may have a breach of contract cause of action against A's estate. *See* McGovern § 4.9.

> *Most states that have not enacted the Uniform Probate Code have statutes similar to UPC § 2-603. See McGovern § 8.3.*

> **Answers (A) and (C) are incorrect** for the reasons given.

> **Answer (D) is incorrect.** It is arguable that A's promise to B not to revoke the 2000 will was not supported by any consideration. However, C will likely argue that A's promise was supported by consideration, if relevant law permits a joint tenant to unilaterally sever a joint tenancy.

15.   Although a testator has the power in a will to declare how the individual wishes his or her property to be distributed after the individual's death, that authority is effectively limited to the individual's probate estate. Nonprobate assets pass to their designated beneficiaries. Thus, Blackacre will pass to A, and the insurance will be payable to B. *See* McGovern § 5.5 (p. 303, 304).

16.   No, for the same reason discussed in the immediately preceding question. *See* DUKEMINIER pp. 469–474. If the will had included a specific devise of the insurance policy or proceeds, the Restatement takes the position the proceeds should be paid to the devisee. *See* RESTATEMENT, THIRD, OF PROPERTY: WILLS AND OTHER DONATIVE TRANSFERS § 7.2 comment e (2003) (hereinafter "Restatement, Third, Property § ____").

17. **Answer (D) is correct.** Since S did not survive O, and there was not an alternative designated beneficiary of the policy, the proceeds become part of the probate estate and pass pursuant to the provisions of the will. *See* RESTATEMENT, THIRD, PROPERTY § 7.1.

Answers (A), (B), and (C) are incorrect for the reasons given.

18. B would have an election. B could retain the $1,000,000 as the designated beneficiary of the policy. However, if B accepts any benefits under the will, B will be required to assign the $1,000,000 to A. *See* Atkinson § 138.

19. **Answer (C) is correct.** In community property states, the first spouse to die has testamentary power over that spouse's separate property and one-half of the community property. The surviving spouse retains his or her separate property and half of the community property. *See* Andersen § 28(A).

Answers (A), (B), and (D) are incorrect for the reasons given.

20. S2 would have an election to make. S2 can retain Greenacre and a one-half interest in Whiteacre by disclaiming the residuary estate (*e.g.*, Blackacre). However, if S2 elects to "accept" under the will in order to receive the residuary estate, including Blackacre, S2 will need to convey S2's half of Whiteacre to C. *See* Atkinson § 138 and McGovern § 3.8 (p. 196).

1. Generally, a will is a testamentary instrument that directs how the testator's property is to be distributed after the testator's death. It may also be used to designate who the testator wishes to serve in fiduciary capacities (*e.g.*, executor, trustee, etc.). A will is not valid unless it was executed by the testator who had testamentary capacity following required statutory formalities. If not revoked by the testator prior to death, the will can be admitted to probate by a court of competent jurisdiction to be effective as a testamentary disposition. *See* McGovern Ch. 4. A few states permit ante-mortem probate. *See* McGovern § 13.3.

2. **Answer (B) is correct.** A testator must be at least 18 years of age and be of sound mind in order to validly execute a will. *See* UPC § 2-501. In a contested probate proceeding, F will have the burden to prove the facts of (i) O's death, (ii) the court's venue, and (iii) the due execution of the will. However, A will have the burden to prove O did not have testamentary capacity. *See* UPC § 3-407.

    In some jurisdictions, F would have the burden to prove O had testamentary capacity at the time O executed the will. See Atkinson §§ 100, 101.

    Answer (A) is incorrect. A diagnosis of Alzheimer's alone is not likely to be considered prima facie evidence of the lack of O's testamentary capacity.

    Answer (C) is incorrect. According to the Uniform Probate Code, the burden of proof on the issue of testamentary capacity is on the contestant.

    Answer (D) is incorrect. The test for the capacity necessary to execute a will differs from the test for incapacity in a guardianship or conservatorship proceeding. In order to determine whether a testator had testamentary capacity, courts typically look at various factors, such as the testator's ability to understand the nature of a testamentary act, to remember the "natural" objects of the testator's bounty, and to understand the nature and extent of the testator's property. *See* McGovern § 7.1.

3. **Answer (B) is correct.** A has the burden to prove O lacked testamentary capacity when the will was executed. *See* UPC § 3-407. However, introduction of evidence that O had previously been found to be incapacitated in a guardianship proceeding may be evidence that O lacked testamentary capacity. *See* McGovern § 7.2.

    In some non-UPC jurisdictions, the burden of proof is on F to prove O had testamentary capacity. See Atkinson §§ 100, 101.

    Answers (A), (C), and (D) are incorrect for the reasons given.

4. **Answer (B) is correct.** A has the burden to prove O lacked testamentary capacity when the will was executed. *See* UPC § 3-407. The fact that O was found to be incapacitated in a guardianship proceeding after the will was executed may be evidence of incapacity but is not conclusive. Different tests for capacity are used in guardianship proceedings and probate

proceedings.

F would have the burden to prove O had testamentary capacity in some non-UPC jurisdictions. See Atkinson §§ 100, 101.

Answers (A), (C), and (D) are incorrect for the reasons given.

5.   **Answer (C) is correct.** The will of a testator with the requisite testamentary capacity can still be denied probate if the devisee improperly influenced the testator during the execution of the will. Accordingly, A has the burden to prove F's undue influence. *See* UPC § 3-407.

States that have not enacted the Uniform Probate Code typically place the burden on the contestant for the issue of undue influence. See McGovern § 7.3.

Answers (A) and (B) are incorrect. Undue influence is an issue separate and distinct from testamentary capacity, although evidence of one is relevant to the other.

Answer (D) is incorrect. The burden of proof is typically on the contestant even in a state where the burden of proof on capacity is on the proponent.

6.   A will must be in writing and signed by the testator. *See* UPC § 2-502. However, a testator does not need to sign the testator's legal name or even the name typically used by the testator. If whatever was actually written on the will by the testator was intended by the testator to be a signature, the will has been signed by the testator. Accordingly, if O wrote O's first name and intended it to be O's signature, the will was signed; if the evidence shows O intended to write both the first and last names, but was unable to complete the task, some courts have held the will was not signed. *See* McGovern § 4.2.

The same result is typically reached in states that have not enacted the Uniform Probate Code.

7.   **Answer (C) is correct.** Whatever a testator intends to be a signature can be a signature. It is not unusual for a testator to make a "mark" on the will rather than sign the testator's name. If the "mark" was intended to be a signature, the will has been signed. *See* McGovern § 4.2. Accordingly, B has the burden to prove due execution, including the signature requirement. *See* UPC § 3-407.

States that have not enacted the Uniform Probate Code typically place the burden of proof on the proponent of the will. See Atkinson §§ 100, 101.

Answers (A), (B), and (D) are incorrect. If B can prove O intended the mark to be O's signature, the will can be admitted to probate.

8.   **Answer (C) is correct.** UPC § 2-502(a)(2) authorizes what is commonly called a "proxy signature." If the testator's name is signed by another in the testator's conscious presence and at the testator's direction, the will can be admitted to probate. Accordingly, B has the burden to prove the requisites of a "proxy signature."

While most states that have not enacted the Uniform Probate Code permit "proxy signatures," they may differ on what is required for a "proxy signature" to be effective. See McGovern § 4.2.

Answer (A) is incorrect. A will can have a proxy signature.

Answer (B) is incorrect. B will have to prove by a preponderance of the evidence that the witness signed O's name at O's direction and in O's conscious presence.

Answer (D) is incorrect. UPC § 2-502 (a)(2) requires that the witness sign O's name at O's direction in O's conscious presence.

In some non-UPC states, the "proxy signature" may need to have been done in O's "visual presence" or "line of sight." If so, since O could not see the witness sign the will, the will may not be valid.

9.   UPC § 2-502 does not require that the testator "publish" the document as a will. Accordingly, it is not necessary to prove that the witnesses were aware the document they were signing was O's will. If G can prove that the witnesses signed after they observed O sign the document, or that the witnesses signed after O acknowledged O's signature, the will can be admitted to probate, even if they were not aware what they signed was actually a will.

In states that have not enacted the Uniform Probate Code, the technical requirements for will execution vary. For example, the testator may be required to "publish" the will; in others, the testator must at a minimum acknowledge to the witnesses that the document is the testator's document. Some states require that the testator request the witnesses sign the document. See McGovern § 4.3.

10.   **Answer (C) is correct.** UPC § 2-502(a)(3)(A) does not require the witnesses observe a testator signing the will. If it can be established that the witnesses signed the will within a reasonable time after they observed the testator acknowledging the testator's signature or the will itself, the will can be admitted to probate.

In a state that has not enacted the Uniform Probate Code, the state's attestation requirements may be significantly different. See McGovern § 4.3.

Answers (A) and (B) are incorrect for the reasons given.

Answer (D) is incorrect. Not a good answer to give the client! The Uniform Probate Code only requires that each witness observe one of the following: (i) the testator sign the will, (ii) the testator acknowledge the testator's signature, or (iii) the testator acknowledge the document as the testator's will.

In a state that has not enacted the Uniform Probate Code, the state's attestation requirements may be significantly different, and the will may not be valid.

11.   The Uniform Probate Code does not require that each witness sign in the presence of the other witnesses so long as they otherwise comply with UPC § 2-502 (a)(3)(A).

Some states which have not enacted the Uniform Probate Code may require the witnesses to sign in each other's presence. See McGovern § 4.3.

12.   **Answer (B) is correct.** UPC § 2-502(a)(3)(A) does not require that the witnesses sign the will in the presence of the testator. Assuming the other requirements of UPC § 2-502 can be proven by F, the will can be admitted to probate. *See* UPC § 3-407.

Many states which have not enacted the Uniform Probate Code require that the witnesses sign the will in the presence of the testator. See McGovern § 4.3.

Answers (A) and (C) are incorrect for the reasons given.

Answer (D) is incorrect. The Uniform Probate Code does not require that the testator observe the witnesses sign the will.

In those jurisdictions that require the witnesses sign in the presence of the testator, research may be necessary to determine if the law of the state requires "conscious" presence or "visual" or "line of sight" presence. If so, the will may not be valid.

13.   The Uniform Probate Code does not require that the witnesses sign the will in the testator's presence, and the comments to UPC § 2-502 suggests that they can even sign the will after the testator's death. Accordingly, if F can prove that the witnesses did sign within "a reasonable time" after they observed O sign the will, or O acknowledge O's signature, or O acknowledge the document as O's will, the will may be admitted to probate.

> *The statutes in most states which have not enacted the Uniform Probate Code require that the witnesses sign in the testator's presence, and many courts have rejected wills signed by witnesses after the testator's death. See McGovern § 4.3.*

14.   **Answer (B) is correct.** The Uniform Probate Code only requires two witnesses. *See* UPC § 2-502(a)(3). If the will is otherwise valid, the will can be admitted to probate with only two witnesses. The Uniform Probate Code was amended in 2008 to allow notarized wills without any witnesses. *See* McGovern § 4.3.

   Answers (A, (C), and (D) are incorrect. The Uniform Probate Code does not require three witnesses.

> *In those jurisdictions that do require more than two witnesses, research may be necessary to see if the state has a "harmless error" statute, or if the courts have otherwise relaxed the doctrine of "strict compliance."*

15.   **Answer (C) is correct.** Unlike statutes in some states, the Uniform Probate Code does not require that the testator sign the will at the end of the document. *See* UPC § 2-502(a)(2). B must prove that O intended the writing of O's name in the first line to be O's signature. *See* UPC § 3-407.

> *The result may be different in a non-UPC state. See McGovern § 4.2.*

   Answers (A) and (B) are incorrect. The fact that the testator did not sign at the end is not necessarily a bar to the will's probate. Nevertheless, the fact the testator wrote the testator's name in the body of the will may not constitute a "signature."

   Answer (D) is incorrect. The Uniform Probate Code does not require the testator's signature to be at the end of the will.

> *In a state that has not enacted the Uniform Probate Code, research may be necessary to determine if the applicable statute requires the testator's signature to appear at the end of the will. If so, the will may not be valid.*

16.   C1 will likely inherit the entire estate. O did not comply with the statutory requirements of revocation or execution. Thus, the 2000 will was not revoked by O prior to O's death. It is generally accepted that a will may be revoked by either a subsequent valid will or an authorized act done to the will. UPC § 2-507 confirms this principle. Accordingly, notwithstanding O's expressed intent to revoke the 2000 will and leave O's property to G, O's intent was not expressed in a writing that met the requirements of a valid will. *See* UPC § 2-502. The e-mail did not meet the statutory requirements of a will.

> *The result is likely to be the same in a state that has not enacted the Uniform Probate Code. See McGovern § 5.1.*

17.   **Answer (B) is correct.** The 2000 will was not revoked by O. It is generally accepted that a will may be revoked by either a subsequent valid will or an authorized act done to the will.

UPC § 2-507 confirms this principle. Accordingly, notwithstanding O's expressed intent to revoke the 2000 will and leave O's property to G, O's intent was not expressed in a writing that meets the requirements of a valid will. *See* UPC § 2-502.

The result is likely to be the same in a state that has not enacted the Uniform Probate Code. See McGovern § 5.1.

Answers (A) and (D) are incorrect for the reasons given.

Answer (C) is incorrect. The letter was not a valid will unless the court finds UPC § 2-503 is applicable and G meets the burden of proof required by the statute.

18.   **Answer (C) is correct.** UPC § 2-502(b) provides that a will that is not properly witnessed can still be valid if the material provisions of the will are in the testator's handwriting. Accordingly, if the letter manifests "testamentary" or "revocatory" intent (*i.e.*, the letter indicates it was intended to have a dispositive effect and not just a casual expression of what a future will should contain), it is a will that revokes the old will and devises O's probate estate to G. Proof of the testator's intent can be made with extrinsic evidence. *See* UPC § 2-502(c). In a significant departure from the generally accepted view, UPC § 3-407 places on the contestants the burden of establishing O's lack of testamentary intent.

Some states that have not enacted the Uniform Probate Code do not recognize unwitnessed holographic wills. See McGovern § 4.4. Some states place the burden of proof on the proponent. See Atkinson §§ 100, 101.

Answers (A), (B), and (D) are incorrect for the reasons given.

19.   **Answer (B) is correct.** The 2000 will was not revoked. The document found in the safe deposit box is not a valid will. UPC § 2-502(b) provides that a will that is not properly witnessed must be acknowledged by the testator before a notary public or be in the testator's handwriting.

The result is likely to be the same in a state that has not enacted the Uniform Probate Code. See McGovern § 5.1.

Answers (A) and (D) are incorrect. O was survived by both children but did not die intestate.

Answer (C) is incorrect. The document in the safe deposit box is not a valid will unless the court finds UPC § 2-503 is applicable and G meets the burden of establishing O intended the document to be O's will.

20.   Delivery is not a prerequisite. UPC § 2-502(b) provides that a will that is not properly witnessed can still be valid, if the material provisions of the will are in the testator's handwriting. Accordingly, the new will may have impliedly revoked the old will due to the inconsistent dispositive provisions and devised O's probate estate to G.

Some states that have not enacted the Uniform Probate Code do not recognize unwitnessed holographic wills. See McGovern § 4.4.

21.   **Answer (C) is correct.** UPC § 2-502(b) requires that only the "material portions" of the will be in the testator's handwriting.

In some non-UPC states, the 2000 will was not revoked since the new will was not properly witnessed. In other states, a court may determine that O intended for the date to be part of the new will and that the new will is, therefore, not wholly in the testator's handwriting and invalid. Another state may find that the name of the hotel and the date were "surplus" and that the new will was wholly in the testator's handwriting and valid. See McGovern § 4.4.

Answers (A), (B), and (D) are incorrect for the reasons given.

22. O died intestate. The 2010 will was revoked by O. It is generally accepted that a testator can revoke a will by lining through the testator's signature, and since the 2010 will was found in O's safe deposit box, most courts would presume that O placed the "X" on O's signature with an intent to revoke, thereby revoking the will. *See* McGovern § 5.2. UPC § 2-507 adopts this principle. This answer assumes O had testamentary capacity at all relevant times.

23. **Answer (B) is correct.** The 2000 will was not revoked. While it is generally accepted that a will can be revoked by the testator destroying the same or another individual destroying the same at the direction of the testator, a "proxy" revocation must be done in the "presence" of the testator. UPC § 2-507(a)(2) adopts this principle. It is doubtful that the lawyer's destruction of the 2000 will be found to have been done in O's presence.

Like the Uniform Probate Code, the law in some non-UPC states adopts a "conscious" presence test; other states use a more conservative "visual presence" or "line of sight" test. See McGovern § 5.2.

Answers (A) and (D) are incorrect. The will was not destroyed in O's presence. C2 may argue that the proxy revocation was done in O's presence, if the lawyer destroyed it while O was on the phone and O heard the lawyer destroy it. If C2 is successful, C1 may argue for the application of the "doctrine of dependent relative revocation" to negate the revocation since O's intent to devise O's estate to G cannot be carried out. *See* comment to UPC § 2-507.

Answer (C) is incorrect. There is no writing documenting O's intent to devise the probate estate to G.

24. It appears that O revoked the most current will in favor of G, causing O's probate estate to pass by intestate succession to C1 and C2. The 2010 will would not likely be revived by the revocation of the later will under these circumstances. *See* UPC § 2-509. However, G will likely argue that O did not have the requisite mental capacity to revoke the will. Alternatively, the common law doctrine of "dependent relative revocation" may be applicable, if G can prove that O's mistaken belief of G's death caused O to revoke the will. *See* comment to UPC § 2-507 and Andersen § 9(E). If either argument is successful, the new will could be probated notwithstanding its destruction. A will that cannot be produced may be admitted to probate in most jurisdictions upon adequate proof of its contents and the execution. *See* McGovern § 5.2.

Some states, which have not enacted the Uniform Probate Code, have held that the revocation of a revoking document does have the effect of reviving the earlier revoked will. See McGovern § 5.3.

25. **Answer (B) is correct.** According to UPC § 2-509(a), the 1990 will is likely to have been revived since it is evident from the circumstances and O's contemporary declarations that O intended the 1990 will to take effect at O's death.

The result may be different in a state which has not enacted the Uniform Probate Code. Some courts have held that, because a will is ambulatory, the earlier will is not actually revoked until the testator dies and the later will is admitted to probate. Other courts follow the rule that the earlier will was revoked when the later one was executed. The rule in some states distinguishes between express and implied revocations. See Atkinson

§ 92.

Answer (A) is incorrect. UPC § 2-509(a) is likely to revive the 1990 will, so O did not die intestate.

However, in some non-UPC states, the 1990 will is not revived and O died intestate.

Answer (C) is incorrect. The 2000 will was revoked.

Answer (D) is incorrect. Even if O died intestate, the cousins would not be considered heirs despite the estrangement between O and C.

26. **Answer (B) is correct.** The 1990 will was "impliedly" revoked by the execution of the 2000 will due to the wills' inconsistent provisions. *See* UPC § 2-507(c). Since the 2000 will was revoked, UPC § 2-509(a) is likely to revive the 1990 will.

    In some non-UPC states, the 1990 will was not revoked by the execution of the 2000 will, since the 2000 will was revoked before O died. In other states, the 1990 will was revoked by the execution of the 2000 will and was not revived when the 2000 will was revoked. The rule in some states distinguishes between express and implied revocations. See Atkinson § 92.

    Answers (A), (C), and (D) are incorrect for the reasons given.

27. **Answer (B) is correct.** The 1990 will was revoked by the execution of the 2000 will but is likely to have been revived by O's destruction of the 2000 will. *See* UPC § 2-509(a). It is irrelevant that the 2000 will was a holographic will. *See* UPC §§ 2-502(b), 2-507.

    Non-UPC states which recognize holographic wills are likely to adopt the same rule. See Atkinson §§ 87, 92. If the state does not recognize holographic wills, the 1990 will was never revoked.

    Answers (A), (C), and (D) are incorrect for the reasons given.

28. A is likely to inherit the entire estate. The 1990 will is likely to have been revived by the revocation of the 2000 will under the circumstances. *See* UPC § 2-509(a). The fact that the 1990 will was destroyed by the lawyer is not determinative, if its contents can otherwise be established. *See* McGovern § 5.2. The lawyer's destruction of the will was not a "proxy revocation." *See* UPC § 2-507(a)(2).

    The result may be different in a non-UPC state. Some might hold that the 1990 will was revoked when the 2000 will was executed. Some might hold that the 1990 will was not revived by the revocation of the 2000 will. Atkinson § 92.

29. **Answer (A) is correct.** It is generally accepted that, if a will was last known to have been in the testator's possession, the will is presumed to have been revoked by the testator destroying the same when it cannot be found after the testator's death. *See* McGovern § 5.2. Without proof of when and why O destroyed the 1990 will, O likely died intestate.

    Answer (B) is incorrect for the reasons given.

    Answers (C) and (D) are incorrect. Even if O died intestate, the siblings would not be considered heirs.

30. **Answer (A) is correct.** The 1990 will was revoked by the nurse at O's direction and in O's presence. UPC § 2-507(a)(2) adopts the generally accepted concept of "proxy revocation." O died intestate.

Answer (B) is incorrect for the reasons given.

Answers (C) and (D) are incorrect. Even if O died intestate, the siblings would not be considered heirs.

31. Since the will was not executed, it cannot be admitted to probate. The comment to UPC § 2-503 seems to indicate that the situation described is not one that could be corrected by the court admitting the unexecuted will to probate. However, G may be successful in requesting the court to impose a constructive trust on C1 and C2 due to C1's wrong doing in order to prevent unjust enrichment by both C1 and C2. Even though only one of the heirs did anything wrong, a court may impose the constructive trust on both the "guilty" and the innocent parties, since the innocent party would not have inherited any part of the estate had it not been for the bad acts of the "guilty" person. *See* McGovern § 6.1.

32. **Answer (B) is correct.** C has the burden to prove O's lack of testamentary intent. Upon proof of the circumstances surrounding its execution, the will is not likely to be admitted to probate. Although the document was executed with the requisite testamentary formalities, it did not express O's actual testamentary intent. *See* Atkinson § 55.

In some jurisdictions, the proponent has the burden of proof on testamentary intent. See Atkinson §§ 100, 101.

Answers (A), (C), and (D) are incorrect. The will did not reflect O's actual testamentary intent so it should not be admitted to probate.

33. **Answer (A) is correct.** Although the will was destroyed, it was not revoked since O lacked the requisite intent to revoke the will due to C1's coercion. *See* Atkinson § 86. The comments to UPC § 2-507 confirm this principle.

Answers (B), (C), and (D) are incorrect. O lacked the intent to revoke when O destroyed the will.

34. **Answer (C) is correct.** Since the will was not revoked, it can be admitted to probate. However, due to G1's wrongdoing, C may be successful in requesting the court to impose a constructive trust on G1 and G2 to prevent their unjust enrichment. *See* McGovern § 5.2.

Answers (A) and (B) are incorrect. The will can be admitted to probate, but the court may impose a constructive trust on both G1 and G2.

Answer (D) is incorrect. The court may impose a constructive trust on both G1 and G2 to prevent their unjust enrichment due to G1's wrongdoing.

35. Like the law in all states, UPC § 2-507(a)(2) provides that a will may be revoked by the testator performing a revocatory act with the intent and for the purpose of revoking the will. In order to have the required intent, the testator must have testamentary capacity. UPC § 3-407 places the burden on a will's contestant to prove that the testator revoked a will; this rule suggests that the contestant must establish that O had the requisite mental capacity to revoke the will; however, that same section requires a will's contestant to prove that the testator lacked testamentary intent or capacity. That section fails to expressly describe who has the burden of proof where the issue is the testator's capacity to revoke a will. The overall intent of the Uniform Probate Code suggests that testators are presumed to have the capacity to both execute and revoke wills.

The common law typically placed the burden of the capacity issue on the party trying to establish a will had been executed or revoked. The law in some non-UPC states places the burden on a will's proponent to prove the will was not revoked.

36. **Answer (D) is correct.** Since its material provisions are in the testator's handwriting, the note is a valid will even though it was not signed by any witnesses. *See* UPC § 2-502(b). The earlier will was revoked even though it was signed by two witnesses. *See* UPC § 2-507(a)(1).

In a non-UPC state that does not recognize holographic wills, the earlier will would not have been revoked absent the application of a "harmless error" statute, such as UPC § 2-503. However, in most non-UPC states that allow holographic wills, a holographic will can revoke an attested one. See McGovern § 5.1.

Answer (A) is incorrect. The earlier will has been revoked.

Answer (B) is incorrect. O did not die intestate. The note not only revoked the earlier will but also devised O's probate estate to C1.

Answer (C) is incorrect. O did not die intestate, and even if O had died intestate, O was survived by C1 and C2.

37. **Answer (B) is correct.** UPC § 1-201(57) defines the term "will" to include a testamentary instrument that merely revokes another will, and UPC § 2-507 says a will can be revoked by a subsequent will. Because the new will did not contain a new disposition of O's estate, O's probate estates passes to O's heirs at law.

The same result is likely to occur in states which have not enacted the Uniform Probate Code.

Answers (A), (C), and (D) are incorrect for the reasons given.

38. O's marriage to S after the execution of the will did not revoke the will. *See* UPC § 2-508. However, S is generally entitled to what S would have received had O died intestate. *See* UPC § 2-301. The amount is deducted from the augmented estate to determine S's elective share amount as defined in UPC § 2-202. In addition, S will be entitled to assert any rights S might have under local law in or to the homestead, homestead allowance, exempt property, and family allowance.

In a community property state, the surviving spouse is generally entitled to half of any community property. The rights of the "forgotten" or "pretermitted" spouses, if any, in other non-UPC states will vary from state to state. In some states, the will may have been revoked by operation of law. See Atkinson § 85.

39. **Answer (C) is correct.** O generally has the right to devise O's estate to whomever O chooses, subject to S's elective share percentage amount. *See* UPC § 2-202. In addition, S will be entitled to assert any rights S might have under local law in or to the homestead, homestead allowance, exempt property, and family allowance.

In a community property state, a surviving spouse generally retains half of any community probate property. In states which have not adopted the Uniform Probate Code and which are not community property states (other than Georgia), surviving spouses have a right to some share of the estate. See McGovern § 3.7.

Answer (A) is incorrect. S will be entitled to an elective share amount as described above. In addition, S will be entitled to assert any rights S might have under local law in or to the homestead, homestead allowance, exempt property, and family allowance.

Answers (B) and (D) are incorrect. The will is valid; O did not die intestate.

40. According to UPC § 2-804(b), the divorce revoked any dispositive provision of O's will in

favor of S. Since the will devised all of O's probate estate to S, the probate estate passes by intestate succession to O's heirs. If S is named as the executor of O's estate, the divorce also revoked O's nomination of S as executor.

Statutes in most non-UPC states would produce the same result, and in some states, even without a statute, case law may work a revocation by operation of law due to the change of circumstances. In a few states, a divorce revokes the entire will and not just the provisions in favor of the former spouse. See McGovern § 5.4.

1.   The term "will interpretation" is frequently used to refer to the evidentiary process of attempting to determine a testator's actual intent by examining the language of the will, as well as any other admissible extrinsic evidence. "Will construction" is the term frequently used to describe the process to determine the deemed intent of the testator when the testator's actual intent cannot be ascertained. It is a legal concept; interpretation is factual in nature. *See* Atkinson § 146.

2.   **Answer (A) is correct.** O's probate estate passes to O's devisee subject to the rights of O's creditors, as well as any expenses incurred in the administration of O's estate. *See* UPC § 3-101.

     In states that have not enacted the Uniform Probate Code, a personal representative typically discharges the decedent's debts out of the probate estate. See McGovern § 13.5.

     Answers (B), (C), and (D) are incorrect for the reasons given.

3.   C may have a right to an amount payable out of O's probate estate equal to $22,500 as a homestead allowance. *See* UPC § 2-402. In addition, C may be entitled to $15,000 in household furnishings, furniture, automobiles, and personal effects. *See* UPC § 2-403. In addition, if O had an obligation to support C prior to O's death, C may also be entitled to a reasonable allowance for maintenance for a period not to exceed one year. *See* UPC §§ 2-404, 2-405. The balance of the estate will be used to satisfy the debts and expenses.

     A minor child's right to these types of allowances will vary considerably in those states that have not enacted the Uniform Probate Code. See McGovern § 3.4.

4.   **Answer (A) is correct.** Absent a provision in relevant state law (*e.g.*, the state constitution) that either (i) grants a decedent's surviving spouse a right to occupy the home owned by the deceased spouse regardless of the solvency of the estate or who actually inherits the home and/or (ii) exempts the family home from the claims of unsecured creditors and estate administration expenses, if the owner is survived by a spouse, the home will likely be sold to raise cash to pay allowances and the obligations. *See* UPC §§ 2-401, 2-402.

     The availability of the homestead to satisfy a decedent's general obligations will vary from state to state. See McGovern § 3.4.

     Answers (B), (C), and (D) are incorrect. Unless relevant state law creates a homestead right in S as described above, the home will be sold to pay expenses and debts.

5.   **Answer (A) is correct.** UPC § 2-607 provides that a specific devise passes subject to any indebtedness secured by the property unless the will provides otherwise.

     In those states that have not enacted the Uniform Probate Code, or a statute similar to UPC § 2-607, the common law rule of exoneration creates a presumption that a testator intends a devisee to inherit a specific devise, free of indebtedness. In those states, half of the stock would be sold to raise the cash to pay the note. See

McGovern § 8.4.

Answers (B) and (C) are incorrect. The Uniform Probate Code creates a presumption of "nonexoneration." Jurisdictions that still follow the common law rule of "exoneration of liens" grant S the right to receive the home free of debt.

Answer (D) is incorrect. In some jurisdictions the secured creditor can elect either to have the debt paid in due course of administration or pursuant to the terms of the creditor's contract with the decedent. This decision should not affect whether S or D bears the burden of the debt.

6.   **Answer (A) is correct.** Because the will does not direct the order of "abatement," the debt should be paid out of the residuary devise. *See* UPC § 3-902.

Many non-UPC states have abatement statutes that are similar to UPC § 3-902; other states follow common law abatement which would produce the same result under these circumstances. See McGovern § 8.4.

Answers (B) and (C) are incorrect. The debts paid by the executor should be paid out of the residuary devise.

Answer (D) is incorrect. The source of the debt payment depends on the relevant abatement rule.

7.   An executor will typically use the most liquid non-exempt asset of the estate which has not been specifically devised by the testator in the will. If the cash is used, the executor may also need to sell the stocks and bonds to raise the cash necessary to satisfy the pecuniary bequest owing to B. *See* UPC § 3-902. In this situation, C is not likely to receive anything upon final settlement of O's estate since the executor must distribute to B either $100,000 in cash, or stocks and bonds worth $100,000 on the date distributed to B. B can demand cash. *See* UPC § 3-906.

States that have not enacted the Uniform Probate Code are likely to have statutes or common law rules that reach a similar result. However, some states' laws will require the executor to satisfy the pecuniary bequest in cash unless the devisee agrees to a distribution "in-kind." See McGovern § 12.3 (p. 585).

8.   **Answer (A) is correct.** Absent a provision in the will that provides otherwise, UPC § 3-902 prescribes how the probate estate abates in order to satisfy the decedent's debts.

States that have not enacted the Uniform Probate Code will typically have a similar statute or a common law rule that reaches a similar result. See McGovern § 8.4.

Answer (B) is incorrect. If the executor uses the cash to pay the debts, the home and its contents may have to be sold to raise the $100,000 to satisfy the bequest to B.

Answer (C) is incorrect. C was specifically devised all of the stocks and bonds.

Answer (D) is incorrect. UPC § 3-902 prescribes how the probate estate abates in order to satisfy the decedent's debts.

9.   **Answer (A) is correct.** The executor will typically use the most readily available liquid non-exempt asset available to pay the creditors. Pursuant to UPC § 3-906(a)(2), the executor may need to sell other assets, like the stocks and bonds, to raise the cash necessary to satisfy B's pecuniary bequest. *See* McGovern § 8.4.

States that have not enacted the Uniform Probate Code will typically have a similar statute or a common law rule that reaches a similar result. See McGovern § 8.4.

Answers (B), (C), and (D) are incorrect for the reasons given.

10.   **Answer (A) is correct.** UPC § 2-605 directs that A is entitled to the ExxonMobil stock. UPC § 2-606(a)(5) directs that Whiteacre passes to B.

   The results may differ in states that have not enacted the described provisions of the Uniform Probate Code or similar statutes. Under the common law, the rule of "ademption by extinction" may cause the entire probate estate, including the stock and land, to pass to C. See McGovern § 8.2.

   Answer (B) is incorrect. UPC § 2-606(a)(5) directs that B is entitled to Whiteacre since O acquired it as a replacement for Blackacre.

   Many non-UPC states have enacted statutes similar to UPC § 2-605, but not statutes like UPC § 2-606. In those states, Answer (B) would be correct.

   Answers (C) and (D) are incorrect. The Uniform Probate Code has replaced the common law's strict "identity" test with a more liberal "change in form" rule.

11.   UPC § 3-902 directs that the debts are to be paid from the residuary devise, and if it is not sufficient, from the general devises. After the debts and expenses are paid, specific devises are distributed, general devises are paid to the extent assets are available, and if there is anything remaining, it is delivered to the residuary devisee. Accordingly, after the home and the stocks and bonds are sold to pay the debts, A will receive the proceeds paid by the insurance company for the damage to the car. *See* UPC § 2-606(a)(3). B will receive the balance. C will receive nothing.

   In states that have not enacted the Uniform Probate Code or similar statutes, the common law rule of "ademption by extinction" may limit A to only $1,000, the value of the car at the time of O's death, and the balance would pass to B. See Atkinson § 134.

12.   **Answer (A) is correct.** An inter vivos gift to a person named as a devisee in the donor's will is not treated as the "satisfaction" of the testamentary devise unless the will provides for a deduction of the gift or there is a written document in which the donor or donee indicates that the gift is to be taken into account at the time of the donor's death. *See* UPC § 2-609.

   States that have not enacted the Uniform Probate Code or similar statutes may still follow the common law rule which presumes a gift to a general or residuary devisee is either a partial or total "satisfaction" of the testamentary devise. See Atkinson § 133.

   Answers (B) and (C) are incorrect. Where applicable, the doctrine of satisfaction generally applies to both general and residuary devises.

   Answer (D) is incorrect. Absent written evidence to the contrary in the will or another written document, the gifts are not to be taken into account when O dies.

13.   **Answer (B) is correct.** An executor has a duty to expend reasonable efforts to collect any valid debts due and owing the decedent, including one owed by a devisee, particularly if the estate is insolvent. *See* Atkinson § 117.

   Answer (A) is incorrect. O's death does not extinguish the debt.

   Answer (C) is incorrect. Since the estate is insolvent, B is obligated to repay the entire $10,000.

   Answer (D) is incorrect. Since the estate is insolvent, A, B, and C do not receive any part of O's estate.

14. **Answer (D) is correct.** Since the estate's assets exceed the debts by more than $10,000, the executor has enough non-exempt liquid assets on hand to pay the creditors what they are owed and to pay A the pecuniary bequest of $10,000. From a practical perspective, there is no reason for the executor to collect the $10,000 from B since B, in effect, owes half of that amount to himself or herself as a residuary devisee. *See* UPC § 3-903.

The result is likely to be the same in a non-UPC state pursuant to the common law concept of "retainer." See Atkinson § 141.

Answers (A), (B), and (C) are incorrect for the reasons given.

15. **Answer (A) is correct.** The debt cannot be collected by the executor since it appears to be barred by the statute of limitations. *See* Atkinson § 117.

Answers (B) and (C) are incorrect for the reasons given.

Answer (D) is incorrect. Since the estate is insolvent, B does not have a residuary share to reduce by the amount of the debt.

16. **Answer (A) is correct.** UPC § 3-903 provides that, while a debt of a devisee is to be offset against the devisee's share of the estate, the devisee has the benefit of "any defense" that would be available in a proceeding for recovery of the debt, including the statute of limitations.

In states that have not enacted the Uniform Probate Code or similar statutes, the result may be different. See Atkinson § 141.

Answers (B) and (C) are incorrect. The debt is not collectible due to the statute of limitations.

Answer (D) is incorrect. UPC § 3-903 grants B "any defense," including the statute of limitations.

In some non-UPC states, B's share of the residuary may be reduced by half of the debt.

17. Since a will is a disposition of property that becomes effective at the testator's death, the common law required a devisee to survive the testator by an "instant" of time. Most states have enacted statutes that require devisees to survive testators by 120 hours unless the will provides otherwise. The Uniform Probate Code has adopted this rule. *See* UPC § 2-702. UPC § 2-604 adopts the common law rule that a lapsed specific devise becomes part of the residuary devise. *See* Atkinson § 140. Accordingly, only C survived O by 120 hours, and the entire estate, including the two tracts of land, passed (subject to formal administration of C's estate) to C's spouse.

18. **Answer (D) is correct.** UPC § 2-702 requires that a devisee survive the testator by 120 hours unless the will provides otherwise. Because A and B did not survive O by 120 hours, their devises "lapsed." However, UPC § 2-604 is not applicable, and the two tracts do not become part of the residuary devise. UPC § 2-603 directs that the two tracts pass to the children of A and B.

Most states that have not enacted the Uniform Probate Code have similar "antilapse" statutes. See McGovern § 8.5.

Answers (A), (B), and (C) are incorrect. They fail to take into consideration both UPC §§ 2-702 and 2-603.

19. **Answer (D) is correct.** UPC § 2-604 does not address what happens if the residuary beneficiary does not survive the testator. Because all three children died before O, their devises lapsed, and O's probate estate probably passes by intestate succession to O's intestate heirs under the "no residue of the residue" rule. O's closest relatives that survived O were the cousins. *See* McGovern § 8.5 (p. 404).

    Answers (A), (B), and (C) are incorrect. The devisees named in O's will died before O; their gifts lapsed. UPC § 2-603, or a similar statute in a non-UPC state, is not applicable because the children did not have descendants.

20. The devise to A, B, and C lapsed because they died before O. The antilapse provisions of UPC § 2-603 apply only to certain categories of devisees. No part of O's estate passes to the spouses or children of A, B, and C. O's probate estate passes by intestate succession to D.

    In a state which has not enacted the Uniform Probate Code, the result may differ depending on the terms of the applicable "antilapse" statute. However, most states have statutes which would create the same result as UPC § 2-603 under these circumstances. See McGovern § 8.5.

21. **Answer (C) is correct.** A died before O; B is deemed to have died before O because of the 120-hours rule. *See* UPC § 2-702. Their gifts lapsed, but the "antilapse" provisions of UPC § 2-603 direct that the two thirds of the estate they would have received pass equally to their children.

    Most states that have not enacted the Uniform Probate Code have similar statutes. See McGovern § 8.5.

    Answers (A), (B), and (C) are incorrect. The testamentary gifts to A and B "lapsed," but their children succeed to what they would have been entitled had they survived O by 120 hours.

22. **Answer (A) is correct.** Because A and B did not survive O by 120 hours, their gifts lapsed. *See* UPC § 2-702. According to UPC § 2-604(b), the interests in O's probate estate they would have received pass to C.

    In states that have not enacted the Uniform Probate Code or similar statutes, the result may be different. The common law typically applied the "lapsed fractional gift" rule to this type of situation, and the two thirds of the estate devised to A and B would pass by intestate succession to O's heirs. See Atkinson § 140.

    Answers (B) and (C) are incorrect. The gifts to A and B lapsed.

    Answer (D) is incorrect. The gifts to A and B lapsed, and the two thirds of O's probate estate they would have received pass to C. The common law rule typically resulted in the two-thirds passing to O's heirs, C and D.

23. **Answer (A) is correct.** O's will devised O's probate estate to three individuals, not including E. Only "omitted children," not omitted grandchildren, have rights under UPC § 2-302.

    "Pretermission" statutes in some non-UPC states may afford rights to descendants of omitted children. See McGovern § 3.5.

    Answers (B), (C), and (D) are incorrect. E is not entitled to any portion of O's probate estate.

24. **Answer (A) is correct.** A testator may devise property to a "class" of beneficiaries rather than to several named individuals. According to UPC § 2-603(b)(2), the "antilapse" provisions

apply to certain class gifts. So, A1 and B1 succeed to the interests A and B would have had they survived O by 120 hours.

In states which have not enacted the Uniform Probate Code or similar statutes, the result may differ. See McGovern § 8.5.

Answers (B), (C), and (D) are incorrect for the reasons given.

25.   **Answer (D) is correct.** The "class" of devisees opened at O's death and included E and C, as well as the substituted takers, A1 and B1. *See* UPC § 2-603(b)(2).

The same result would occur in states that have not enacted the Uniform Probate Code but have a similar "antilapse" statute that applies to "class" gifts. See McGovern § 8.5.

Answers (A), (B), and (C) are incorrect. These answers do not take into account both the nature of "class gifts" and the applicable "antilapse" statute.

In a state that does not extend its "antilapse" provisions to class gifts, C and E would share the estate equally. McGovern § 8.5.

26.   The "antilapse" provisions of UPC § 2-603 prescribe a rule of construction to apply in the absence of a contrary intention expressed in the testator's will. However, UPC § 2-603(b)(3) also provides that words of survivorship like "my surviving children" are not, in the absence of additional evidence, a sufficient indication of "contrary intention." Accordingly, A1 and B1 may take the two-thirds their parents would have received had they survived O by 120 hours, and C takes the balance.

The view in many states that have not enacted the Uniform Probate Code, or a statute similar to UPC § 2-603(b)(3), is that words of survivorship attached to a devise, like "who survive me," are sufficient to negate the applicable "antilapse" statute. In those states, C would inherit the entire estate. See McGovern § 8.5 (p. 394).

27.   **Answer (A) is correct.** At the time of O's death the "class" of devisees "opened" and "closed." C was the only member of the class that survived O. *See* McGovern § 10.2.

Answers (B) and (C) are incorrect for the reasons given.

Answer (D) is incorrect. A and B did not survive O by 120 hours.

28.   **Answer (D) is correct.** A died before O; B is deemed to have died before O because of the 120-hours rule. *See* UPC § 2-702. Their gifts lapsed, and according to UPC § 2-603, stepchildren of the testator's children are not included among the devisees whose gifts can be saved by the antilapse statute. UPC § 2-604(b) directs that C succeed to the entire residuary estate.

States that have not enacted the Uniform Probate Code typically do not extend their "antilapse" provisions to stepchildren. However, in some non-UPC states, the two thirds of the estate that A and B would have received pass to O's heir, D, pursuant to the common law's "lapsed fractional gift" rule. See Atkinson § 140.

Answers (A), (B), and (C) are incorrect. The testamentary gifts to A and B "lapsed," and their children do not succeed to what they would have been entitled had they survived O by 120 hours.

29.   The initial question is who were the intended beneficiaries of O's estate? Absent evidence of contrary intent in the will, stepchildren of a child would normally be excluded from the class of defined beneficiaries in the will — testator's grandchildren (unless they were adopted by

the child). The Uniform Probate Code appears to have adopted this prevailing view. *See* UPC § 2-705. However, UPC § 2-705(c) creates an exception for relatives by marriage. It is arguable that A, B, and C are to be considered O's grandchildren under the will. See comment to UPC § 2-705. The result may differ in a state that has not adopted UPC § 2-705 or a similar statute. *See* Atkinson § 60.

30. Modern statutes, such as UPC § 2-1105, authorize heirs and devisees to disclaim their interests in decedents' estates. However, the law varies from state to state on the effect a disclaimer has on the rights of the disclaimant's creditors. Federal law will control, if the disclaimant is in bankruptcy. *See* McGovern § 2.8. In any event, Blackacre passes (subject to any rights G's creditors may retain) as if G had predeceased O to the charity under the residuary clause pursuant to UPC § 2-604.

31. **Answer (B) is correct.** A will may dispose of property by incorporation by reference or reference to facts that have significance independent from their effect on the disposition made by the will. Accordingly, the stocks pass to A, and the jewelry passes to B. UPC §§ 2-510, 2-512 codify these generally accepted concepts. *See* McGovern § 6.2. The described items of other tangible personal property will pass to C even though the memo was not executed with testamentary formalities because the will refers to it. *See* UPC § 2-513.

   Results may differ in states that have not enacted the Uniform Probate Code or similar statutes. Absent a statute similar to UPC § 2-513, such items may pass to the residuary devisee, D. See McGovern § 6.2.

   Answers (A), (C), and (D) are not correct for the reasons given.

32. Because the will makes no reference to the intended trust, a testamentary trust was not created. *See* RESTATEMENT, THIRD, OF TRUSTS § 17. If F does not volunteer to perform as agreed, the court will admit evidence of the oral agreement in order to impose a constructive trust on F in favor of C and G to prevent F from being unjustly enriched. F will ordinarily be ordered to transfer the property to another person who will carry out the intended purposes of the oral agreement. *See* RESTATEMENT, THIRD, OF TRUSTS § 18.

33. **Answer (D) is correct.** An express inter vivos trust was not created when the agreement was signed or during O's lifetime because property had not been transferred to F. *See* RESTATEMENT, THIRD, OF TRUSTS §§ 2, 3, 10. Because the will makes no reference to the intended trust, a testamentary trust was not created. *See* RESTATEMENT, THIRD, OF TRUSTS § 17. However, the court would likely impose a constructive trust on F in favor of C and G. *See* RESTATEMENT, THIRD, OF TRUSTS § 18. Also, see answer to the immediately preceding question.

   Answer (A) is incorrect. An express inter vivos trust was not created when the agreement was signed because property had not been transferred to F during O's lifetime. Because the will makes no reference to the intended trust, a testamentary trust was not created. The comment to UTC § 401 notes that a trust instrument signed during the settlor's lifetime is not invalid because the trust was not funded until after the settlor's death. Accordingly, it is arguable that an express trust was created when O devised Blackacre to F. However, the Restatement takes the position that an express trust is not created if the settlor fails during life to complete the contemplated transfer. *See* RESTATEMENT, THIRD, OF TRUSTS § 16.

   Answer (B) is incorrect. Equity will not allow F to be unjustly enriched.

   Answer (C) is incorrect. The situation does not fit the limited circumstances that justify the imposition of a resulting trust.

34. **Answer (D) is correct.** Although O's will manifests an intent to create an express trust, other elements essential to the creation of a testamentary trust are not in the will. Accordingly, a testamentary trust was not created. *See* Restatement, Third, of Trusts § 17. The Restatement takes the position that the court should impose a constructive trust on F in favor of C and G, if F does not volunteer to perform as agreed. *See* Restatement, Third, of Trusts § 18. However, some courts may impose a resulting trust on F in favor of the charity notwithstanding the modern trend adopted by the Restatement. *See* comment c to Restatement, Third, of Trusts § 18.

     Answer (A) is incorrect. Because the will failed to identify the beneficiaries, an express trust was not created.

     Answer (B) is incorrect. The modern trend appears to impose a constructive trust in favor of C and G.

     Answer (C) is not correct. The situation does not fit the circumstances that justify the imposition of a resulting trust in favor of O's heirs.

35. **Answer (B) is correct.** Obviously, O did not intend for F to inherit fee simple title, but the will did not create an express trust because the terms of the intended trust were not included in the will. A constructive trust is not available because there is no evidence of the intended beneficiaries or the purpose of the trust. When a settlor's attempt to create an express trust fails, the courts will typically impose a resulting trust on the intended trustee in favor of the settlor or the settlor's successor in interest. In this case, the charity will likely succeed to Blackacre. *See* Restatement, Third, of Trusts §§ 8, 18.

     Answer (A) is not correct. An express trust was not created because the will did not name the beneficiaries or describe the terms of the intended trust. Further, there is no evidence of any pre-existing agreement between O and F.

     Answer (C) is not correct. The charity, not O's heir, is O's successor in interest and has standing to seek the imposition of the resulting trust.

     Answer (D) is not correct. Obviously, O did not intend for F to acquire fee simple title.

36. Although O's will manifests the intent to create an express trust, other elements essential to the creation of a testamentary trust, such as the purposes of the trust, are not in the will. Further, the purposes of the trust cannot be inferred from the will. *See* Restatement, Third, of Trusts § 17. Accordingly, an express testamentary trust was not created. However, evidence of the oral agreement is admissible to impose a constructive trust on F in favor of C and G in order to carry out O's intent if F does not volunteer to perform as agreed. *See* Restatement, Third, of Trusts § 18. If evidence of the oral agreement is not admissible, or if the oral agreement is not proven, even if admissible, the trust is "passive," and the intended beneficiaries, C and G, are entitled to the property. The statute of uses, or a similar statute, may merge legal and equitable titles in C and G. *See* Restatement, Third, of Trusts § 6.

37. **Answer (D) is correct.** The trust is "passive," and the legal and equitable titles merge in C and G. UTC § 402 has codified this common law concept that a trustee must have duties to perform in order to have a valid, express trust. *See* Restatement, Third, of Trusts § 6.

     In a state that does not have a statute of uses, or a similar statute, the intended beneficiary is entitled to possession upon demand to the person in possession. See McGovern § 9.3.

Answer (A) is not correct. An express trust was not created since the will did not impose on F any affirmative duties.

Answer (B) is not correct. The charity, as the residuary beneficiary, inherits only those probate assets which have not been specifically or generally devised.

Answer (C) is not correct. O did not die intestate.

38. **Answer (D) is correct.** Because C died before O, only G has standing to seek the imposition of a constructive trust, if F does not volunteer to convey Blackacre to G pursuant to the oral agreement. *See* Restatement, Third, of Trusts § 18.

Answer (A) is not correct. Because the will makes no reference to the intended trust, a testamentary trust was not created. *See* RESTATEMENT, THIRD, OF TRUSTS § 17.

Answer (B) is not correct. Equity will not allow F to retain the property upon proof of the oral agreement between O and F.

Answer (C) is not correct. In view of the oral agreement between O and F, a constructive trust in favor of G is the appropriate remedy.

39. **Answer (C) is correct.** Because (i) O's attempt to create an express trust failed, and (ii) the trust intention does not appear in the will, O's successor in interest, the charity, will have the court impose a constructive trust on F to prevent F from being unjustly enriched. *See* Restatement, Third, of Trusts § 18.

Answers (A) and (B) are not correct. Since G did not survive O, neither GS nor GG has standing to impose a constructive trust.

Answer (D) is not correct. Although it appears from the will that F has inherited Blackacre, equity will not allow F to retain the property once satisfactory evidence of the oral agreement is produced.

40. **Answer (D) is correct.** F died before O devised Blackacre to F; neither F's spouse nor F's child acquired an interest in Blackacre. The gift to F lapsed, and Blackacre passed to the charity upon O's death. *See* UPC § 2-604. C and G will argue that the court should impose a constructive trust in their favor on the charity to avoid the charity from being unjustly enriched. A constructive trust typically arises out of an intended express trust that is unenforceable because of the failure to satisfy the applicable wills act. *See* RESTATEMENT, THIRD, OF TRUSTS § 18. The imposition of a resulting trust is not appropriate since O's successor in interest, the charity, already has acquired title.

Answers (A) and (B) are not correct. Because F died before O, neither F's spouse nor F's child acquired an interest in Blackacre.

Answer (C) is not correct. C is not O's successor in interest and does not have standing to seek a resulting trust.

41. **Answer (C) is correct.** F should be able to accept the specific devise of Blackacre and convey the property to C and G, if they are both competent adults. After accepting the deed, C and G, as the intended beneficiaries, can decide the ultimate disposition of the property. Because an express trust was not created, UPC § 2-707 should not be applicable. If UPC § 2-707 is applicable, G's remainder interest is contingent on G surviving C, and the charity may have inherited O's reversionary interest. If C and G do not agree to the proposed

conveyance, or if either is not a competent adult, F should consider asking for court authority to convey the property to another party who would agree in writing to carry out the purposes of the original oral agreement. Alternatively, F may want to consider disclaiming the property.

Answer (A) is not correct. F can refuse to accept Blackacre by filing a qualified disclaimer. If F disclaims, Blackacre would vest in the charity, and C and G will have to deal with the charity concerning the oral agreement. They may have to incur expenses in convincing a court to impose a constructive trust on the charity to avoid its unjust enrichment. *See* RESTATEMENT, THIRD, OF TRUSTS § 18.

Answer (B) is not correct. If F disclaims, Blackacre passes to the charity. *See* UPC § 2-1106.

Answer (D) is incorrect. An express trust was not created. *See* RESTATEMENT, THIRD, OF TRUSTS § 17.

42. Whether the devise to you was real or personal property is irrelevant. Because the will makes no reference to the intended trust, a testamentary trust was not created. *See* RESTATEMENT, THIRD, OF TRUSTS § 17. If you accept the stock under the will, equity will not allow you to retain it for your own use. Parol evidence is admissible to explain the oral agreement. C and G will likely seek to impose a constructive trust, if you accept the stock and do not assign it to C and G. *See* RESTATEMENT, THIRD, OF TRUSTS § 18.

1. Yes, the devisees named in the will may elect not to have the will admitted to probate. The will may not effectively devise the entire probate estate. The devisees could disclaim their interests in the estate. Even if admitted to probate, the devisees may not have survived the testator by the required period of survivorship. In addition, a will can still be a valid testamentary instrument even if it does not contain directions concerning the distribution of the estate. *See* Andersen § 3.

2. **Answer (A) is correct.** The parties with standing to contest the probate of a will include the decedent's heirs at law. Generally, *see* McGovern § 13.3. M and D were O's parents and O's only heirs at law absent extraordinary circumstances. *See* UPC §§ 2-103, 2-114.

    The result is likely to be the same in a non-UPC state.

    Answers (B) and (C) are incorrect. Absent disclaimers by O's parents, O's siblings are not heirs of O since both of O's parents survived O. *See* UPC § 2-103. It does not matter if the siblings were born of the same, or a prior, marriage of O's parents.

    Answer (D) is incorrect. One's status as an heir is not dependent upon the actual personal relationship that existed prior to the decedent's death. *But see* UPC § 2–114.

3. **Answer (D) is correct.** The parties with standing to contest the probate of a will include the decedent's heirs at law. Generally, *see* McGovern § 13.3. Notwithstanding their divorce, H and W were O's parents and O's only heirs at law absent extraordinary circumstances. *See* UPC §§ 2-103, 2-114.

    The result is likely to be the same in a non-UPC state.

    Answer (A) is incorrect. Other than a decedent's surviving spouse, a person related to the decedent only by marriage is not an heir at law.

    Answers (B) and (C) are incorrect. Since H and W both survived O, neither the ancestors of H and W nor the descendants of those ancestors are O's heirs at law.

4. **Answer (D) is the correct answer.** W and H2 are the heirs. H would not have a right to inherit from O, if O died intestate. *See* UPC §§ 2-118, 2-119. Accordingly, H would not have standing to contest the probate of the will.

    The same result is likely to occur in a non-UPC state. See McGovern § 2.10.

    Answers (A) and (C) are incorrect. The adoption process typically eliminates the biological parent's status as an heir of the adopted child.

    Answer (B) is incorrect. H2 is treated as a parent of O. Consequently, W is not O's sole heir at law.

5. **Answer (A) is correct.** Notwithstanding (i) the divorce of H and W and (ii) O's adoption by

W's second husband, H2, O is still considered to be a child of H for intestacy purposes. *See* UPC §§ 2-118, 2-119.

The same result may occur in a non-UPC state. See McGovern § 2.10.

Answers (B), (C), and (D) are incorrect. Because H was survived by O, H's parents and siblings are not heirs.

6.   Because H2 is also the father of children of a prior marriage, H2 is W's sole heir only if the value of the probate estate is less than $225,000. *See* UPC § 2-102 and its comments. If the value of W's probate estate exceeds $225,000, O is entitled to a share of W's probate estate. Having been adopted by H2, O is the child of W and H2 for intestacy purposes. W's stepchildren, S1 and S2, are excluded. O and H2 will share equally the estate in excess of $225,000. *See* McGovern § 2.10. In states that have not adopted the Uniform Probate Code, H2 may be the sole heir due to H2's adoption of O.

In some community property states, the decedent's half of the community property passes to the surviving spouse only if all the decedent's descendants are also descendants of the surviving spouse.

7.   **Answer (D) is correct.** *See* UPC § 2-102.

The statutory results will likely differ in a non-UPC state.

Answers (A), (B), and (C) are incorrect for the statutory reasons given.

8.   **Answer (B) is correct.** O's siblings, who are either born to, or adopted by, either H or W, are O's heirs at law and will share equally in the estate. *See* UPC §§ 2-103, 2-107.

In some non-UPC states, siblings of the half-blood inherit only half of what siblings of the whole blood inherit. See McGovern § 2.2 (p. 66).

Answer (A) is incorrect. S4 is related to O by marriage and excluded as an heir unless W adopted S4.

Answer (C) is incorrect. S3 is a child of W and is an heir.

Answer (D) is incorrect. S2 and S3, children of H and W, respectively, are also heirs of O per UPC § 2-107.

However, in some non-UPC jurisdictions, Answer (D) is correct because siblings of the half-blood are not heirs unless there are no siblings of the whole blood. See McGovern § 2.2 (p. 66).

9.   **Answer (D) is correct.** Because O was survived by children, O's heirs are C1 and C2, who would share O's probate estate equally. C3 is a stepchild and excluded, unless O had adopted C3 (or unless the intestate is not survived by a spouse, issue, parents, grandparents or their issue). *See* UPC §§ 1-201(5), 2-103.

The result is likely to be the same in a non-UPC state. See McGovern § 2.2 (p. 56).

Answers (A), (B), and (C) are incorrect. Neither P nor C3 is an heir at law. P is excluded because O was survived by children.

10.   C4 is likely to be an heir. *See* UPC § 2-117. State statutes which have excluded non-marital children from inheriting from their biological fathers in the past have been held to violate the equal protection clause of the 14th Amendment of the U. S. Constitution. *See Trimble v. Gordon*, 430 U.S. 762, 776 (1977). UPC § 2-115(5) directs that the parent-child relationship

may be established under relevant state law, such as the Uniform Parentage Act (2000, as amended).

States typically have procedures which allow a child to establish that a man was the child's biological father either before or after the man's death. These statutes typically allow the child to establish paternity after the father dies even if the father never acknowledged the child as his own. See McGovern § 2.9.

11.   **Answer (D) is correct.** C4 is O's only heir. The identity of a child's other parent or the parent who was awarded custody is irrelevant. However, in order to be an heir, one must not only survive the intestate, but survive by 120 hours. If one survives the intestate but dies within 120 hours, that person is deemed to have died before the intestate. *See* UPC §§ 2-103, 2-104.

Some states which have not enacted the Uniform Probate Code have statutes that require an heir to survive by 120 hours. See McGovern § 2.2 (p. 57).

   Answer (A) is incorrect. C1 did not survive O.

Even if applicable state law did not require an heir to survive by 120 hours, the common law required an heir to survive the intestate by an "instant" of time.

   Answers (B) and (C) are incorrect. Typically, state statutes require heirs to survive the decedent by 120 hours. Prior to the enactment of statutes that require survivorship by 120 hours, many states had statutes that would have created the presumption that C2 died before O. Absent proof to the contrary, in those states, C3 and C4 would be O's heirs.

12.   **Answer (C) is correct.** Because of the "120-hour rule" of UPC § 2-104, C4 would appear to be O's only heir. However, the "representation rule" of UPC § 2-106 would substitute G2 and G3 as heirs in place of C2 and C3. Accordingly, O's probate estate would be delivered equally to G2, G3, and C4's devisee, S4. If G2 and G3 are minors, their respective shares would be delivered to a guardian or other surrogate pursuant to local law.

The result would be the same in most states that have not enacted the Uniform Probate Code. See McGovern § 2.2 (p. 57).

   Answers (A) and (B) are incorrect. The "120-hour rule" excludes C2 and C3 as heirs. Consequently, their devisees are not entitled to any part of O's estate.

   Answer (D) is incorrect. C4 survived O by 120 hours and was one of the heirs. At C4's death, C4's interest passed to S4 subject to formal administration of C4's estate.

13.   **Answer (C) is correct.** An individual in gestation at the time of the intestate's death is treated as living at the time of the intestate's death, if the individual lives for at least 120 hours after birth. *See* UPC § 2-104. G6, having been adopted by C3, is an heir of O as well. *See* UPC §§ 2-118, 2-119. Consequently, G5 and G2, as well as G6 and G3, succeed to the one-third interests that their parents would have been entitled to had the parents survived O by 120 hours. *See* UPC §§ 2-104, 2-106, 2-118, 2-119.

The result would be the same in some states that have not enacted the Uniform Probate Code. See McGovern §§ 2.2, 2.10.

   Answers (A), (B), and (D) are incorrect for the reasons given.

14.   G2, G5, G3, G6, and G4 will share the estate equally. None of the children of O survived O. UPC § 2-106(b) adopts the system of representation called "per capita at each generation"

(i.e., equal shares to those equally related). Consequently, the grandchildren share equally in O's probate estate since none of the children survived O.

The result is likely to differ in a non-UPC state that has not enacted a statute similar to UPC § 2-106. Some state statutes provide for a "per stirpes" system of representation; other states have enacted different systems (such as an earlier Uniform Probate Code approach — "per capita with representation"). If the applicable statute is a strict "per stirpes," one third would pass to G2 and G5, one-third would pass to G3 and G6, and one-third would pass to G4. See McGovern § 2.2 (p. 57).

15.   **Answer (D) is correct.** According to UPC § 2-106, O's probate estate is divided into five equal shares for each grandchild who survived O (G2, G3, G5, G6) and for the deceased grandchild who left a descendant who survived O (G4).

The result may differ in a non-UPC state. See McGovern § 2.2 (p. 57).

Answers (A) and (B) are incorrect. GG succeeded to the interest in O's estate that G4 would have inherited had G4 survived O.

Answer (C) is incorrect. This answer would be correct in a state with a strict "per stirpes" system of representation.

16.   **Answer (D) is correct.** O's probate property passes ("escheats") to the state where O resided since there are no heirs as defined in UPC §§ 2-102, 2-103. *See* UPC § 2-105. *See* McGovern § 2.2 (p. 67).

Some states that have not enacted the Uniform Probate Code have adopted a similar "parentelic" system; however, not all parentelic systems are the same. Other states have adopted a "next of kin" system to apply in this situation. See McGovern § 2.2 (p. 63).

Answers (A), (B), and (C) are incorrect. Neither A nor B is an heir.

However, in some states both A and B would be the heirs of O. In other states, only A would be an heir.

17.   **Answer (C) is correct.** According to UPC § 2-103, a descendant of deceased grandparents takes by representation. Accordingly, C would inherit O's probate estate.

The result may differ in a non-UPC state. See McGovern § 2.2 (p. 63).

Answers (A) and (B) are incorrect. The state takes only if there is no taker under UPC § 2-103.

Answer (D) is incorrect. The cousin died before O died.

18.   Early common law prohibited aliens from acquiring land by descent, a rule followed in some states. The modern view is that non-citizens can acquire property unless a state's statute provides otherwise. *See* Atkinson § 24. UPC § 2-111 does not disqualify an heir because he or she is an alien.

The result may differ in a non-UPC state. However, even if a state statute purports to limit an alien's inheritance, federal law may override it, if the United States has a treaty with the alien's country. See Atkinson § 24.

19.   Both A and B are O's heirs; however, in the absence of a statute, the gift may be presumed to be an advancement of B's inheritance and would be taken into account in determining B's share of O's probate estate. If so, the value of Blackacre would be added to the value of the probate estate to determine the "hotchpot estate," and B's share of the probate estate would

be reduced using the "hotchpot" method. B would not be required to reimburse A or to restore Blackacre to the probate estate. *See* McGovern § 2.6. However, UPC § 2-109 and similar statutes enacted in most non-UPC states require written evidence of the intent that a gift is to be treated as an advancement. *See* McGovern § 2.6.

20.   **Answer (C) is correct.** C2 would appear to be O's only heir. However, the "representation rule" of UPC § 2-106 would substitute G1 as an heir in place of C1. If G1 is a minor, G1's share would be delivered to a guardian or other surrogate pursuant to state law. *See* McGovern § 2.2.

   Answers (A), (B), and (D) are incorrect for the reasons given.

21.   **Answer (C) is correct.** C2's spouse acquired C2's interest in O's estate. The "representation rule" of UPC § 2-106 substitutes G1 as an heir in place of C1. Accordingly, O's probate estate should be delivered equally to G1 and C2's devisee, S2. If G1 is a minor, G1's share would be delivered to a guardian or other surrogate pursuant to state law.

   The result would be the same in most states that have not enacted the Uniform Probate Code. See McGovern § 2.2 (p. 57).

   Answers (A), (B), and (D) are incorrect for the reasons given.

22.   **Answer (A) is correct.** Absent written evidence that O intended the conveyance to be an advancement (or that C2 acknowledged the gift was an advancement), S2 not only inherited Blackacre when C2 died but also succeeded to C2's interest in O's probate estate. *See* UPC § 2-109.

   The result may differ in states that have not enacted the Uniform Probate Code or a statute similar to UPC § 2-109. See McGovern § 2.6.

   Answers (B) and (C) are incorrect. In order for the gift to be treated as an advancement and either reduce or eliminate C2's interest in O's probate estate, written evidence of O's intent to treat the gift as an advancement (or that C2 acknowledged that the gift was an advancement) must be produced.

   In a non-UPC state, the gift may be presumed to be an advancement.

   Answer (D) is not correct. Even if the gift is treated as an advancement, Blackacre was owned by C2 and passed to S2 at C2's death subject to formal administration of C2's estate. Neither C2 nor S2 is under a legal obligation to reimburse O's other heirs or restore Blackacre to O's probate estate.

23.   **Answer (A) is correct.** Even if there is written evidence of O's intent to treat the gift as an advancement to C1, C1 died before O, and G1 succeeded to the interest in O's probate estate that C1 would have inherited had C1 survived O. *See* UPC §§ 2-103, 2-106. Accordingly, Blackacre is not taken into account in determining G1's share of O's probate estate. *See* UPC § 2-109(c).

   The result may differ in states that have not enacted the Uniform Probate Code or a statute similar to UPC § 2-109. See McGovern § 2.6.

   Answers (B) and (C) are incorrect. Absent written evidence that O not only intended for the gift to C1 to be an advancement but that O also intended for the advancement to be taken into account in the event C1 predeceased O, the gift is not treated as an advancement.

In non-UPC states, G1 may be "burdened by representation."

Answer (D) is incorrect. Even if the gift was an advancement, neither C1, C1's heirs and devisees, nor C1's descendants taking by representation have a legal obligation to restore Blackacre to O's probate estate.

24.   **Answer (A) is correct.** Since the gift was to G2, it has no effect on C2's inheritance from O that passed to S2 when C2 died. The gift is not an advancement. *See* UPC § 2-109. *See* McGovern § 2.6.

Answers (B), (C) and (D) are incorrect. The facts do not create an advancement situation under the Uniform Probate Code, similar statutes in non-UPC states, or the common law. Even a written agreement between O and G2 defining the transaction as an advancement may not be binding on C2. Had C2 been a party to the agreement and agreed the gift would be taken into account in determining C2's share of O's probate estate, S2 may be bound by the agreement, or estopped to deny that the advancement to G2 should not be taken into account in determining C2's share of O's probate estate.

25.   Absent written evidence that O intended the gift to be an advancement to G2, the gift is not taken into account in determining G2's share of O's probate estate. *See* UPC § 2-109.

The same result is likely to occur in a state that has not enacted the Uniform Probate Code because the presumption of advancement may not be applicable since G2 was not an "heir apparent" at the time of the gift. At common law, the gift had to have been made to one who would have been an heir at the time of the gift in order to create the presumption of advancement. See Atkinson § 129.

26.   **Answer (A) is correct.** At the time of the assignment, C1 did not have a property interest in O's probate estate that C1 could transfer; C1 had an expectancy, not a property interest. O still owned fee simple title. *See* Atkinson § 131. When C2 died, C2's interest in O's estate passed to C2's spouse.

The same result would likely occur in states that have not enacted the Uniform Probate Code.

Answers (B) and (C) are incorrect. C1 did not own a property interest in O's property that could be given or sold to the assignee. Had C1 survived O by more than 120 hours, the assignee may have been able to enforce the assignment against C1 and C1's estate, if the assignment had been supported by fair consideration.

Answer (D) is incorrect. The assignee may be a creditor of C1 or C1's estate, but O's estate is not legally obligated to C1's assignee.

27.   **Answer (B) is correct.** As soon as O died, O's heirs succeeded to their respective interests in O's estate subject to the 120-hour rule, as well as the debts and other obligations of O and O's estate. *See* UPC § 2-101. Accordingly, C2's expectancy in O's property became a property interest at the time of O's death and could be assigned by C2 to the third party. Of course, the assignee could not acquire an interest greater than the one C2 owned at the time of the assignment.

Answer (A) is incorrect. C2 has assigned C2's interest in O's probate estate.

Answer (C) is incorrect. An assignment does not need good and valuable consideration to be effective. It may have been a gift.

Answer (D) is incorrect. The third party is not a creditor of O; the third party acquired whatever interest in O's probate estate that C2 inherited.

28. At the time of the assignment, C2 had an expectancy in O's property. Such an expectancy is not a future interest in O's property; it's not even a property interest. Therefore, the assignment did not transfer any property interest in O's property to the assignee. At O's death, C2's expectancy, in effect, matured into a property interest. State law may provide the third party with a remedy to enforce the assignment as a contract, if the third party paid good and valuable consideration. If no consideration was paid by the third party to C2, the transaction may be viewed as an unenforceable promise of C2. *See* Atkinson § 131. If the assignment was a conveyance of real property, the doctrine of "after acquired title" may be applicable. *See* ROGER A. CUNNINGHAM, WILLIAM B. STOEBUCK AND DALE A. WHITMAN, THE LAW OF PROPERTY § 11.5 (2d ed. 1993).

29. **Answer (A) is correct.** Because C1 predeceased O, C1 is not an heir and did not acquire a property interest in O's probate estate that could be attached by a creditor of C1. *See* McGovern § 2.2.

Answers (B), (C), and (D) are incorrect for the reasons given.

30. **Answer (A) is correct.** Because C1 did not survive O by 120 hours, C1 is not an heir. Thus, no part of O's probate estate is reachable by C1's creditor. *See* McGovern § 2.2.

Answers (B) and (C) are not correct for the reasons given.

Answer (D) is not correct. The creditor is not a creditor of O and does not have to follow the procedures required of O's creditors.

31. **Answer (B) is correct.** Because C1 survived O by 120 hours, the lien can attach to C1's interest in O's probate estate that passed to S1 when C1 died. *See* McGovern § 2.2. However, C1's interest in O's estate is still subject to administration by O's personal representative, as well as O's debts and other obligations. The creditor cannot acquire an interest greater than the one C1 inherited.

Answer (A) is not correct. The lien can attach to C1's interest in O's probate estate.

Answer (C) is not correct. The nature of the debt is irrelevant.

Answer (D is not correct. The creditor is not a creditor of O and does not have to follow the procedures required of O's creditors.

32. The early common law did not allow a decedent's heirs to refuse to accept their inheritances. Modern statutes in most states, such as UPC §§ 2-1102, 2-1105, 2-1106, authorize an heir to disclaim the heir's interest in the decedent's estate so that the property to which the heir would have been entitled passes as if the heir had predeceased the decedent. Statutes in some states, such as UPC § 2-1105, permit an heir's court-appointed surrogate, guardian, conservator, or personal representative to execute the disclaimer. However, the law varies from state to state on the effect the disclaimer will have on the disclaimant's creditors. *See* UPC § 2-1113 and its comments. Federal law will control if the disclaimant is in bankruptcy. *See* McGovern § 2.8.

33. **Answer (A) is correct.** Assuming the disclaimer satisfied the requirements of both applicable state law and the relevant provisions of the Internal Revenue Code, the interest in

O's probate estate that C2 would have inherited had it not been for the disclaimer passes from O to G2. *See* UPC § 2-1106(b)(3). No part of the disclaimed property is included in C2's gross estate for estate tax purposes, and C2 is not deemed to have made a gift to G2 for gift tax purposes. *See* IRC § 2518. *See* McGovern § 2.8.

Answers (B), (C), and (D) are incorrect for the reasons given.

34.   In most states, if O's probate estate is otherwise solvent (*i.e.*, the assets exceed the liabilities), whether or not the debt is valid and enforceable, the concept of "retainer" provides that C1's share of O's estate should be reduced by $6,000 so that the other heir's share of the probate estate is increased by a like amount in order to create equality among the heirs. *See* Atkinson § 141. However, UPC § 3-903 gives the borrower the benefit of any defense which would be available in a direct proceeding for recovery of the debt. If O's estate is insolvent (*i.e.*, the liabilities exceed the assets) and the debt is a valid and enforceable obligation of C1, C1 should pay into O's estate $12,000 in order for the personal representative to have funds to pay O's debts. If C1 does not pay what is owed, O's personal representative should pursue the $12,000 debt against C1. *See* Atkinson Ch. 13. If the debt is no longer enforceable (*i.e.*, collection is barred by the statute of limitations), C1 has no obligation to pay any amount into O's estate.

35.   **Answer (A) is correct.** It is generally accepted that delivery and acceptance are necessary for a valid inter vivos gift. Neither the cash nor the deed was delivered to C1 during O's lifetime. Accordingly, unless relevant state law relaxes the delivery and acceptance requirements of a gift under "gift causa mortis" theory, both the house and cash would pass to O's heirs. *See* Atkinson § 45.

Answers (B) and (D) are not correct. The concept of "gift causa mortis" has been limited in most jurisdictions to gifts of personal property only.

Answer (C) is incorrect. If the described assets were still part of O's probate estate, the assets would pass to O's heirs. However, if O made an inter vivos gift of the assets prior to O's death, the assets would have already been owned by the donee prior to O's death. Delivery during the donor's lifetime is an essential element of a gift. Since the deed was not delivered while O was alive, the house is still part of the probate estate. However, states that recognize the concept of "gift causa mortis" may relax the delivery and acceptance requirements. Accordingly, in those states the cash may have been given to C1.

36.   **Answer (B) is correct.** UPC § 2-803(b) provides that an heir who feloniously and intentionally kills the intestate forfeits the heir's intestate share. It also provides that the intestate's probate estate passes as if the killer disclaimed the killer's interest in the intestate's estate. Accordingly, the interest C1 would have received passes from O to G1.

A number of states that have not enacted the Uniform Probate Code have similar statutes. See McGovern § 2.7.

Answer (A) is not correct. Since C1 is deemed to have disclaimed the interest, the interest is not forfeited to the state.

Answer (C) is incorrect. UPC § 2-803(b) provides that C1's interest passes as if C1 had disclaimed C1's interest.

However, in some states, the applicable "slayer's rule" directs that C1's interest might be forfeited and C1's interest would pass to O's other heirs. Accordingly, in those states, G2 would take C1's interest, and G1 is excluded since C1, in fact, survived O. See McGovern § 2.7.

Answer (D) is incorrect. UPC § 2-803(b) provides a legal remedy that avoids having to resort to equitable principles.

However, in states that do not have a "slayer's rule" statute, the other heirs may be able to resort to the constructive trust as a remedy to prevent unjust enrichment.

1.   False. An express trust is a fiduciary relationship with respect to property that subjects the person who has legal title to legally enforceable duties to deal with the property for the benefit of another. *See* RESTATEMENT, THIRD, OF TRUSTS § 2.

2.   **Answer (B) is correct.** If the only proof of the oral trust is G's testimony of what O told G about the conveyance after the alleged transaction took place, it is likely that F will retain the fee simple title. G's testimony may not even be admissible under relevant rules of evidence. *See* RESTATEMENT, THIRD, OF TRUSTS § 18.

    Answers (A), (C), and (D) are not correct because there is no admissible evidence of the actual transaction that took place between O and F.

3.   The Uniform Trust Code permits the creation of an express oral trust if its terms can be established by clear and convincing evidence. However, the relevant statute of frauds may require a writing for the creation of an inter vivos trust of real property. If so, the oral express trust may not be enforceable if F is not willing to perform as agreed, notwithstanding the willingness of the friends to testify as to the oral agreement. *See* RESTATEMENT, THIRD, OF TRUSTS § 24. Traditionally, F would be allowed to retain Blackacre unless G was able to prove that F acquired Blackacre by fraud, undue influence, or duress, or that F, at the time of the transfer, was in a confidential relationship with O. In which event, the imposition of a constructive trust for G was the appropriate remedy. There appears, however, to be a modern trend developing toward the use of a resulting trust or a constructive trust to prevent F's unjust enrichment under these circumstances. Some cases favor the intended beneficiaries; others favor the settlor, or his or her successor in interest. *See* comment h to RESTATEMENT, THIRD, OF TRUSTS § 24.

4.   **Answer (B) is correct.** The relevant statute of frauds may require a writing for the inter vivos creation of enforceable express trusts of interests in real property. *See* RESTATEMENT, THIRD, OF TRUSTS § 22. Since there is no writing evidencing the trust, F may be able to retain Blackacre, notwithstanding F's acknowledgment of the oral agreement, unless G can prove that F procured the transfer by fraud, duress, or undue influence, or that O and F were in a confidential relationship at the time of the transfer. *See* answer to previous question.

    Answers (A), (C), and (D) are incorrect. Assuming there is no other evidence of F's intent at the time of the conveyance or of a special relationship existing between O and F at the time of the conveyance, a constructive trust may not be appropriate. The traditional view is a constructive trust can be imposed on a grantee of a deed only if the grantee did not intend to perform as agreed when the promise was made. *See* McGovern § 6.4. There are, however, cases in some jurisdictions suggesting the use of a constructive trust is appropriate to prevent the unjust enrichment of a grantee who orally agrees but later refuses to act in accordance with the agreement. *See* comment h to RESTATEMENT, THIRD, OF TRUSTS § 24.

5.   **Answer (C) is correct.** Because of the pre-existing fiduciary relationship that existed between O and F, a court is likely to impose a constructive trust on F in favor of G to avoid unjust enrichment by F. *See* Restatement, Third, of Trusts § 24.

    Answers (A), (B), and (D) are not correct. Because of the pre-existing fiduciary relationship between O and F, equity will not likely permit F to retain Blackacre.

6.   **Answer (B) is correct.** The testimony of the friends is likely to be the evidence needed to prove the creation of the oral express trust and its terms. Most states do not require a writing to create or enforce an inter vivos express trust of personal property under these circumstances. *See* Restatement, Third, of Trusts §§ 20, 21. However, UTC § 407 does require "clear and convincing evidence" of the creation of the oral trust and its terms.

    Some states that have not enacted the Uniform Trust Code may require only a "preponderance of the evidence." See Bogert § 21.

    Answer (A) is not correct. Assuming G has "clear and convincing" evidence of the oral agreement, G can simply bring an action to enforce the express trust.

    Answer (C) is not correct. O's attempt to create the express trust did not fail for lack of a beneficiary or for failure of the trust's purpose.

    Answer (D) is not correct. Sufficient evidence is available to prevent F from retaining the stock for F's own use.

7.   **Answer (C) is correct.** The oral trust agreement does not satisfy a statute of frauds that requires a writing for inter vivos trusts of real property. Thus, G cannot enforce the express trust. *See* Restatement, Third, of Trusts §§ 22, 24. However, it is apparent that O did not intend F to take Blackacre for F's own use, thereby leading to the imposition of a resulting trust in favor of C, as O's successor in interest. Other cases suggest a constructive trust for G is the appropriate remedy. *See* comment i of Restatement, Third, of Trusts § 24.

    Answer (A) is not correct. In order to satisfy the requirements of the statute of frauds, the writing must not only manifest trust intention, but also identify the trust property, the beneficiaries, and the purposes of the trust.

    Answer (B) is not correct. In some states, C, as O's successor in interest, has standing to require F to return the property. *See* Restatement, Third, of Trusts § 24.

    Some states may allow G to impose the constructive trust to avoid C's unjust enrichment. See comment i to Restatement, Third, of Trusts § 24.

    Answer (D) is not correct. Equity will not allow F to retain the property.

8.   **Answer (B) is correct.** F can carry out the terms of the oral express trust, if the creation and the terms of an oral trust can be proven by clear and convincing evidence. Only F can assert the statute of frauds as a defense and take advantage of the oral express trust being unenforceable. *See* Restatement, Third, of Trusts § 24. If F elects to take advantage of the statute of frauds or cannot prove the existence of the oral agreement, the trust is "passive," and G can demand the transfer of the property to G. If the statute of uses, or a similar statute, is applicable, F's legal title merges with G's equitable interest, and G already owns fee simple title. *See* Restatement, Third, of Trusts § 6.

    While UTC § 407 requires clear and convincing evidence to prove an oral trust, many non-UTC states require proof by only a preponderance of the evidence.

Answers (A), (C), and (D) are incorrect for the reasons given.

9. If a valid, enforceable trust has been created, Blackacre is not subject to the personal obligations of T. *See* RESTATEMENT, THIRD, OF TRUSTS § 42. UTC § 507 has codified this generally accepted principle. However, because there is not a written evidence of the trust, UTC § 407 requires that the creation of the trust and its terms be proven by "clear and convincing evidence." Will the court accept T's acknowledgment of the trust as sufficient proof of the existence of the trust and its terms? If T and G fail to meet the burden of proof, the creditors can attach the property.

In states that have not enacted the Uniform Trust Code, the creation of the trust and its terms may have to be proven by only a preponderance of the evidence.

10. Even if the terms of the trust agreement can be established by G, T could plead the statute of frauds as an affirmative defense, thereby making the trust unenforceable and allowing the creditor to attach Blackacre unless G can intervene and meet the burden of proof to have a constructive trust imposed on T in favor of G. *See* RESTATEMENT, THIRD, OF TRUSTS § 24. Alternatively, T can acknowledge the oral trust, not plead the statute of frauds, and prevent Blackacre from being attached, if there is clear and convincing evidence of the oral trust. *See* UTC § 407.

In states that have not enacted the Uniform Trust Code, the creation of the trust and its terms may have to be proven by only a preponderance of the evidence.

11. **Answer (A) is correct.** If you allow the creditor to attach Blackacre, you will breach your fiduciary duties to G. *See* McGovern § 12.1. A valid, enforceable express trust exists. Since an express trust exists, Blackacre is not subject to the personal obligations of T. *See* RESTATEMENT, THIRD, OF TRUSTS § 42. UTC § 507 codifies this generally accepted principle.

    Answer B is not correct. Because a valid, enforceable express trust has been established, the trust property is not subject to the personal obligations of T.

    Answers (C) and (D) are not correct. Since an express trust exists, Blackacre is not subject to the personal obligations of T.

12. **Answer (A) is correct.** An enforceable express trust was created; the death of G did not terminate the trust. At common law, conditions of survivorship were not implied with respect to future interests. *See* comment to UPC § 2-707. However, UPC § 2-707 provides that a future interest under the terms of a trust is contingent on the beneficiary surviving the distribution date. Since G was not survived by any lineal descendants, the property passed to O's heir, C, at O's death. *See* UPC § 2-707.

    Answers (B) and (C) are not correct. Because G predeceased O, neither C nor M inherited G's interest in the trust.

In a state that has not enacted UPC § 2-707, or a similar statute, the result is likely to differ. G's interest would likely be inherited by G's heirs, C and M, unless the express trust failed. See RESTATEMENT, THIRD, OF TRUSTS §§ 8, 55.

    Answer (D) is not correct. In any event, F does not retain the property for F's personal use.

13. **Answer (B) is correct.** Absent additional evidence of O's intentions, UPC § 2-707 directs

that the trustee deliver the property to C as O's heir.

In states that have not enacted the Uniform Probate Code, G's contingent remainder failed, and O's reversionary interest passed to C, as O's heir. See RESTATEMENT, THIRD, OF TRUSTS §§ 8, 55. However, if G would have been survived by a child, the child would have acquired G's interest notwithstanding the "survivorship" language. According to UPC § 2-707, words of survivorship are not, in the absence of additional evidence, a sufficient indication of contrary intent to negate the "substitute gift" rule of UPC § 2-707. See comment to UPC § 2-707. In a state that has not enacted the Uniform Probate Code, the result will likely differ. See comment a to RESTATEMENT, THIRD, OF TRUSTS § 55.

Answer (A) is not correct. The death of the surviving trust beneficiary does not generally pass fee simple ownership to the trustee.

Answers (C) and (D) are not correct. G's contingent remainder interest failed; the purpose of the trust has become frustrated.

14. **Answer (D) is correct.** An express trust is created in a will only if the testator manifests the intent to impose on the devisee legally enforceable duties to manage the property for another. However, only such manifestations of intent which are admissible as proof in a judicial proceeding may be considered. *See* RESTATEMENT, THIRD, OF TRUSTS § 13. The Uniform Trust Code has codified these generally accepted common law principles. *See* UTC § 402 and commentary. Accordingly, without additional proof of O's intent, the language in O's will is likely to be found to be "precatory" rather than "mandatory."

Answer (A) is not correct. The use of the words "with the request" by O generally is considered to be "precatory" rather than "mandatory."

Answer (B) is not correct. Either C has fee simple title or an express trust was created for the benefit of G.

Answer (C) is not correct. Either an express trust was created for the benefit of G or C owns the stock.

15. **Answer (A) is correct.** It is evident that O did not intend C to acquire the stock for C's personal use and benefit. All of the elements of an express trust are present. *See* RESTATEMENT, THIRD, OF TRUSTS § 17. The Uniform Trust Code has codified these generally accepted common law principles. *See* UTC §§ 401, 402.

Answer (B) is not correct. An express trust has been created. G will seek to enforce the terms of the express trust.

Answer (C) is not correct. All of the elements of an express trust are present.

Answer (D) is not correct. C inherited the legal title only; G inherited an equitable interest in the stock.

16. **Answer (B) is correct.** Because G died before O, an express trust was not created. *See* Restatement, Third, of Trusts § 17. The devise to C fails, and O's executor should deliver the stock to O's residuary beneficiary, the charity. *See* RESTATEMENT, THIRD, OF TRUSTS § 8. The Uniform Probate Code has codified this generally accepted common law principle. *See* UPC § 2-604.

Answer (A) is not correct. O's attempt to create an express trust for the benefit of G failed because G died before the trust was created. G's heirs did not acquire any interest in the stock.

Answer (C) is not correct. The executor should not deliver the stock to C. If C already has the stock, the charity may need to seek the imposition of a resulting trust to acquire the stock as O's successor in interest.

Answer (D) is not correct. It is evident that O did not intend C to acquire the stock for C's personal use and benefit.

17. An express trust can be created by the settlor's declaration that the settlor holds identifiable property for another. *See* RESTATEMENT, THIRD, OF TRUSTS § 10. The Uniform Trust Code has codified this generally accepted common law principle. *See* UTC § 401. The fact that O's declaration of trust was oral is problematic. However, the Uniform Trust Code has adopted the view that, absent a statute to the contrary, an express trust does not need to be evidenced by a trust instrument, if the creation of the oral trust and its terms can be established by clear and convincing evidence. *See* UTC § 407. Assuming there is no such statute and that the friends' testimony will be accepted by the court as "clear and convincing" evidence of the creation of the express trust, an express trust was created, and the court should appoint a successor trustee to manage Blackacre until G attains age 21.

The result will differ in a state where the statute of frauds requires a signed writing in order for trusts of real property to be enforceable. The statute of frauds in many jurisdictions requires oral declarations of trust to be in writing. In those states, C, as O's heir, would likely retain Blackacre. See RESTATEMENT, THIRD, OF TRUSTS § 22. However, a possible exception exists that may permit G to seek a constructive trust on C to prevent C's unjust enrichment. See comment j to RESTATEMENT, THIRD, OF TRUSTS § 24.

18. **Answer (A) is correct.** An express trust can be created by the settlor's declaration that the settlor holds identifiable property for another. *See* RESTATEMENT, THIRD, OF TRUSTS § 10. The Uniform Trust Code has codified this generally accepted common law principle. *See* UTC § 401. The fact that O's declaration of trust was oral is problematic. However, the Uniform Trust Code has adopted the view that, absent a statute to the contrary, an express oral trust does not need to be evidenced by a trust instrument, if its creation and terms can be established by clear and convincing evidence. *See* UTC § 407.

The result will differ in a state where the statute of frauds requires a signed writing for declarations of trusts of personal property. See RESTATEMENT, THIRD, OF TRUSTS § 22.

Answer (B) is incorrect. Assuming that the friends' testimony will be accepted by the court as "clear and convincing" evidence of the creation of the trust, an express trust was created.

The statute of frauds in some jurisdictions requires oral declarations of trust to be in writing. In those states, C, as O's heir, would likely retain the stock.

Answer (C) is incorrect. The traditional view is that a constructive trust is an appropriate remedy when a transferee committed a fraud, exerted undue influence, or breached a confidential relationship. Neither O nor C committed any of those acts. However, a possible exception exists that may permit G to seek a constructive trust on C to prevent C's unjust enrichment. *See* comment j to RESTATEMENT, THIRD, OF TRUSTS § 24.

Answer (D) is incorrect. It is not the role of a personal representative to manage the settlor's inter vivos trust.

19. **Answer (A) is correct.** An express trust can be created by the settlor's declaration that the settlor was holding identifiable property for the benefit of another. *See* RESTATEMENT, THIRD, OF TRUSTS § 10. The Uniform Trust Code has codified this generally accepted common law

principle. *See* UTC § 401.

The same result is likely to occur in a non-UTC state since the writing requirement of an applicable statute of frauds is satisfied. See RESTATEMENT, THIRD, OF TRUSTS § 23.

Answer (B) is incorrect. All of the elements of a valid, enforceable express trust are present.

Answer (C) is incorrect. If C has possession and refuses to cooperate when G seeks to enforce the express trust, the court may need to impose a constructive trust.

Answer (D) is incorrect. It is not the role of a personal representative to manage the settlor's inter vivos trust.

20.   **Answer (A) is correct.** Assuming the Uniform Trust Code was in effect at the time the express trust was created, the settlor may revoke the trust unless the terms of the trust provide the trust is irrevocable. *See* UTC § 602. The Uniform Trust Code has reversed the generally accepted common law rule that trusts are presumed to be irrevocable. *See* RESTATEMENT, THIRD, OF TRUSTS § 63. Presumably, a court would likely find that O's conveyance to F was evidence of O's intent to revoke the trust.

The result is likely to be different in a state that does not presume inter vivos trusts are revocable.

Answers (B) and (C) are incorrect. O retained the power to revoke the trust. In a state that has not adopted the Uniform Trust Code approach, or if the trust was created before the state adopted that approach, G can file suit for breach of fiduciary duty by O. If successful, the court may be able to impose a constructive trust on F since F was not a good-faith purchaser.

Answer (D) is incorrect. While a court may impose a constructive trust on a third party who participates in a trustee's breach of trust, the third party is generally not personally liable to the beneficiary, if the third party is not aware of the trust. *See* UTC § 1012.

21.   **Answer (D) is correct.** It appears as if a valid, enforceable express trust was created during O's lifetime, even though title remained in O's name until O died. *See* UTC §§ 401, 402. At O's death, Blackacre is a nonprobate asset, and F's equitable remainder interest became possessory.

The result is likely to be the same in states that have not enacted the Uniform Trust Code. See RESTATEMENT, THIRD, OF TRUSTS § 10.

Answers (A) and (B) are incorrect. An express inter vivos trust does not need to be executed with testamentary formalities. Blackacre passes pursuant to the terms of the trust, not by the will or by intestate succession.

Answer (C) is incorrect. Because O did not change the title to Blackacre when the trust was created, Blackacre still appears to be a probate asset, and F will need to take steps to establish the existence of the trust and F's ownership under the trust.

22.   **Answer (D) is correct.** The facts that there was no transfer of title before O's death and that O retained the power to revoke the trust do not affect the trust's validity. *See* UTC §§ 401, 402. *See* RESTATEMENT, THIRD, OF TRUSTS § 10. Since O did not revoke the apparently valid, enforceable express trust prior to O's death, the terms of the trust control the disposition of Blackacre. Since the trust was created by O's declaration of trust, at O's death, Blackacre is

a nonprobate asset, and F's equitable remainder interest became possessory.

The result is likely to be the same in states that have not enacted the Uniform Trust Code. See comment to UTC § 401.

Answers (A) and (B) are incorrect. An express inter vivos trust does not need to be executed with testamentary formalities.

Answer (C) is incorrect. Since O did not change the title to Blackacre when the trust was created, Blackacre still appears to be a probate asset, and F will need to take steps to establish the existence of the trust and F's ownership under the trust.

23. **Answer (C) is correct.** If the creation and funding of the trust were in fraud of O's creditors, the creditors can pursue their claims against the trust estate pursuant to the relevant state's law on fraudulent transfers. The transfer may also constitute a voidable preference in bankruptcy. *See* comment to UTC § 505. If O did not become insolvent by reason of the creation and funding of the trust, the trust estate is not reachable to satisfy O's debts. UTC § 505 adopts this generally accepted principle. *See* Bogert § 48.

Answers (A) and (B) are incorrect. If the creation and funding of the trust were in fraud of the creditors, they can still reach the trust estate.

Answer (D) is incorrect. The trust assets are not reachable by the creditors unless the creation and funding of the trust were in fraud of the creditors.

24. **Answer (D) is correct.** During the lifetime of the settlor, the trust estate of a revocable trust is subject to claims of the settlor's creditors. *See* UTC § 505(a)(1).

The result is likely to be the same in a state that has not adopted the Uniform Trust Code. See comment e to RESTATEMENT, THIRD, OF TRUSTS § 25.

Answers (A), (B) and (C) are incorrect for the reasons given.

25. **Answer (D) is correct.** Following the settlor's death, the trust estate of a revocable trust continues to be subject to claims of the settlor's creditors. UTC § 505(a)(3) adopts this widely accepted principle.

The result may differ in a non-UTC state. See Bogert § 148.

Answers (A), (B), and (C) are incorrect for the reasons given.

26. **Answer (C) is correct.** Assuming the terms of the trust, including its irrevocability, can be established by clear and convincing evidence, the fact that the express trust was created pursuant to an oral agreement should not be determinative of the issue. *See* UTC § 407. If the transfer to T had been in fraud of O's creditors, the creditors can pursue their claims against the property transferred. If not, the property is not reachable to satisfy O's debts. *See* UTC § 505.

The same result is likely to occur in a non-UTC state. See Bogert § 48.

Answers (A), (B), and (D) are incorrect for the reasons given.

27. **Answer (A) is correct.** The trust property is not subject to the personal obligations of the trustee. UTC § 507 has codified this generally accepted principle. *See* RESTATEMENT, THIRD, OF TRUSTS § 42. If you use the trust estate to satisfy your creditors, you will breach your duty of

loyalty to the trust's beneficiaries. *See* McGovern § 12.1.

Answers (B), (C), and (D) are not correct. Trust property is not subject to the trustee's personal debts.

28.   As long as the creation of the oral trust and its terms can be established, the trust property cannot be reached by the trustee's personal creditors. *See* Restatement, Third, of Trusts § 42. Since the trust is oral, the UTC requires "clear and convincing evidence" of the terms of the trust. *See* UTC § 407. The lack of a writing does not affect the validity of the trust as to the real property, and the trustee can properly perform notwithstanding the statute of frauds. *See* RESTATEMENT, THIRD, OF TRUSTS § 24.

In a state that has not adopted the UTC approach, the existence of the trust may need to be proven by only a "preponderance of the evidence."

29.   **Answer (B) is correct.** Absent a "spendthrift" or "forfeiture" provision in the trust agreement, the court may authorize a creditor to reach a beneficiary's interest in the trust by attachment of either present or future distributions. UTC § 501 has codified this generally accepted common law principle. *See* McGovern § 9.8.

Answer (A) is not correct. C's interest is limited to the income the trust generates during C's lifetime.

Answer (C) is not correct. It doesn't matter whether the debt is tortious or contractual in nature.

Answer (D) is not correct. To the extent a beneficiary's interest is not subject to a "spendthrift" or "forfeiture" provision, it is generally available to satisfy the beneficiary's creditors. *See* Bogert § 39.

30.   **Answer (D) is correct.** Generally, the interest of a beneficiary is liable to be taken by a beneficiary's creditors. The process varies from state to state. *See* Bogert §§ 39, 41. Whether or not the trust agreement contains a "spendthrift" or "forfeiture" provision, a creditor of a beneficiary generally does not have standing to compel a trustee to make a discretionary distribution from the trust to the creditor or the beneficiary. *See* UTC § 504. *See* McGovern § 9.8. However, the creditor may be able to attach the beneficiary's interest, and although the interest is not subject to execution sale, the trustee may be held personally liable to the creditor for any amount paid by the trustee to the beneficiary if the trustee has been served with notice of the attachment. *See* Comment c to RESTATEMENT, THIRD, OF TRUSTS § 60.

Answer (A) is not correct. C's interest is effectively limited to whatever income, if any, is distributed to C in T's discretion.

The Restatement takes the position that the creditor is entitled to "judicial protection from abuse of discretion by the trustee." However, it also acknowledges that the trustee's refusal to make a distribution under these circumstances may not be an abuse of discretion. See Comment e to RESTATEMENT, THIRD, OF TRUSTS § 60.

Answer (B) is not correct. C does not have a mandatory right to the income.

Answer (C) is not correct. Generally, the only creditor that may be excepted from the general rule is a child, spouse, or former spouse of the beneficiary with a judgment or order against C for support. *See* UTC § 504(c)(2).

31.   **Answer (D) is correct.** See the answer to the previous question. UTC § 504 applies to

distributions defined by an ascertainable standard.

See comment c to RESTATEMENT, THIRD, OF TRUSTS § 60. The result may differ in a state that has not adopted the UTC or the Restatement, Third, of Trusts approach since C's interest in the trust estate is limited to whatever income is necessary for C's health, education, maintenance, or support, and when C dies, G is entitled to the income not properly distributed to C. See McGovern § 9.8.

Answers (A), (B), and (C) are not correct. The only creditor that may be excepted from the general rule is a child, spouse, or former spouse of a beneficiary with a judgment or order against C for support. *See* UTC § 504(c)(2).

32. **Answer (D) is correct.** See the answer to the previous question. A creditor of a beneficiary cannot compel a discretionary distribution from a trust, even if the trustee has failed to comply with a standard of distribution. *See* comment to UTC § 504.

The result may differ in a state that has not adopted the Uniform Trust Code approach. Here, C's interest is limited to whatever income is distributed to C pursuant to the described standard of distribution. Because the hospital rendered medical services, it is arguable that it should be able to garnish C's interest in the trust. See McGovern § 9.8.

Answers (A), (B), and (C) are not correct for the reasons given.

While UTC § 504 appears to prohibit the creditor from compelling a distribution, states that have not adopted the Uniform Trust Code approach may allow the hospital to collect from the trustee out of the trust's income if the trust agreement does not contain a "spendthrift" or "forfeiture" provision. See McGovern § 9.8.

33. **Answer (B) is correct.** Absent a "spendthrift" or "forfeiture" provision in the trust agreement, the court may authorize a creditor to attach a beneficiary's future interest in the trust estate. The Uniform Trust Code codifies this generally accepted common law principle. *See* UTC § 501. The court may even order a sale of the beneficiary's future interest. *See* McGovern § 9.8. However, the value of G's remainder interest is diminished by it being contingent on G surviving C. *See* UPC § 2-707.

Answer (A) is not correct. The creditor cannot divest C's interest in the trust.

Answer (C) is not correct. While a creditor, in theory, may force a judicial sale of a beneficiary's interest, such a sale cannot adversely affect the interests of other beneficiaries.

Answer (D) is not correct. Only G's future interest can be attached.

34. In most jurisdictions, a settlor has the power to include as part of the terms of the trust a provision that prevents a creditor from reaching a beneficiary's interest in the trust or a distribution by the trustee before its actual receipt by the beneficiary. *See* Bogert § 40. This so-called "spendthrift" provision is generally valid in most states so long as it prohibits both voluntary and involuntary transfers of beneficial interests. *See* McGovern § 9.8. These generally accepted principles have been codified in UTC § 502. Accordingly, if the agreement prohibits both voluntary and involuntary alienation, the creditor cannot attach the beneficiaries' interests in the trust, and the creditor must wait until there are actual distributions to the beneficiaries. *See* McGovern § 9.8. If valid under state law, the spendthrift provision will be effective in bankruptcy. *See* comment a to RESTATEMENT, THIRD, OF TRUSTS § 58.

Apparently, a few states still do not recognize the effectiveness of "spendthrift" provisions. See McGovern § 9.8.

35. **Answer (C) is correct.** Even in jurisdictions that do not accept the effectiveness of "spendthrift" provisions, a settlor can generally place a "condition subsequent" on a beneficiary's interest, causing the beneficiary's interest to terminate or change, if there is an attempted involuntary or voluntary alienation. Sometimes the condition subsequent converts the beneficiary's interest into a discretionary interest. *See* Bogert § 44 and McGovern § 9.8.

Answer (A) is not correct. C's interest is not affected by the termination of G's interest.

Answer (B) is not correct. C's interest is not enhanced by the termination of G's interest.

Answer (D) is not correct. Most jurisdictions accept the effectiveness of these so-called "forfeiture" provisions.

36. **Answer (A) is correct.** As a general rule, a court may authorize an assignee of a beneficiary's interest to reach the beneficiary's interest by attachment of present or future distributions. *See* Restatement, Third, of Trusts § 51. The Uniform Trust Code has codified this generally accepted common law principle. *See* UTC § 501. *See* Bogert § 38.

Answers (B), (C) and (D) are not correct. As a general rule, to the extent a beneficiary's interest is not subject to a "spendthrift" provision or a "forfeiture" provision, or a statute limiting the beneficiary's power of alienation, the interest is assignable.

37. **Answer (D) is correct.** Absent a "spendthrift" or "forfeiture" provision, or a state statute limiting the beneficiary's power of alienation, a court may authorize an assignee to reach the beneficiary's interest by attachment of present or future distributions to or for the benefit of a beneficiary. *See* UTC § 501. In other words, the assignee is generally entitled to receive any distributions the trustee makes, or is required to make, after the trustee has knowledge of the transfer. However, an assignee cannot acquire an interest greater than the one owned by the beneficiary prior to the assignment, and the court should limit the award to such relief as is appropriate under the circumstances. *See* UTC § 501. G is entitled to whatever is not properly distributed to or for the benefit of C's health, support, education or maintenance. *See* Bogert § 48.

Answers (A) and (B) are not correct. An assignee cannot acquire an interest greater than the one the assignor owned prior to the assignment.

Restatement, Third, of Trusts takes the position that "support" trusts are discretionary trusts and that the assignee is entitled to "judicial protection from abuse of discretion by the trustee." However, it also acknowledges that the trustee's refusal to make a distribution under these circumstances may not be an abuse of discretion, suggesting that the balancing process typical of discretionary issues is weighted against assignees. Comment e to Restatement, Third, of Trusts § 60.

Answer (C) is not correct for the reasons given.

However, the law in some states may prohibit assignments of support interests unless they were made for the purpose of acquiring goods or services for C's support, assuming that the interests were not limited by a "spendthrift" or "forfeiture" provision, or a statute limiting the beneficiaries' powers of alienation. See Bogert §§ 38, 42.

38. Absent a "spendthrift" or "forfeiture" provision, or a state statute that limits the beneficiary's power of alienation, a beneficiary's assignee has a right to receive discretionary distributions to which the beneficiary would otherwise be entitled. *See* Restatement, Third, of Trusts § 60. However, the assignee cannot compel the trustee to make a distribution, if the beneficiary could not do so. In a discretionary trust, the assignee would have to prove the

trustee abused its discretion after consideration of the beneficiary's circumstances and the effect the decision will have on G in light of the purposes of the trust. *See* comment e to RESTATEMENT, THIRD, OF TRUSTS § 60. Traditionally, the assignment is only effective if and when the trustee elects to make a distribution. *See Bogert § 41.*

39. **Answer (C) is correct.** Assuming the trust agreement did not contain a "spendthrift" or "forfeiture" provision, and state law does not limit the beneficiary's power of alienation, the assignment of a beneficiary's future interest is valid. *See* RESTATEMENT, THIRD, OF TRUSTS § 51. UTC § 501 has codified this generally accepted common law principle. At C's death, the trust estate should be delivered to Q, if G survives C. *See* UPC § 2-707. *See Bogert § 38.*

    Answer (A) is not correct. A beneficiary of a trust owns an interest in property which, as a general rule, is assignable.

    Answer (B) is not correct. The assignee cannot acquire an interest greater than that owned by the beneficiary.

    Answer (D) is not correct. As a general rule, the assignment is enforceable against the trustee.

40. **Answer (A) is correct.** The terms of the trust include a "spendthrift" provision. Accordingly, G cannot assign G's interest in the trust estate to Q. *See* RESTATEMENT, THIRD, OF TRUSTS § 58. UTC § 502 codifies this widely accepted principle of trust law. However, the comment to UTC § 502 notes that the trustee may choose to honor the assignment unless G revokes the assignment. *See Bogert § 40.*

    Answer (B) is not correct. In most jurisdictions, a beneficiary may not transfer an interest in a trust in violation of a valid "spendthrift" provision.

    Answer (C) is not correct. Whether the assignee paid consideration for the assignment is irrelevant.

    Answer (D) is not correct. The spendthrift provision made it impossible for G to make a legally binding transfer. However, G may be estopped to deny the assignment once the property is delivered to G.

41. **Answer (D) is correct.** As a general rule, the beneficiaries of an express trust can assign their interests to assignees, including the person serving as the trustee. *See* Restatement, Third, of Trusts § 51. However, this particular assignment is problematic even in the absence of a "spendthrift" or "forfeiture" provision, or a statute limiting the beneficiary's power of alienation. Because of the fiduciary relationship existing between C, G, and T, the transaction is suspect, and if there was improper conduct by T, or if C and G were not aware of all of the material facts, the assignment may be set aside. *See* comment b to RESTATEMENT, THIRD, OF TRUSTS § 51.

    Answer (A) is not correct. In most states, O is a "stranger" to the trust because the trust is irrevocable and O did not retain any interest in, or power over, the trust estate. However, in a state that has adopted UPC § 2-707, G's remainder interest is a contingent interest, and if G does not survive C, G's descendants, or O, may have an interest in the property. Does this interest give O standing to challenge the transaction?

    Answer (B) is not correct. If the assignment is valid, legal title and equitable title merged, and the trust no longer exists, subject to the possible interests of G's descendants and O.

Answer (C) is not correct. Answer (C) would be correct if the assignment is valid.

42.   A trustee has the fiduciary duty to act impartially, giving due regard to interests of all of the beneficiaries. In addition, T has a fiduciary duty to exercise a discretionary power in good faith and in accordance with the terms and purposes of the trust and the interests of the beneficiaries. Accordingly, either beneficiary has standing to bring a cause of action to remedy a breach of trust. *See* Bogert §§ 153, 157. The Uniform Trust Code has codified these generally accepted principles of trust law. *See* UTC §§ 803, 814, 1001.

43.   **Answer (D) is correct.** Because T is still a fiduciary, the terms of the trust are not interpreted literally and the burden of proof is typically on the beneficiary to plead and prove that the trustee "abused" the trustee's exercise or non-exercise of the discretionary power by not acting in good faith or in accordance with the purposes of the trust. *See* UTC § 814(a). *See* Bogert § 89.

      Answers (A), (B), and (C) are not correct. The determinative issue is whether T "abused" the discretion granted by the settlor. The trier of fact is not to substitute its judgment, or even the judgment of a reasonably prudent trustee, for the decision of the trustee.

44.   **Answer (D) is correct.** The Restatement treats "support" trusts as a category of discretionary trusts. Accordingly, the issue is whether the trustee abused its discretion. *See* Restatement, Third, of Trusts § 50.

      The burden of proof may differ in states that have not adopted the Restatement view. See Bogert §§ 89, 109.

      Answers (A), (B), and (C) are incorrect. In states that have not adopted the Restatement view, the burden may be on the beneficiary to prove what amount was actually necessary for C's health, support, education, or maintenance.

1. A donee with a general power of appointment has the authority to appoint the appointive property to (i) the donee or the donee's estate or (ii) the creditors of the donee or the donee's estate. The donee of a non-general power of appointment does not have such authority. *See* Andersen § 37(C)(1); RESTATEMENT, THIRD, OF PROPERTY § 17.3.

2. **Answer (C) is correct.** A owns the equitable life estate and is the donee of a non-general power of appointment, and the charity owns an equitable remainder interest that is subject to divestment, if A validly exercises the testamentary power. The children, as permissible appointees, are not beneficiaries of the trust. It will not be known until A dies if the power is exercised and the charity is divested. *See* UTC § 103(3) and comment c to RESTATEMENT, THIRD, OF PROPERTY § 19.7.

    Answer (A) is not correct. A owns an equitable life estate and is the donee of a testamentary non-general power of appointment. A is a beneficiary of the trust in both capacities according to the Uniform Trust Code.

    Answers (B) and (D) are not correct. A's exercise of the power will not be effective until A's death. Until the power is exercised, the objects of the power have expectancies and are not beneficiaries.

3. **Answer (B) is correct.** A was the donee of a non-general testamentary power of appointment. Since such a power is presumed to be "exclusionary" or "exclusive," A can appoint to any one or more of the objects of the power or permissible appointees. *See* Andersen § 39(B). When the will is admitted to probate, the charity is divested.

    Answer (A) is not correct. The charity's remainder interest has been divested.

    Answer (C) is not correct. Because the power was "exclusionary" or "exclusive," A was not required to include C3.

    Answer (D) is not correct. C3 does not acquire an interest in the trust estate.

4. **Answer (A) is correct.** It is widely accepted that a general disposition of a testator's property in a will does not exercise a non-general power of appointment. *See* Andersen § 39(A). The Uniform Probate Code has codified this principle. *See* UPC § 2-608.

    Answers (B), (C), and (D) are not correct for the reasons given.

5. In order for the charity's remainder interest to be divested, A, as the donee of the power, must validly exercise the power. A testamentary power can only be exercised in a document which is formally sufficient to be admitted to probate. *See* Andersen § 37(C). Thus, the charity was not divested. UPC § 2-503 *(or a similar statute in a non-UPC state)* may provide the opportunity to probate the defective will, if there is clear and convincing evidence that A intended the document to be A's will.

6.   The charity is not divested because A's attempt to exercise the non-general power was invalid in that S was not a permissible appointee. *See* Andersen § 37(C). C1 and C2 may argue for the application of the doctrine of dependent relevant relation. If successful, the earlier will may still be valid to exercise the power. *See* Andersen § 9(E).

7.   **Answer (A) is correct.** A failed to exercise the power. Consequently, the charity was not divested.

      Answers (B), (C), and (D) are not correct. A was not under any legal obligation to exercise the power. The permissible appointees have no standing to complain about A's inaction.

8.   **Answer (B) is correct.** A expressly exercised the general testamentary power in A's will. *See* Andersen § 39.

      Answer (A) is not correct. The charity was divested.

      Answers (C) and (D) are not correct. Because A was not the donor of the power, the value of A's augmented estate in order to determine S's elective share amount does not include property over which A had a testamentary general power of appointment. *See* RESTATEMENT, THIRD, OF PROPERTY § 23.1. The UPC adopts this position. *See* UPC § 2-205(1)(A).

      The result may differ in a non-UPC state. See McGovern § 10.5 (p. 513).

9.   **Answer (C) is correct.** Because O's will contained a "gift over" in the event the power was not exercised, the charity's remainder interest was not divested. *See* UPC § 2-608. A did not expressly or impliedly exercise the testamentary general power of appointment. *See* McGovern § 10.5 (p. 515); RESTATEMENT, THIRD, OF PROPERTY § 19.4.

      Answer (A) is not correct. A did not have a legal obligation to exercise the power and did not manifest an intent to exercise the power.

      Answers (B) and (D) are not correct. Because A did not hold an inter vivos general power, Blackacre is not included in A's augmented estate for S's elective share determination. *See* UPC § 2-205(1)(A).

      The result may differ in a non-UPC state.

10.   Because A did not effectively exercise the power, Blackacre passes to the taker in default, the charity. *See* Andersen § 39(C).

11.   **Answer (A) is correct.** A attempted to exercise the power in favor of a permissible appointee who predeceased A. However, the antilapse provisions of UPC § 2-603(b)(5) create a substitute gift in favor of CC.

      The result may differ in states that have not enacted the Uniform Probate Code or similar legislation.

      Answer (B) is not correct. C died before A and could not devise Blackacre to CS.

      Answer (C) is not correct. S did not acquire any interest in Blackacre.

      Answer (D) is not correct. The charity has been divested.

12.   RESTATEMENT, THIRD, OF PROPERTY § 22.3 takes the position that the property subject to a general testamentary power is subject to the claims of the donee's creditors to the extent the donee's probate estate is insufficient to satisfy the donee's creditors. However, the states

seem to be divided on this issue. Absent a specific statute on point, the majority view reaches a similar result. Since the general testamentary power was exercised, the donee's creditors can reach the property subject to the power. Courts in some states, however, have held the creditors of the donee cannot reach the property, even if the power was exercised. *See* McGovern § 10.5.

13. **Answer (D) is correct.** It is generally accepted that, during the settlor's lifetime, the settlor's creditors may reach the maximum amount that can be distributed to, or for the benefit of, the settlor even if the initial creation and funding of the trust did not amount to a fraudulent transfer. The Uniform Trust Code has codified these principles. *See* UTC § 505(a)(2). *See also* comment e to RESTATEMENT, THIRD, OF TRUSTS § 58.

    Answers (A), (B), and (C) are not correct. A settlor who is also a beneficiary cannot use a trust as a shield against the settlor's creditors under these circumstances.

14. RESTATEMENT, THIRD, OF TRUSTS § 60, comment g, takes the position that the creditors of a donee of a power who has the authority to appoint to the donee can reach the property over which the donee has the power, even if the power is exercised in a fiduciary capacity and whether or not it is limited by an ascertainable standard. The Uniform Trust Code has been amended to negate the possible application of the Restatement position if the beneficiary/trustee's power is limited by an ascertainable standard as defined in the Internal Revenue Code. *See* UTC § 504(e). Spendthrift statutes in some states also maintain the "spendthrift" protection if the donee's power is limited to the donee's health, education, maintenance and support. However, the result may differ in other jurisdictions.

15. **Answer (D) is correct.** If, under applicable state law, A's power to appoint to A was limited to the ascertainable standard of health, education, maintenance or support, the trust estate described in Question 14 would not be included in A's gross estate. *See* I.R.C. § 2041. The trust estate of the trust described in Question 13 will be included in A's gross estate because A was the settlor of the trust. *See* IRC §§ 2036, 2037.

    Answers (A), (B), and (C) are incorrect for the reasons given.

1. The use of the term "death tax" is misleading. Some states impose inheritance and/or estate taxes. Some states impose neither. The federal government has an estate tax. An estate tax is an excise tax on a decedent's privilege of transferring property at death. An inheritance tax is imposed on the recipient of the property. *See* Andersen § 59.

2. **Answer (D) is correct.** Any property over which the decedent possessed a general power of appointment (*i.e.*, the authority to appoint to the donee, the donee's estate, the donee's creditors, or the creditors of the donee's estate), either immediately prior to or at the time of death, is included in the decedent's gross estate. *See* IRC § 2041. A only had a non-general power over Blackacre, so it is not included in A's gross estate. However, A did possess a general testamentary power over the trust estate.

    Answers (A), (B), and (C) are not correct. A did not have the power to appoint Blackacre to A's estate or creditors, so Blackacre is not included in A's gross estate. Because A had the power to appoint the trust estate to A's probate estate, the power is a general power, and the trust estate is included in A's gross estate.

3. **Answer (D) is correct.** Any property over which the decedent possessed a general power of appointment, either immediately prior to or at the time of death, is included in the decedent's gross estate even if the decedent does not exercise the power. *See* IRC § 2041.

    Answers (A), (B), and (C) are not correct. A did not have the power to appoint Blackacre to A's estate or creditors, so Blackacre is not included in A's gross estate. Because A had the power to appoint the trust estate to A's probate estate, the power is a general power, and the trust estate is included in A's gross estate.

4. No, even though the trust estate is included in A's gross estate, because A did not exercise the general testamentary power over the trust estate, the trust estate passes to the taker in default, Big State University, and qualifies for the charitable deduction. *See* IRC § 2055.

5. **Answer (A) is correct.** A decedent's gross estate includes the decedent's entire probate estate (*i.e.*, any assets passing by will or intestate succession). *See* IRC § 2033.

    Answers (B) and (C) are incorrect for the reasons explained.

    Answer (D) is incorrect. Whether or not a probate asset is subject to administration under state law is irrelevant.

6. My answer would not change. The identity of the heirs or devisees is irrelevant for determining the value of the gross estate. *See* IRC § 2033. The devise to the surviving spouse will qualify for the marital deduction and reduce the value of the taxable estate by the value of what was devised to S. *See* IRC § 2056.

7. **Answer (D) is correct.** If a decedent had the power immediately prior to the decedent's death to appoint the property to the decedent, the power would be classified as a general power, and the value of the appointive property would be included in the decedent's gross estate unless the power was limited by an "ascertainable" standard. *See* Treas. Reg. § 20.2041-1(c)(2). B's power over trust one was limited by an ascertainable standard, and the trust estate is excluded. However, B's power over trust two was not limited by an ascertainable standard. The value of trust two is included in B's gross estate.

    Answers (A), (B), and (C) are not correct. An "ascertainable" standard is one that limits distributions for the purposes of the health, education, maintenance, or support of the donee. A standard defined by the words "comfort or welfare" may not be considered to be "ascertainable" and is likely to cause inclusion of trust two in B's gross estate.

8. **Answer (B) is correct.** B's interests in both trusts terminated at B's death, and B did not possess any power (directly or indirectly) over either trust estate. The federal estate tax is an excise tax on a decedent's privilege to transfer property at death. *See* IRC § 2033.

    Answers (A), (C), and (D) are not correct. Since B was not the settlor, did not possess a power of appointment, and did not have the right to transfer any part of the trust estates when B died, neither trust estate is included in B's gross estate.

9. All probate assets, whether real, personal, tangible or intangible, are included in the decedent's gross estate. Accordingly, the fair market value of any property of S1's passing by will or intestate succession by reason of S1's death is included in S1's gross estate. *See* IRC § 2033. The fact that a spouse may have a right to an elective share does not affect the makeup of the decedent's gross estate. *See* IRC § 2034. The fact that the assets were devised to S2 does not affect the makeup of the gross estate, but the net value of the assets devised to S2 will qualify for the marital deduction and be deducted from the value of the gross estate to determine the value of the taxable estate. *See* IRC § 2056. Accordingly, since $6,000,000 is the value of the gross estate and it was devised to S2, it qualifies for the marital deduction, and there is no estate tax liability.

    If any of the described assets were community property according to relevant state law, only the decedent's half interest would be included in S1's gross estate.

10. Assuming S1's executor elected "portability" in S1's federal estate tax return, when S2 died, S2's estate of $8,000,000 (S2's $2,000,000, plus S1's $6,000,000) will not generate any estate tax liability because of S2's 2013 exemption equivalence of $5,250,000 and S1's unused 2013 exemption (exclusion) amount of $5,250,000. In 2014, the exemption amount was increased to $5,340,000. *See* IRC § 2010(c).

11. **Answer (A) is correct.** The gross estate includes the value of all property transferred by the decedent during life if the decedent retained for life the possession or enjoyment of, or the right to receive the income from, the property transferred. *See* IRC §§ 2036, 2037.

    Answers (B), (C), and (D) are incorrect. It does not matter whether O's retained interest is a life estate or a fee simple interest subject to an executory interest.

12. **Answer (A) is correct.** Nonprobate assets are also included in the decedent's gross estate. *See* IRC §§ 2033, 2036, 2038.

    Answers (B) and (C) are not correct. One cannot avoid inclusion in the gross estate by making this type of nonprobate disposition of the property.

Answer (D) is not correct. Even though the checking account is in the names of both O and B, 100% of the account is included in O's gross estate because O created and funded the account.

13. **Answer (A) is correct.** An insurance policy on the decedent's life is included in the decedent's gross estate if (i) the policy is payable to the decedent's probate estate or (ii) the decedent owned the policy immediately prior to death. *See* IRC § 2033, 2042.

    Answers (B), (C), and (D) are not correct. O owned both policies at the time of death. Accordingly, the proceeds of each policy are included in the gross estate.

14. O did not own either policy at the time of death, and neither policy was payable to O's estate. Accordingly, neither policy is included in the gross estate under IRC § 2042. However, the whole-life policy is included in the gross estate under IRC § 2035 because O transferred the policy to A within three years of O's death. The proceeds of the term policy are excluded from the gross estate, but the value of the policy on the date of the assignment (in excess of any available annual exclusion for gift tax purposes) will be added to O's taxable estate to determine the tax base. *See* IRC § 2001.

15. **Answer (B) is correct.** Since O did not own the stock at the time of death, the stock is not included in the gross estate. The estate tax is an excise tax on the transfer of property at death. *See* IRC § 2033.

    Answers (A), (C) and (D) are not correct. O did not own the stock at the time of death. However, the value of the stock on the dates of the gifts (in excess of any available annual exclusion for gift tax purposes) will be added to O's taxable estate to determine the tax base as an adjusted taxable gift. *See* IRC § 2001.

16. **Answer (A) is correct.** The amount of any debt legally owed by O and payable out of the assets included in O's gross estate is properly deducted from the gross estate to determine the taxable estate. *See* IRC § 2053.

    Answers (B), (C), and (D) are not correct. It does not matter whether the debts are secured or unsecured. However, if O is not personally liable for a secured debt, the debt is subtracted from the fair market value of the asset securing the debt to determine the amount to include in the gross estate. *See* Treas. Reg. § 20.2053-1(a)(1)(iv).

17. There will be no tax owing. In addition to the $700,000 debts owed by O prior to O's death, expenses of last illness, funeral expenses, and administration expenses are also deductible. *See* IRC § 2053. These expenses total $50,000, creating deductions of $750,000 and reducing O's tax base to the 2013 applicable exclusion amount of $5,250,000. In 2014, the exemption amount was increased to $5,340,000. *See* IRC § 2010.

18. **Answer (C) is correct.** The amount devised to S1's child is not deductible. The devise to S2 qualifies for the "marital deduction," and the devise to the charity qualifies for the "charitable deduction." *See* IRC §§ 2055, 2056.

    Answers (A), (B), and (D) are not correct. Congress, for public policy reasons, encourages testamentary gifts to decedents' spouses and to qualified charities.

19. **Answer (B) is correct.** The $1,000,000 devised to the first described trust would not qualify for the marital deduction because S2 was given a "non-deductible terminable" interest in the trust. *See* IRC § 2056(b)(1). The $5,000,000 devised to the second trust appears to meet the requirements of a "qualified terminable interest property" trust ("QTIP trust") in that S2 is entitled to all of the trust's income for the remainder of S2's lifetime. *See* IRC § 2056(b)(7).

     Answer (A) is not correct. However, if the second trust does not meet the requirements of a "QTIP" trust, or if S1's executor does not make the "QTIP election," this answer would be correct.

     Answer (C) is not correct. The first trust does not qualify for the marital deduction.

     Answer (D) is not correct. In any event, whatever amount passes to the charity qualifies for the charitable deduction, assuming the devise to the charity meets the requirements of IRC § 2055.

20. The trust estate of the first trust will not be included in S2's gross estate when S2 dies. At S2's death, S2's life estate simply terminates, and the child's remainder interest becomes possessory. Whether the trust estate of the second trust will be included in S2's gross estate depends on two factors. First, did the trust meet the requirements of a "QTIP" trust? Second, did S1's executor make the "QTIP election"? *See* IRC § 2056(b)(7). If the answer is yes to both questions, the trust estate of the second trust is included in S2's gross estate. *See* IRC § 2044.

1. The probate exception to federal jurisdiction is a long-standing principle that reserves to state probate courts the probate and contests of wills, the determination of heirship and the administration of decedents' estates. Federal courts do have jurisdiction to hear certain estate-related matters. *See* McGovern §§ 12.8, 13.3.

2. **Answer (D) is correct.** According to general principles of conflict of laws, the substantive law of a decedent's domicile normally governs rights of succession to the decedent's personal property. *See* McGovern § 1.2 (p. 33). Because all of the described assets are personal property, the law of the state of X will determine whether these assets will pass (i) by intestate succession to O's heirs determined under the law of X or (ii) to devisees described in a will of O that is admitted to probate in accordance with the law of the state of X. *See* UPC §§ 1-301, 1-302.

    Answer (A) is incorrect. Even though the heirs may reside in different states and certain assets of O are located in different states, these facts do not trigger the application of any federal statutes to determine who owns what.

    Answer (B) is incorrect. While federal banking laws govern many of the practices of the bank, the succession of the checking account is a matter of state law. While (i) the state of Y may have jurisdiction over the shares of stock due to the corporation being a Y corporation and (ii) the state of Z has jurisdiction over the tangible personal property located in Z, the succession of those assets is a matter of the law of the state where O was domiciled, the state of X.

    Answer (C) is incorrect. While (i) the state of Y may have jurisdiction over the shares of stock due to the corporation being a Y corporation and (ii) the state of Z has jurisdiction over the tangible personal property located in Z, the succession of those assets is still a matter of the law of X.

3. **Answer (B) is correct.** UPC § 1-201 (38) defines the term "property" to include both real and personal property, and UPC §§ 1-301 and 1-302 appear to give the state of X the authority to determine the rights of succession to the real property in the states of Y and Z. However, conflict of laws principles provide that the substantive law of the decedent's domicile normally governs the rights of succession to the decedent's personal property, but the law of the situs of real property usually governs the rights of succession to the real property. *See* McGovern § 1.2 (p. 31).

    Answer (A) is incorrect. Conflict of laws principles generally provide that the law of the decedent's domicile governs the succession to the decedent's personal property, but the law of the situs of real property governs the succession of the real property. A state statute may permit the probate of a will that is valid under another state's law even if the will was not executed in accordance with the formalities of the state's applicable wills act. *See* UPC § 2-506.

Answers (C) and (D) are incorrect for the reasons given.

4.   **Answer (C) is correct.** A proceeding to settle a decedent's estate is an in rem action. Accordingly, any state has territorial jurisdiction over the property of a decedent physically located in the state even though the decedent was domiciled in another jurisdiction. In addition, the state where the decedent was domiciled at the time of death also has jurisdiction over the personal property of the decedent located in another jurisdiction. *See* McGovern §§ 1.2, 13.4.

Answers (A), (B), and (D) are incorrect. Conflict of laws principles dictate that the situs state has jurisdiction over property, both real and personal, located in that state. The domiciliary state also has jurisdiction over the decedent's personal property wherever located.

5.   **Answer (C) is correct.** Conflict of laws principles dictate that the situs state has territorial jurisdiction over property, both real and personal, located in that state. The domiciliary state also has jurisdiction over the decedent's personal property wherever located. Conflict of laws principles presume that the law of the decedent's domicile governs the rights of succession to the decedent's personal property, but the law of the situs of real property governs the rights of succession to the real property. *See* McGovern § 1.2.

Answers (A), (B), and (D) are incorrect. Conflict of laws principles generally provide that the law of the decedent's domicile governs the succession of the decedent's personal property, but the law of the situs of real property governs the succession of the real property.

6.   **Answer (D) is correct.** In general, the lawyer's duty of confidentiality continues after the death of a client. Accordingly, a lawyer ordinarily should not disclose confidential information following a client's death. However, if consent is given by the client's personal representative, or if the deceased client had expressly or impliedly authorized disclosure, the lawyer who represented the deceased client may provide an interested party with information regarding a deceased client's estate plan and intentions. *See* ACTEC Commentaries on the Model Rules of Professional Conduct Section 1.6 (4th ed. 2006) (hereinafter "ACTEC Commentary_____"). In this situation, the client did not authorize the disclosure. Thus, consent by the bank would be required.

Answer (A) is incorrect. Upon the client's death, the personal representative has the legal rights of the client, which include the rights to any confidential information held by the deceased client's lawyer.

Answer (B) is incorrect. A has no right to authorize the disclosure of the information held by the client's lawyer, even if he is the "object" of such information. Only the client and the client's personal representative have this right.

Answer (C) is incorrect. Spouses have no greater rights than any other third party to any confidential information held by the deceased client's lawyer.

7.   **Answer (B) is correct.** A lawyer is impliedly authorized to disclose otherwise confidential information to the courts, administrative agencies and other individuals and organizations as the lawyer believes is reasonably required by the representation. This authority includes making arrangements, in case of the lawyer's death or disability, for another lawyer to

review the files of his or her clients. It is assumed that reasonable clients would likely not object to, but rather approve of, efforts to ensure that their interests are safeguarded. *See* ACTEC Commentary 1.6.

Answer (A) is incorrect. It is not necessary that clients expressly authorize disclosure of information since there are situations in which they do so by implication. As explained above, this is one of those situations.

Answer (C) is incorrect. While a lawyer does have implied authorization to share confidential information with partners, associates and employees to the extent reasonably necessary to the representation, as explained above, the lawyer also has implied authorization to make arrangements with lawyers who are not partners or associates in case of the lawyer's death or disability.

Answer (D) is incorrect. The authorization from the client is implied, so it is not necessary for it to be express. Further, there is no requirement that a lawyer seek court approval for the arrangement.

8. **Answer (A) is correct.** When a lawyer reasonably believes that a client is at risk of substantial harm unless action is taken and that a normal client-lawyer relationship cannot be maintained because the client lacks sufficient capacity to make decisions, the lawyer can take protective measures deemed necessary and disclose information to the extent necessary. These measures include seeking a court-appointed guardian or similar representative or consulting with family members, support groups, adult-protective agencies or others who have the ability to protect the client. *See* ABA Model Rules of Professional Conduct 1.14 (hereinafter "Model Rule ____"); ACTEC Commentary 1.6. In this situation, because L reasonably believes that C is going to suffer substantial harm if no one else intervenes, L may take the steps L believes reasonably necessary to protect C.

Answer (B) is incorrect for reasons explained above.

Answer (C) is incorrect. A lawyer does not need approval by a court prior to taking the protective steps discussed above.

Answer (D) is incorrect. The protective alternatives available to the lawyer are not limited to court actions. The lawyer may take less formal alternatives, such as contacting family members or adult-protective agencies.

9. **Answer (C) is correct.** A client may wish to have family members or other persons participate in discussions with the lawyer. When necessary to assist in the representation, the presence of such persons generally does not affect the applicability of the attorney-client evidentiary privilege. C's participation was necessary for A to understand M's directions, so the privilege should not be affected. *See* comment 3 to Model Rule 1.14.

Answers (A), (B), and (D) are incorrect. The attorney-client relationship between A and M is independent of A's relationship with C. C's participation in the discussions did not affect the formation of the relationship between M and A, nor does a pre-existing relationship with C and A affect the applicability of the attorney-client privilege for information M provides.

10. Due to (i) the obvious confidential relationship that exists between C and M and (ii) A's pre-existing relationship with C, A should not proceed any further in the matter. Because of C's

participation in the meeting, C will be presumed to have exerted undue influence on M in any future will contest. *See* McGovern § 7.3 (p. 359). A should advise M to seek independent legal counsel. *See* ACTEC Commentary 1.6.

11.   **Answer (A) is correct.** Absent an agreement otherwise, when multiple parties consult with a lawyer on a matter, the presumption is that the lawyer represents the clients jointly rather than separately. *See* ACTEC Commentary 1.6. The best practice, of course, is to detail the terms of representation in writing.

   Answer (B) is incorrect. The presumption is that the representation is joint.

   Answer (C) is incorrect. Representation is either joint or separate, never both.

   Answer (D) is incorrect for the reasons explained.

12.   Joint representation means the lawyer represents both clients. What one client discusses may be disclosed to the other, if the discussion is legally relevant to the representation. The lawyer cannot withhold legally relevant information from either client. The lawyer cannot give legal advice or take any actions without the clients' mutual knowledge and consent. If a conflict arises between the clients, all the lawyer can do is point out the "pros" and "cons" of the positions, opinions and alternatives. If a conflict arises that makes it impossible for the lawyer to perform impartially, it would be necessary for the lawyer to withdraw from being either client's lawyer. *See* ACTEC Commentary 1.6.

13.   **Answer (B) is correct.** In deciding how to respond to a private communication with one spouse when a lawyer represents the spouses jointly, the lawyer must consider the relevance and significance of the information. If the information is irrelevant to the legal representation, then it need not be communicated to the other. A disclosure of prior adultery may be considered irrelevant under the circumstances. Merely knowing one spouse's secret does not mean the attorney must inform the other spouse. The attorney's obligation is only with respect to relevant and significant information. Unless S1's prior adultery seems likely to affect their joint estate planning, L need not disclose it. *See* ACTEC Commentary 1.6.

   Answers (A) and (D) are incorrect for the reasons given.

   Answer (C) is incorrect. One of the consequences of joint representation is that matters disclosed by one of the joint clients may be disclosed by the attorney to the other client. ACTEC Commentary 1.6.

14.   **Answer (B) is correct.** Since the information is inherently relevant and significant, L should discuss the consequences with S1. L should explain to S1 that L has ethical duties to both clients. L may encourage S1 to tell S2 or to consent to L telling S2. If S1 refuses, L likely will have to withdraw from representation. Before withdrawing, L should use professional judgment as how best to limit the negative consequences to both clients.

   Answer (A) is incorrect. One of the consequences of joint representation is that matters disclosed by one of the joint clients may be disclosed by the attorney to the other client. *See* ACTEC Commentary 1.6.

   Answers (C) and (D) are incorrect. In deciding how to respond to a private communication with one spouse when a lawyer represents the spouses jointly, the lawyer must consider the relevance and significance of the information. *See* ACTEC Commentary 1.6. Since the estate plan involves coordinating the nonprobate and probate assets, the information about the beneficiaries of the nonprobate assets is inherently relevant and significant even though the lawyer was not retained to review the nonprobate designations.

15. **Answer (B) is correct.** A lawyer may accept a gift from a client. However, a substantial gift may be voidable by the client under the doctrine of undue influence, which treats client gifts as presumptively fraudulent. *See* McGovern § 7.3. In no event should a lawyer suggest a gift. *See* ACTEC Commentary 1.8.

   Answers (A), (C), and (D) are incorrect for the reasons given.

16. L should explain that it is not professional for a lawyer to prepare a will including a substantial gift to the lawyer. *See* ACTEC Commentary 1.8.

17. A lawyer is not prohibited from serving as a fiduciary for the client so long as the client is properly informed of the consequences of naming the lawyer, including the apparent conflict of interest for the lawyer to draft the document. The discussion should be memorialized in a writing signed by the client. *See* ACTEC Commentary 1.7.

18. **Answer (A) is correct.** The general rule is that the personal representative is the lawyer's client. What duties, if any, are owed by the lawyer to the beneficiaries of the estate vary among jurisdictions, but the fiduciary is the client in most jurisdictions. *See* ACTEC Commentary 1.13.

   Answer (B) is incorrect. A minority of cases and ethics opinions have adopted the so-called "entity approach" under which the estate is characterized as the lawyer's client. Generally, however, an estate (unlike a corporation or partnership) is not considered an entity.

   Answers (C) and (D) are incorrect. While a lawyer may owe certain duties to those interested in an estate (beneficiaries), the general rule is that the executor (or other fiduciary) is the lawyer's client, unless the lawyer, expressly or impliedly, agrees to some sort of joint representation.

19. An executor is a fiduciary who has a duty to administer the estate solely in the interests of the estate's beneficiaries. Placing the interests of anyone else above the interests of the beneficiaries is a breach of that duty. A should refuse to accept the work absent the informed consent of the beneficiaries. *See* McGovern § 12.1.

20. While an executor is generally free to retain the services of a lawyer of his or her own choice, E still has a conflict of interest-divided loyalties between the estate beneficiaries and E's law partners. The testator may have expressly or impliedly authorized the retention of E's law partners in the will. Absent such authorization, A should advise E to obtain the consent of the estate's beneficiaries. *See* McGovern § 12.1.

21. **Answer (C) is correct.** The rules do not prohibit the drafting lawyer from being named as a fiduciary in a will. Generally, it is best for the lawyer not to suggest being named and to provide written information to the client explaining his or her options and how executor's fees and other compensation are determined. The objective is to make it clear (and preserve as evidence) that the client understood the advantages and disadvantages, and the costs and benefits before making a decision. *See* ACTEC Commentary 1.7.

Answers (A), (B), and (D) are incorrect for the reasons given.

22. No, unless A establishes that the clause was fair and that its existence and consequences were adequately communicated to C. In determining whether the clause was fair, the court will consider: (1) the extent of the prior relationship between A and C; (2) whether C received independent advice; (3) C's sophistication with respect to business and fiduciary matters; (4) A's reasons for inserting the clause; and (5) the scope of the particular provision inserted. *See* comment to UTC § 1008(b).

23. L may retain the will subject to C's later instructions. L should provide C with a letter or other writing confirming that L is holding the document for safekeeping subject to C's future instructions. Of course, the will should be properly identified and appropriately safeguarded while in L's possession. *See* ACTEC Commentary 1.8.

PRACTICE FINAL EXAM: ANSWERS

PRACTICE FINAL EXAM

1. UPC § 2-804(b) revokes any disposition to a relative of the divorced individual's former spouse. In a non-UPC state, a careful review of the relevant statute is necessary to determine if the terms of the statute revoke only the disposition as to the former spouse or to the former spouse and the former spouse's relatives.

2. **Answer (D) is correct.** As B1's joint tenant, B2 succeeded to complete ownership of the real estate when B1 died. *See* Andersen § 18(A). Furthermore, in some states, B1's creditors may not be able to attach the interest B1 owned in the real estate during B1's lifetime because B1's interest terminated at death. The general rule in those states is that a creditor must attach a joint tenant's interest during the tenant's lifetime. Thus, B2 is now the sole owner of the real estate, free and clear of any of claims of B1's creditors. In other states, B1's interest may pass nonprobate subject to B1's debts. *See* McGovern § 13.6.

   Answers (A), (B), and (C) are incorrect. The joint tenants had rights of survivorship. A joint tenant in real estate cannot devise his or her share by will. When B1 died, he had no interest in the real estate that could be devised by his will. If B1 wanted to devise the property in his will, he would have had to sever the joint tenancy with B2, converting it into a tenancy in common. However, he had no power to sever the joint tenancy at his death in his will. *See* McGovern § 5.5 (p. 304–306).

3. **Answer (D) is correct.** The deed does not need to have been executed in compliance with the statutory formalities required for wills because the deed created an inter vivos trust, not a will. The property subject to S's trust is not probate property at death because it was no longer owned by S, individually, but rather by the successor trustee and the beneficiary. An inter vivos trust (unlike a will) is a means to presently transfer ownership during the settlor's lifetime. The fact that B's interest was subject to S's power to revoke or amend the trust did not make the trust a will (*i.e.*, the trust instrument need not comply with the statutory formalities for wills). *See* Andersen § 2(B).

   Answers (A), (B), and (C) are incorrect for the reasons explained.

4. **Answer (C) is correct.** Wills are revocable dispositions of property that take effect upon the testator's death. The execution of a joint will does not create a presumption of a contract not to revoke the will. *See* UPC § 2-514. Accordingly, absent written evidence of a contract, A had the power and the right to revoke the 2000 will, which A did by the execution of the 2010 will. *See* UPC §§ 2-507(c), 2-514.

   Many non-UPC states have similar statutes. Absent a statute, the common law of a state may create a presumption that the parties intended to have a contractual will when they executed the joint will. See McGovern § 4.9.

   Answer (A) is incorrect. The 2000 document was intended by A and B to be a will. In order for it to be effective, the 2000 will must be admitted to probate. However, it was apparently revoked by A when A executed the 2010 will.

Answer (B) is not correct. The 2000 will was revoked. Further, there is no evidence that A ever revoked the 2010 will.

Answer (D) is not correct. UPC § 2-514 creates a presumption that the 2000 will was not executed pursuant to a contract not to revoke it. Accordingly, unless B can establish that a contract existed pursuant to UPC § 2-514, B is without a cause of action. Even if a contract can be established, A revoked the 2000 will, and B's remedy is typically limited to a breach of contract action. *See* McGovern § 4.9 (p. 279).

5. **Answer (A) is correct.** Since O's will devised all of O's estate to their surviving parent, C1 and C2 will not receive an interest in O's probate estate even though they were omitted from the will. *See* UPC § 2-302 (a) (1). Their births did not revoke the will. *See* UPC § 2-508.

In almost every state that has not enacted the Uniform Probate Code, statutes grant "omitted" or "pretermitted" children certain rights in their parents' estates under some circumstances; the details vary from state to state. See McGovern § 3.5.

Answers (B), (C), and (D) are incorrect for the reasons given.

6. **Answer (B) is correct.** When a devisee disclaims, the property disclaimed passes as if the disclaimant had predeceased the testator. *See* UPC § 2-1106(b)(3). The "antilapse" provisions of UPC § 2-603 create a "substitute gift" in favor of the disclaimant's descendants, if any. C was correct — it is not deemed to be a gift by him for tax purposes. *See* IRC § 2518.

The same result is likely to occur in a state that has not enacted the Uniform Probate Code. See McGovern §§ 2.8, 8.5, 15.4.

Answers (A), (C), and (D) are incorrect for the reasons given.

7. **Answer (A) is correct.** When a devisee disclaims, the property disclaimed passes as if the disclaimant had predeceased the testator. *See* UPC § 2-1106(b)(3). The "antilapse" provisions of UPC § 2-603 provide a "substitute gift" in favor of the disclaimant's descendants. However, a stepchild of the testator's child does not qualify as a devisee whose death before the testator qualifies for "antilapse" treatment. The entire estate passes to O's only heir, D.

The same result may occur in a state that has not enacted the Uniform Probate Code. Antilapse statutes vary considerably from state to state. See McGovern §§ 2.8, 8.5.

Answers (B), (C), and (D) are incorrect for the reasons given.

8. **Answer (D) is correct.** O died intestate. The Uniform Probate Code requires wills to be in writing. O's oral statements as to O's testamentary wishes do not control the disposition of any of O's probate estate. *See* UPC § 2-502. The home and its contents are part of O's probate estate and pass subject to formal administration equally to O's heirs, C1 and C2.

The same result is likely in states that have not enacted the Uniform Probate Code. However, there are limited situations in some states which may give rise to a valid oral will of personal property. See Atkinson § 76 and McGovern § 4.4 (p. 239).

Answers (A), (B), and (C) are not correct. Whether real or personal property, testamentary dispositions require a writing executed pursuant to the requisite testamentary formalities.

9.   **Answer (A) is correct.** O died intestate. UPC § 2-502 requires that testamentary wishes be reduced to a writing executed with the requisite testamentary formalities. It is irrelevant how many witnesses heard O's oral statements and when they heard the statements.

The same result is likely in states that have not enacted the Uniform Probate Code. There are limited situations in some states which may give rise to a valid oral will of personal property. See Atkinson § 76 and McGovern § 4.4 (p. 239).

Answers (B), (C), and (D) are not correct. A testamentary disposition requires a writing executed with testamentary formalities.

10.   Because there is no writing signed by O evidencing the contract, UPC § 2-514 would appear to prevent C1 from enforcing the terms of the oral agreement assuming the contract was agreed to after the effective date of the Uniform Probate Code. Thus, since O died intestate, the probate estate, including the home and its contents, passed to C1 and C2. However, because C1 rendered good and valuable consideration to O during O's lifetime, C1 may seek recovery against O's estate in quantum meruit for the value of the services rendered. *See* comment to UPC § 2-514.

The result may differ in states that have not adopted UPC § 2-514 or a similar statute. See McGovern § 4.9. For example, C1's partial performance of the agreement may excuse any writing requirement and allow C1 to enforce the terms of the agreement against O's estate.

11.   **Answer (D) is correct.** O still died intestate. However, because of C1's performance, C1 appears to have a valid, enforceable contract claim to enforce against O's estate. *See* UPC § 2-514. *See* McGovern § 4.9. Accordingly, C1 can possibly seek from O's estate specific performance or the imposition of a constructive trust, or a recovery in quantum meruit. *See* Atkinson § 48.

Answers (A), (B), and (C) are not correct. Even though O died intestate, C1 may wind up with the home and its contents, as provided in the contract.

12.   **Answer (C) is correct.** At common law, conditions of survivorship were not implied with respect to future interests. *See* comment to UPC § 2-707. However, UPC § 2-707 provides that a future interest under the terms of an express trust is contingent on the beneficiary surviving the distribution date. Since G predeceased O, GG is the substituted taker of G's interest pursuant to UPC § 2-707.

In a state that has not enacted the Uniform Probate Code, or a similar statute, the result is likely to differ. See Restatement, Third, of Trusts § 55.

Answers (A) and (D) are not correct. An express trust was created; the death of the beneficiary does not generally extinguish the trust. C may ask for the imposition of a resulting trust if C can convince the court that the trust was fully performed or failed upon the deaths of O and G. *See* Restatement, Third, of Trusts §§ 7, 8. If G had not been survived by any lineal descendants in a UPC state, the property would have passed to O's heir, C. *See* UPC § 2-707.

Answer (B) is not correct. UPC § 2-707 provides that GG acquires G's interest.

However, in some non-UPC states, S would have succeeded to G's vested remainder interest in the trust estate.

13.   **Answer (A) is correct.** O retained a reversionary interest in Blackacre when the trust was

created because the remainder interest was not assigned to G because G was already dead. C inherited O's reversionary interest when O died and has standing to seek the imposition of a resulting trust since the trust now lacks a beneficiary. *See* Restatement, Third, of Trusts §§ 7, 8.

Answer (B) is incorrect. The traditional remedy when a settlor attempts but fails to create an express trust is the resulting trust.

Answers (C) and (D) are not correct. Since G was not alive when the trust was created, G did not own an interest that GG acquired pursuant to UPC § 2-707, or that S inherited in a non-UPC state.

14.   **Answer (A) is correct.** A valid, enforceable express trust has been created. UTC § 401 and § 402 codify the generally accepted principles for the creation of an express trust. *See* Restatement, Third, of Trusts § 22.

        Answers (B), (C), and (D) are not correct. Assuming O had the mental capacity, O transferred the property to F and indicated an intent for F to hold and manage the trust property for O and G.

15.   Assuming the trust document did not address the issue of whether O could revoke the trust, the answer depends on several factors. Most importantly is the law of the state that governs the administration of the trust. In some states, trusts are presumed revocable unless the terms of the trust expressly provide that the trust is irrevocable. The Uniform Trust Code adopts this position. *See* UTC § 602(a). Some states have retained the common law rule that a trust is presumed irrevocable unless the terms of the trust expressly provide that the trust is revocable. *See* Bogert § 148. The second factor is the effective date of the statute, if any, which reversed the common law rule. The third factor may be the date the trust was created, since the law in effect at that time will control whether O retained the right to revoke the trust, thereby requiring the trustee to deliver the property as the settlor directs. If O retained the right to revoke, neither F, O's estate nor X is liable to G. If not, F breached fiduciary duties owing to G. O's estate may also be liable since O conspired with F to breach the terms of the trust agreement. X will probably be treated as a good-faith purchaser.

16.   **Answer (A) is correct.** The donor's intent controls. A was the donee of an exclusive non-general testamentary power of appointment. A can only appoint to any one or more of the objects of the power or permissible appointees. *See* Andersen § 39(B). A's stepchildren were not part of the class of permissible appointees. As the taker in default, the charity is not divested.

        Answers (A), (B), and (C) are not correct for the reasons given.

17.   **Answer (C) is correct.** The amount devised to C is not deductible. The devise to B does not qualify for the "marital deduction" because A and B were not married. The devise to the charity qualifies for the "charitable deduction." *See* IRC §§ 2055, 2056.

        Answers (A), (B), and (D) are not correct. Congress, for public policy reasons, encourages testamentary gifts to decedents' spouses and to qualified charities.

18.   **Answer (D) is correct.** In 2013, the United States Supreme Court in *United States v. Windsor*, 570 U.S. ___, 133 S. Ct. 2675 (2013) held that Section 3 of the Defense of Marriage Act (Public Law 104-199), which defined marriage as between a man and a woman, was

unconstitutional. Later, in Revenue Ruling 2013-17, the IRS ruled it would follow the "place of celebration rule." Thus, the devise to B now qualifies for the marital deduction.

Answers (A), (B), and (C) are not correct for the reasons given.

19. Since a proceeding to settle a decedent's estate is an *in rem* action, the "situs" state has territorial jurisdiction over property, both real and personal, located in that state. The "domiciliary" state also has jurisdiction over the decedent's personal property wherever located. Accordingly, formal administration could be opened in each of the states, X, Y and Z. *See* UPC § 3-815. *See* McGovern § 13.4. Administration proceedings in Y and Z are referred to as "ancillary" administrations; the probate proceeding in X is referred to as the "principal," "primary" or "domiciliary" administration. *See* McGovern § 13.4.

20. **Answer (B) is correct.** While a lawyer may owe certain duties to the beneficiaries of a trust in certain jurisdictions, the general rule is that the trustee is the lawyer's client. *See* ACTEC Commentary 1.13.

Answers (A), (C), and (D) are incorrect for the reasons given.

INDEX
(References are to Topic then Question Number)

INDEX